SHAPING EFFICIENT EMPLOYER BRANDING STRATEGIES TO TARGET GENERATION Y

A CROSS-NATIONAL PERSPECTIVE ON RECRUITMENT MARKETING

ELENA HUBSCHMID

PETER LANG

Bern · Berlin · Bruxelles · Frankfurt am Main · New York · Oxford · Wien

Bibliographic information published by die Deutsche Nationalbibliothek
Die Deutsche Nationalbibliothek lists this publication in the Deutsche Nationalbibliografie; detailed bibliographic data is available on the Internet at ‹http://dnb.d-nb.de›.

British Library Cataloguing-in-Publication Data: A catalogue record for this book is available from The British Library, Great Britain

Library of Congress Cataloging-in-Publication Data

Hubschmid, Elena
Shaping efficient employer branding strategies to target Generation Y: a cross-national perspective on recruitment marketing / Elena Hubschmid.
pages cm
ISBN 978-3-0343-1246-2
1. Employees–Recruiting. 2. Generation Y–Employment. 3. Young adults–Employment. 4. Manpower planning. 5. Target marketing. I. Title.
HF5549.5.R44H83 2012
658.3'11–dc23

2012045897

Cover design/Graphic design: Tim Engel, Bern, www.durchzwei.ch

ISBN 978-3-0343-1246-2 pb. ISBN 978-3-0351-0504-9 eBook

Hochfeldstrasse 32, CH-3012 Bern, Switzerland
info@peterlang.com, www.peterlang.com, www.peterlang.net

TO MY PARENTS

Inaugural dissertation submitted by Elena Hubschmid in fulfillment of the requirements for the degree of Doctor rerum oeconomicarum at the Faculty of Business, Economics and Social Sciences of the University of Bern.

The faculty accepted this work as dissertation on 23rd August 2012 at the request of the two advisors Professor emeritus Dr Prof. h.c. Dr h.c. mult. Norbert Thom and Professor Dr Rudolf Grünig, without wishing to take a position on the view presented therein.

"If we want to attract young talent, we need to fully understand their values [...]. With everyone going for a similar profile, the winners will be those who are able to differentiate themselves."

Hanneke C. Frese[1]

1 Hanneke Frese is an independent consultant active in the field of "think-tank" research, which aims to create a better understanding of the trends that shape the future of work, leadership, the employer value proposition, and similar topics. She has worked for Citibank in Amsterdam, Brussels, London, Zurich, and New York in HRM positions and for Zurich Financial Services in Zurich as Chief Human Resources Officer of Zurich Re, its global reinsurance division.

PREFACE

In a globalised world there is a differentiated demand for the understanding of different employee characteristics that are relevant for defining employer attractiveness. Due to the demographic tendencies that shape our time, it will become more challenging to recruit in the future a sufficient number of qualified and motivated young talents for the company. Especially in the USA, there is extensive literature about the representatives of the so-called young generation Y that is said to have very specific expectations towards their potential employers. However, the statements derived are often not empirically substantiated. Further, in terms of HR perspective, they often lack their relevance for a precise target group (e.g. university graduates that belong to the generation Y).

Dr Elena Hubschmid addresses in her research the following general questions:

- How do national cultures influence employment expectations towards the first employer after graduation?
- Are there any similar attributes within the representatives of the generation Y (so-called Gen Y attitudes) stemming from different national cultures?

Due to her personal cultural background and her specific competences, the author decides to further narrow the research questions. First, she draws her attention to two countries: a highly industrialised Switzerland (its German-speaking part) and an emerging economy of Russia with a specific focus on Moscow. Second, in view of the educational aspect, the research evolves within the target group of the university graduates in Economics and Business Administration (on the level of Master's degree).

The author opts for the quantitative survey. She successfully manages to gain answers from 459 graduates of the target group, whereas 225 are Swiss German master students in Economics (112 female vs. 113 male), and 234 are Russians (154 female vs. 80 male) of the same major. Flexible working conditions, friendly work environment, personal mentoring and coaching as well as high level of corporate social responsibility prove to be especially attractive employer attributes for the representatives of this generational cohort. In the sample studied, nationality has a significant impact on the relationship between the strength of the Gen Y attitudes and the importance of the employer brand attributes in the following cases:

an employer itself is considered to be a good reference for future career; there exists a culture that respects individuality of each employee; further, an organisation has a culture that accepts (underrepresented) minorities; there are opportunities for relocation abroad and international travel; the workplace is situated in an attractive geographic location; the workplace is characterised by a friendly work environment; a performance-related bonus is paid for attainment of pre-set goals; there are good possibilities for rapid promotion.

Based on the empirical findings, the author takes a chance to present practical implications. These include, among others, the necessity of target group segmentation; taking into account of Gen Y attitudes when defining an employer branding strategy (since these Gen Y attitudes exercise a significant influence on the employment expectations of the generational cohort Y); the nationality factor is relevant for certain employer brand attributes and should therefore be considered in the process of adaptation of the suitable recruitment instruments. A simple convergence of national cultures has not been confirmed by the findings of the study regarding the sample examined. Further, it is indispensable to consider the weight of separate employer brand attributes within the holistic employer brand, since there will be differences in weight of single employer brand attributes depending on the target group. An employer branding initiative must be deeply rooted in the strategic orientation of the organisation. As a rule, this cannot be accomplished through the efforts of an HR specialist alone but needs the support of the competent team that stands behind the employer branding efforts. The emphasis should also be put on the authentic communication and the choice of appropriate recruitment channels to reach the specific target group. Moreover, since the representatives of the generation Y network in many ways through electronic channels, this distinctive generational characteristic should be considered when defining an employer branding strategy and adopting concrete recruiting actions.

Previous research conducted on intercultural issues has either underestimated the generational effect or rather has not considered it at all, since the focus was put on surveying the managers of certain categories. Furthermore, certain statements of the existing research on national cultures should be modified due to the change in values that has taken place over the last two decades (e.g. stronger individualism tendencies in modern Russia). These changes are considered to be highly relevant for the younger generation.

Dr Elena Hubschmid had the best prerequisites for the realisation of her research project. She has studied in the international environment (Russia, USA, Switzerland), she is fluent in four languages (Russian, English, German, French), she has supervised the master course "Intercultural Human Resource Management" at the Institute of Organisation and Personnel Management (IOP) of the University of Bern during several years and has managed to acquire the necessary methodological expertise during her doctoral studies. The necessity of the target group differentiation on the basis of systematic empirical evidence provided by Dr Elena Hubschmid deserves special recognition. HR instruments can only be deployed effectively and efficiently, when there is clear empirical evidence about the expectations of the representatives of the target group towards their potential employers of choice.

The results of this study should provide cultural as well as generational researchers with many important and interesting suggestions and support HR practitioners who work for international companies with valuable guidelines for shaping efficient employer branding strategies. I therefore strongly hope that this publication will receive the recognition it deserves by its readership both in academia (HR researchers) and in practice (HR managers).

Bern, December 2012

Professor Dr Norbert Thom
Prof. h.c. Dr h.c. mult.
Former Director of the Institute of Organisation and Personnel Management of the University of Bern

ACKNOWLEDGEMENTS

The three years of my PhD research have been a very challenging and worthwhile journey: a rollercoaster with all the possible ups and downs. Many people have accompanied and strongly supported me during the process of writing my dissertation. I would like to take this opportunity to thank some of them personally.

First and foremost, I would like to express my deepest gratitude to my doctoral advisor, Professor emeritus Dr Prof. h.c. Dr h.c. mult. Norbert Thom, for his constant support and guidance in the course of these past three years of intensive research. My daily scientific discussions with Professor Thom provided me with many insightful remarks and comments in relation to my dissertation project. I have a tremendous admiration and respect for his excellent academic advice, open attitude towards new ideas, and ability to encourage, inspire, and motivate, especially in the difficult moments.

Further, I am very grateful to Professor Dr Rudolf Grünig of the University of Fribourg, Switzerland, for critical discussions and his valuable suggestions during the doctoral seminars Bern-Fribourg in 2009 and 2011 that guided my reflections as the work on this dissertation progressed. I very much appreciate his readiness to take up the role of the second advisor.

My special thanks are due to Dr Kerstin Alfes, senior lecturer of the University of Kingston in London, for her valuable support during the intensive phase of data analysis. Kerstin's fascination for quantitative data analysis became mine, and I will always remember autumn 2011 in London, which apart from challenging work on data analysis was also a lot of fun. Our fruitful, friendly and fair cooperation based on trust and mutual support is a perfect example of academic mentoring for women. Kerstin, I thank you for the inspiration you give me.

Moreover, I would like to thank my fellow PhD colleagues at the University of Bern: Dr David Blatter, Petra Bischofberger, Paul Meyer, Katerina Polinkovska, Dr Katja Leschnikowski – all of you were not only dedicated colleagues on-the-job but good friends outside the university. I also thank junior assistants for their valuable administrative support: Stephanie Jacober, Daniel Schwab, and Philipp Ernst. Stephanie's positive attitude, openness and enthusiasm made our cooperation productive and enjoyable. Without Daniel's IT-support and dedication nothing would be possible. The pink folder called "Elena's Statistics" that Philipp compiled still makes me smile every day. Thank you all very much for providing a respectful, caring and motivating environment during the last few years.

In addition, I thank all the students in Russia and Switzerland who participated in the quantitative study. Their insights made this dissertation possible. Special thanks goes to the professors in Russia and Switzerland who provided me with the opportunity to present my dissertation project at their universities, and thus made the process of data collection more efficient.

I very much appreciate the intense work of Tim Engel on the layout and cover of this book.

Last but not least, the success of this thesis was only possible with the unconditional support of my family and friends. I thank my younger brother Stanislav, for his support and our regular brother-sister skype chats. It has always been an amazing feeling to travel to a different European country every summer just to see him and talk to him whereever he was at that time. Thanks for cheering me up during the hard times and laughing with me during the good ones. Stas, I wish you all the best for your further law studies. I also thank Christian for having been in my life since we were young students and making me smile for many years. Christian, I appreciate your patience and understanding.

Having a lot of friends in my life provides me with balance and happiness. There are too many to name and they know that I highly appreciated the direct and indirect support of each of them during the completion of my dissertation. However, I want to take a chance and thank three of them personally. Elena Hochstrasser is the person who knows me better than I do myself and is always there for me with a ready advice in every life situation. I admire her talent to organise distractions by all possible means which gave me possibility to take my mind off the research when I needed it. Her sense of humour is absolutely unique! Each talk with Nik Ludin makes me admire his wisdom and life experience. Nik, thank you for believing in me and being a dedicated friend throughout all these years. Our friendship means a lot to me. Dr Lyudmila Sankova's creativity and her bright mind were the sources of many useful inputs for my dissertation. Thanks to her support it was possible to conduct an expert interview in Moscow prior to data collection. I am so happy that she moved to Switzerland a year ago and we now get to see each other more often.

The last PhD year was not only a year of intensive research, but also a difficult year in terms of health due to three knee surgeries I had to undergo during 8 months after a bad ski accident. Thank you, Jayne Faulkner, Esther Ackeret, Monika Jans for sharing the bad times with me and cheering me up. In you I found new dedicated friends and regained my faith and optimism. Jayne, I look forward to celebrating our come-back to the mountains as soon as we have fully recovered from our injuries.

Finally, I am especially grateful to my parents, Svetlana and Vladimir, for their continuous support throughout my lifelong educational journey. Despite the physical distance between us, they were always there for me – and I know they will be in the future. My insatiable hunger to learn and dedication to research stem from their deepest respect for academic education. My parents have always encouraged me to explore, never doubt myself, face new challenges with enthusiasm and energy, and believe that the sky is the limit. They have supported me throughout my educational endeavours in more ways that I can ever thank them for. The least I can do in return is to dedicate this dissertation to them.

Zurich, December 2012

TABLE OF CONTENTS

LIST OF FIGURES

LIST OF TABLES

LIST OF ABBREVIATIONS

BFS	Bundesamt für Statistik (Swiss Federal Statistical Office)
BRICS	Brazil, Russia, India, China, South Africa
cf.	confer
CEO	chief executive officer
CSR	corporate social responsibility
DEBA	Deutsche Employer Branding Akademie
DV	dependent variable
EB	employer brand
e.g.	exempli gratia (for example)
EOC	employer of choice
EVP	employer value proposition
gfs.	Gesellschaft für praktische Sozialforschung (Society for practical social research)
Gen Y	generation Y
GLOBE	Global Leadership and Organisational Behaviour Effectiveness
HR	human resources
HRM	human resource management
IBM	International Business Machines
IDV	individualism
IV	independent variable
Jr.	junior
KPIs	key performance indicators
MMR	moderated multiple regression
n/a	not available
oec.	oeconomicarum
OECD	Organisation for Economic Cooperation and Development
PA	Pennsylvania
PD	power distance
PJ	person–job
PO	person–organisation
rer.	rerum
RBV	resource-based view
RJPs	realistic job previews
ROI	return on investment
R&D	research and development
PA	Pennsylvania
sig.	significance

UA	uncertainty avoidance
URL	uniform resource locator
USA/US	United States of America
USP	unique selling proposition
VRIN	value, rarity, inimitability, nonsubstitutability

1

INTRODUCTION

"If you understand the Net Generation, you will understand the future. You will also understand how our institutions and societies need to change today."

Don Tapscott

1.1 Problem statement and the relevance of the topic

The working world has become excessively demanding because of today's highly complex and competitive economic context. This context is characterised by the globalisation of businesses, increasing competition, accelerated technological progress, the ongoing shift towards a service society with more sophisticated and informed customers, and a continuous need to increase innovative abilities to remain competitive (cf. Burke/Cooper 2005: 3; van der Sluis/van de Bunt-Kokhuis 2009: 1). "The move from product-based to knowledge-based economies is a fundamental business transformation impacting the global war for talent" (Beechler/Woodward 2009: 275).

> In a highly competitive economic context, characterized by such phenomena as the globalization of markets, changing customer demands and increasing product-market competition, people and the way they are managed acquire greater importance [...] (De Saá-Pérez/Garcia-Falcón 2002: 123 f.).

In this economic landscape, a company's value is mainly based upon intangible assets (cf. van der Sluis/van de Bunt-Kokhuis 2009: 1), since products and processes are easier to copy and most resources are available across industries (cf. Holland *et al.* 2007: 247). In this regard, the often rare and socially complex nature of intangible assets makes them difficult to imitate and they are thus more likely to produce competitive advantages (cf. Hitt *et al.* 2001: 13). These intangible assets comprise a company's "unique knowledge of production, [...], its knowledge of markets, its relationships with customers and suppliers, [...], and of course its workforce capabilities" (van der Sluis/van de Bunt-Kokhuis 2009: 1). The knowledge, skills, and capabilities of the people within a company, referred to as human capital, represent one part of its intellectual capital (cf. Baron/Armstrong 2007: 6). Owing to the growing emphasis on intellectual capital as a main source of competitive advantage, the importance of recruiting and selecting the right people has become increasingly apparent (cf. Beardwell/Claydon 2007: 189; Leisink/Steijn 2008: 118).

More and more companies are deciding to go international to create additional turnover and profit margin since home markets are stagnating or in decline (cf. Grünig/Morschett 2012: 28). In this respect, a global talent pool in a global economy is able to accelerate the launch of new products and services as well as innovation timelines within companies (cf. Kelley 2012: 2). "Facing a more global marketplace, companies are now placing a high priority on searching for talent in global and emerging markets so they can have the right people in the right jobs in the right locations [...]" (Deloitte 2010: 17).

The findings from the recent surveys carried out by several internationally active consulting firms further substantiate the relevance of the topic in question. In the study conducted by the Boston Consulting Group and the European Association for People Management in 2011[2], managing talent stood out as the most critical for respondents (cf. Strack *et al.* 2011: 4). Interestingly, this is the fourth year in a row that this priority falls in the red zone of the survey: more than one-third of respondents ranked their company as having no talent strategy at all (cf. Strack *et al.* 2011: 12). Five topics that represent the greatest current importance for respondents were defined as follows: improving leadership development, delivering on recruiting, managing talent, managing flexibility and labour costs, and the on-boarding and retention of new recruits. Only 30% to 40% of respondents reported to have structured "on-boarding" activities that are aimed at introducing specific talent segments into the company once hired, and very few companies take seriously managing international talent pools. A total of 60% of respondents said that they leave their employer value propositions (EVPs) to chance, neither attempting to customise their brands to match talent segments' needs nor measuring the attractiveness of their brands on a regular basis (cf. Strack *et al.* 2011: 10, 12).

In the global survey "Talent Edge 2020: Blueprints for the new normal" conducted by Deloitte in 2010 among 334 senior business leaders and human resources (HR) executives in large businesses in the Americas, Asia-Pacific, Europe, the Middle East and Africa, many executives predicted talent shortages across key business units such as R&D and executive leadership. "When asked to list three most pressing talent concerns, 41% of executives named competing for talent globally and in emerging markets, followed by developing leaders and succession planning at 38%"

2 The online survey was carried out from February to April 2011, receiving 2,039 responses from executives in 35 countries. The findings were substantiated by interviewing 58 executives.

(Deloitte 2010: 5). Further, more than seven in 10 respondents (72%) said they would increase their focuses on their brands in the years to come, since most executives (53%) surveyed believed their companies were doing the right thing distinguishing their employer brands (EBs) in the talent marketplace (cf. Deloitte 2010: 15).

In Deloitte's annual report for 2012, which was dedicated to examining important trends in human capital, Adachi *et al.* (2012: 4) provide evidence that one of the driving trends that is boosting change in HR practices is the constantly growing importance of emerging markets, as they represent significant growth opportunities. Developing economies are growing much faster than mature economies and are becoming a primary source of revenue, profits, and talent. Understanding the capabilities, employability, and cultural implications of talent in these markets is critical to effectively prioritizing growth objectives and leveraging the opportunities they present (Adachi *et al.* 2012: 4).

In the survey conducted by Universum in 2011 among 632 global employers about needs and challenges with regard to talent attraction, employers who manage to find the right talent classify their success factors as follows: their employer reputation and image are attractive (76%), the people and culture of the organisation are attractive (61%), organisation knows how and where to target the right talent (54%), organisation made the potential talent aware of itself and its employer offerings (52%), the characteristics of the job appeal to the target group (52%), and remuneration and advancement opportunities are competitive (34%). On the contrary, employers that struggle to recruit the right talent mention the following reasons: potential talents are unaware of organisation and its employer offerings (54%), employer reputation and image are not attractive enough (46%), remuneration and advancement opportunities are not competitive enough (32%), organisation simply does not know how and where to target the right potentials (18%), the characteristics of the job don't appeal to the target group (16%), and the people and culture of the organisation aren't attractive enough (12%). The following distribution of answers among respondents shows that employer image and attractiveness are the most important elements of finding the right talent for the organisation. The majority of employers (54%), further, agree that attracting the right talent is one of the most important benefits of a long-term employer branding strategy (cf. Universum 2011a: 10).

The Global Perspectives Barometer – an online survey conducted by Credit Suisse in cooperation with the St. Gallen Symposium with the assistance of the market research institute gfs.bern – asked 623 young men and women from 60 countries for their views on globalisation. The results of the survey showed that talented young people from around the world apply a different yardstick to the issue of globalisation when it comes to assessing its impact on them personally rather than on their countries of origin or the world as a whole: 81% see the globalisation of the economy as an opportunity for themselves and their careers above all (cf. Kuhn-Spogat 2011: n/a).

From the results presented above, it is generally recognised that intellectual and human capital are the foundations of competitive advantage in the modern economy. "Today, with unprecedented global financial crisis, economic slow-down, and massive restructuring, 'talent' remains a critical agenda item focused on the highest achievers" (Beechler/Woodward 2009: 243). In reality, talent has become a synonym for the entire workforce in many organisations (cf. Beechler/Woodward 2009: 274).

The recent unavailability of university graduates has raised questions about how to create and sustain in companies populations of management and economics graduates that are capable, committed, diverse, and motivated. In the next 20 years, the real winners will be the firms that determine how to reach and recruit generation Y (Gen Y) representatives. The key factor for those firms will be their abilities to adjust their recruiting strategies to the employment expectations of the new generation (cf. Kitces 2005: 16). In order to recruit the right Gen Y representatives, companies should elaborate sound recruitment marketing concepts as an integral part of their talent management strategies, incorporating modern marketing approaches into their human resource management (HRM).

The following arguments of the resource-based view (RBV) are presented to demonstrate the relevance of the topic being studied from the scientific perspective.

1.1.1 RBV perspective

> The resource-based view of the firm emphasizes the role of firm-specific resources, especially firm-specific knowledge resources, in helping a firm to achieve sustainable competitive advantage. However, the deployment of firm-specific knowledge often requires key employees to make specialized human capital investments that are not easily redeployable to other settings (Wang/He/Mahoney 2009: 1265).

The RBV of the firm has its roots in the literature on organisational economics, where theories of profit and competition based on the writings of Ricardo (1817), Schumpeter (1934), and Penrose (1958) focused on the internal resources of the firm as the major determinant of competitive success (see also Wright/McMahan/McWilliams 1994). "Resource-based research has concentrated on clarifying the resource concept, examining the strategic relevance of firm resources and identifying the characteristics of valuable resources" (Grünig/Kühn 2005: 273). The definitions of resources and sustained competitive advantage are central to understanding the RBV of the firm and its interdependence with human capital.

Resources

Wernerfelt (1984: 172) defines a resource as "anything which could be thought of as a strength or weakness of a given firm". Later, Barney (1991: 101) expanded this definition by including in it "all assets, capabilities, organizational processes, firm attributes, information, knowledge, etc. controlled by a firm that enable the firm to conceive and implement strategies that improve efficiency and effectiveness". According to Barney (1991: 101), resources can be divided into three categories: physical capital resources (e.g. plant, equipment, technology, geographic location), organisational capital resources (e.g. organisational structure and a variety of processes and functions), and human capital resources (e.g. knowledge and experience of individual workers and managers).

These resources are viewed as sources of competitive advantage. Grünig and Kühn (2005: 47) argue that: "[...] investment in resources [...] will determine the long-term competitive position of the company. If there is no intended strategy, these investments produce an emergent strategy, and this will contain considerable risks and can threaten the existence of the firm."

Sustained competitive advantage

Barney (1991: 102) alleges that a competitive advantage occurs "when a firm is implementing a value creating strategy not simultaneously being implemented by any current or potential competitors".

The growing acceptance of internal resources as sources of competitive advantage in organisations brought legitimacy to HR's assertion that people should be viewed as strategically important to firm success since they generate a competitive advantage (cf. Wright/Dunford/Snell 2001: 702). Within the RBV, "a competitive advantage is not considered sustained until all efforts by competitors to duplicate the advantage have ceased." (Wright/McMahan/McWilliams 1994: 303).

HR as a firm resource

> [..] One answer to the critical question in strategic management regarding why firms vary in performance is that they differ in human capital. [...] Intangible resources are more likely than tangible resources to produce a competitive advantage. In particular, intangible firm-specific resources such as knowledge allow firms to add value to incoming factors of production (Hitt *et al.* 2001: 13 f.).

Thus, in this challenging business environment organisations are now finding that "sourcing and retaining talent [is becoming] the competitive battleground" (Ulrich 1997: 13). Most organisations today are able to copy the technology, processes, products, and (even the) strategy of other successful organisations (cf. Burke/Cooper 2005: 3), but HR and their interactions within an organisation are hard to imitate (cf. Hitt *et al.* 2001: 113). They, therefore, constitute an exclusive source of competitive advantage (cf. Burke 2005: 17). Hence, successful and highly competitive organisations will be those investing in the recruitment, selection, development, and retention of individuals with the right skills, perspectives, and experiences to drive the organisation to success (cf. Ulrich 1997: 13). Because the skills, knowledge, and engagement of employees form the competitive advantage and therefore significantly contribute to the company's success, it is important that a company manages to attract the right talents (cf. Simon 1993: 763).

Wright, McMahan and McWilliams (1994: 304) define HR as the "pool of human capital under the firm's control in a direct employment relationship. HR practices, on the other hand, are the organizational activities directed at managing the pool of human capital and ensuring that the capital is employed towards the fulfilment of organizational goals"[3]. *Fig. 1* shows the interrelationship among HRM functions, the pool of actual and potential employees, and sustained competitive advantage.

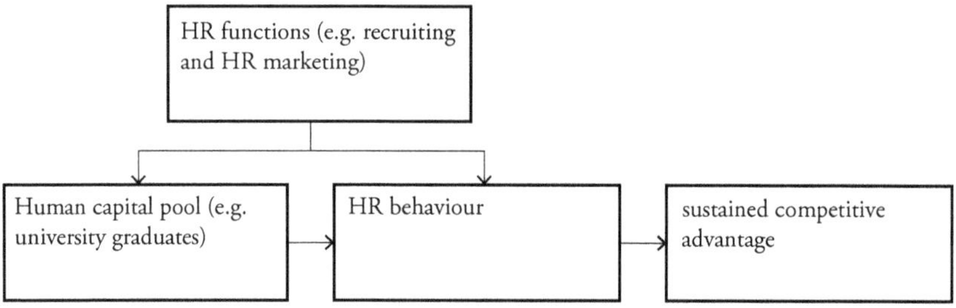

Fig. 1: HR as a source of sustained competitive advantage (based on Wright/McMahan/McWilliams 1994: 318)

As can be seen from *Fig. 1*, HR managers can use HR processes and cross-functions such as HR marketing[4] to attract, identify, and retain high-quality university graduates (cf. Thom 2001: 120 ff.). HR functions moderate the relationship between the human capital pool and firm effectiveness in a way that the pool of employees becomes effective only if HR processes are organised properly, i.e. they capitalise on the advantages by eliciting employee behaviour. In other words, having the correct mix of HR practices is a necessary condition for the maximal effectiveness of the HR capital pool[5] (cf. Wright/McMahan/McWilliams 1994: 320). According to Wright, McMahan and McWilliams (1994: 320), "sustained competitive advantage is achieved only by the interaction between the human capital pool and the HR practices". This means that knowing the initial employment expectations of Gen Y graduates is crucial for recruiting and shaping efficient recruitment marketing strategies. Thus, an organisation that develops a valid selection system, has attractive HR programmes, and

3 In this book, the author refers to human resource practices as functions of HRM (cf. Thom 2001: 119 ff.).
4 Referred to in this book as recruitment marketing.
5 Efficient recruiting schemes and recruitment marketing practices that target university graduates are necessary for setting up the desired Gen Y pool of employees who will bring value to the firm.

promotes them through adjusted employer branding processes can attract, select, and maintain the highest quality pool of employees. Recruitment marketing activities that reach potential employees coupled with effective recruiting procedures that provide a large pool of qualified applicants can ensure that an organisation finds the types of skills needed. HR functions that are deeply embedded in the organisation will be difficult to imitate since it is not easy to identify the precise mechanisms of interaction and value creation between the varieties of HR practices such as recruiting and marketing.

Despite the fact that the relationship among recruiting, recruitment marketing, and competitive advantage is complex, the RBV of the firm points out the potential for HR managers to play an active role in developing such an advantage by focusing on the needs and initial employment expectations of university graduates who are likely to become future employees. Thus, the RBV approach provides a framework for examining the potential of a given Gen Y pool of university graduates to integrate their initial employment expectations into employer branding and recruitment strategies.

Given the growing number of Swiss and Russian firms as well as multinational corporations and multiple international organisations acting in both Swiss and Russian markets, the necessity to build up a pool of efficient employees from both cultural backgrounds becomes obvious. Building on this premise, McWilliams, Van Fleet and Wright (2001: 2 ff.) argue that HR, if defined as the entire pool of employees, present a unique source of advantage in comparison to domestic labour pools in terms of value, rarity, inimitability, and nonsubstitutability (VRIN). Taking into consideration this framework, the author alleges that organisations acting in both Swiss and Russian markets can benefit (if properly attracted, selected, and recruited) from an international workforce in two ways: first, capitalising on the Swiss–Russian labour pools and second, exploiting the cultural synergies of a diverse workforce. A heterogeneous Swiss–Russian pool of graduates potentially provides superior human capital, since firms can draw from a diverse labour pool to match the different needs of an organisation. Furthermore, access to this heterogeneous labour pool increases the quality of international decision-making. However, defining people as the source of sustained competitive advantage requires efficient HR processes that ensure the attraction and recruitment of young Gen Y talent of different nationalities, especially in these times of demographic challenge that the majority of employers are facing.

1.1.2 Demographic challenge

Demographic change, especially in industrialised countries, fosters the importance of HR, since it causes a decline in and aging of the resident population and labour force (cf. Bruch/Kunze/Boehm 2010: 25). The population's increased aging will eventually lead to labour shortages at all levels. This issue (among others) was mentioned as early as 1998 by McKinsey in the famous article "The War for Talent" (cf. Chambers *et al.* 1998). Companies have to handle this shortage partly by recruiting generation Y employees (cf. Cates/Rahimi 2003: 425).

Generation Y represents the latest generational cohort entering the labour market at present (cf. Twenge 2010: 201). The demand and therefore the competition for generation Y increases because of these demographic changes and the aforementioned global economic trends (cf. Lindquist 2008: 56). Organisations have to be aware of the local and global demographic conditions and need to integrate with its societal structure to enable long-term success (cf. Kubicek/Thom 1976: 3988). The quantitative supply of the needed workforce must be considered when planning for long-term business goals. In that respect, the age structure of society is a reliable indicator of the future availability of human capital[6].

Companies should be ready to tackle the problem of their aging workforce.

> For all industrialized nations, long-term demographic change is a powerful and irrepressible force. Population and workforce ageing will reshape our countries in ways that we are only beginning to grasp. Demographic trends in Switzerland are similar to those in the rest of Europe: as people live longer and reproduce at increasingly lower rates, the overall age of the population is rising (Adecco 2008: 2).

6 One of the key findings from the 2008 Swiss Demographic Fitness Survey was that 50% of Swiss firms have taken no action to analyse the age structures of their workforces, indicating that Swiss employers have not yet fully embraced the issue of population aging and its impact on the workforce, i.e. scarcity in the supply of graduates (cf. Adecco 2008: 3).

Since 1950, fewer children have been born in Russia and in western countries including Switzerland than those needed to sustain economic growth. In western countries, the number of employees aged 55 and older has increased by 30%, whereas the number of 25 year olds has only increased by 1% (cf. Clare 2009: 41). By 2020, compared with 2000, there will be over one-third more Swiss workers aged 50 to 64 years and one-fifth fewer workers aged 30 to 44 years (cf. BFS 2006: 7 f.) as well as a 16% drop in the total number of Swiss aged 0–19 years (cf. Adecco 2008: 3). The old age dependency ratio – the proportion of the population older than 64 as a percentage of the 20–64-year-old population within a country – will change from 25% in 2000 to 43% in 2050 (cf. OECD 2006: online).

> Increasing longevity, declining birthrates, and the disproportionate size of the post-war baby boom generation constitute powerful demographic forces that drive an unprecedented shift in the age distribution of the general population worldwide, and are reason for skewed labour pool supply (Beechler/Woodward 2009: 275).

This shortage has created intense competition in recruiting top graduates into the workforce (cf. Lindquist 2008: 56).

> By 2030, an additional 45 million employees will be needed in Western Europe in order to sustain economic growth. In light of current population growth rates, this number will be difficult to reach. At a time of growing talent gaps, when human capital is among the most valuable assets for gaining competitive advantage, too few companies actively manage talent with a sharp focus. Instead, most take big risks by relying on serendipity to address talent scarcity (Strack *et al.* 2011: 5).

At the same time, nowhere in the world is the demographic situation more alarming than in Russia. Of the 140 million people living in Russia today, by 2050 there will be only 100 million left: a decrease of 10 million each decade. Scientists predict enormous depopulation in Russia. The demographic situation is even more dramatic than in western countries since there were no actual Baby Boomers after the Second World War (cf. Lindner 2009: 8). The demographic problem has become even worse as a consequence of the political changes and economic instability in the country during the final decades of the 20th century. In Russia, there is a known "depopulation bomb".

Demographic changes in both Russia and Switzerland mean that employers will be increasingly competing for a smaller pool of young people. Therefore, it is crucial that employers acting in the Swiss–Russian market are able to attract and recruit the right graduate entrants, who can be developed to grow business between these two countries in the future. "Gen Y's entrance into the workplace would seem to present many opportunities in today's ever-more competitive organizations in which high-performing workers are an asset, and demographic shifts point to impending labor shortages" (Eisner 2005: 9). Despite the tendency towards the declining numbers of young employees, the proportion of highly qualified employees required to bring an organisation ahead is increasing. In this respect, talent acquisition, especially recruiting graduates, becomes more important both in Russia and in Switzerland. Hence, demographic security for the sake of cooperation is a common challenge for Russia and Europe, which should push both sides towards closer collaboration (cf. Lindner 2009: 8). Given the expected quantitative decrease of workforce supply and the notorious qualitative shortage in many disciplines, the focus on recruiting strategies for Gen Y is indispensable for long-term success. To compete for future talented graduates, employers also need to be aware of the characteristics of their generation (Gen Y) and engage actively with them so that they can meet their needs effectively. This underlines the importance of exploring the initial employment expectations of potential graduate entrants.

The concept of generation has further gained importance since much attention has been paid to generation Y as a generation revolutionising the working environment (cf. De Hauw/De Vos 2010: 293; Hershatter/Epstein 2010: 211).

1.1.3 Generational paradigm

The concept of generation is used to explain and analyse various phenomena, e.g. in sociology, population study, psychology, anthropology, biology, and educational science (cf. Oertel 2007: 17 f.). In sociology, three concepts of generation with different meanings exist (cf. Hoepflinger 1999: 6). Throughout the book, with its special focus on generation Y, the historic-societal concept of generation is used, which describes a generation as a group of individuals who are born roughly around the same time and experience similar external events during their adolescence and early adulthood years, which constitute their values, attitudes, and preferences (cf. Hoepflinger 1999: 10; Kupperschmidt 2000: 66). This definition and usage of generation is also often used by business studies, e.g. in the scope of management and leadership science, marketing, and HRM.

In business studies, the relevance of the concept of generation has increased only recently. The phenomenon of generation types and their effects on the working environment has thus far been primarily examined in the United States (cf. Oertel 2007: 25). The literature dealing with this topic was mostly coined in a popular scientific manner with inadequate empirical foundation (cf. Bruch/Kunze/Boehm 2010: 91). Thus, statements about generation types were mainly drawn from the authors' own expertise and experience (cf. Oertel 2007: 31). However, the empirical examination of the concept of generation has recently grown in importance (cf. Twenge 2010; Twenge *et al.* 2010).

No other generation and its impact on today's working environment have ever been discussed as intensely as Gen Y has recently (cf. Myers/Sadaghiani 2010: 235). Gen Y has been examined in popular as well as in scientific literature, although popular literature again outnumbers the scientific work available on Gen Y. Much of the popular literature is based on the anecdotal events and personal experiences of consultants, writers, speakers, and trainers (cf. Jorgensen 2003: 43). Little empirical work has been carried out on Gen Y (cf. Twenge *et al.* 2010: 2). The popular literature summarises Gen Y as "[…] the blunt, techno-savvy, contradictory children of Baby Boomers who believe education is key to success, technology is as transparent as the air, diversity is a given, and social responsibility is a business imperative" (cf. Martin 2005: 39). Furthermore, in terms of pay and benefits, advancement, work/life balance, interesting and challenging work, and making a contribution to society, Gen Yers are characterised as "wanting it all" and "wanting it now" (cf. Ng/Schweitzer/Lyons 2010: 282).

Generation Y in the German-speaking world

As previously indicated, the literature on generational differences and generational characteristics that is not formed by US influences is rare. In both Switzerland and Germany, the American typology of generations has often been adapted without questioning (cf. Bruch/Kunze/Boehm 2010: 94 f.).

One of the first systematic typologies for Germany was developed by Oertel (2007: 166). According to Oertel (2007: 168), the German counterparts of Gen Y are the so-called Net children ("Netzkinder") born between 1975 and 1985. Oertel (2007: 168) continues that the situation of these net children is difficult: they are facing problems in the labour market since permanent positions in organisations are hard to obtain. Furthermore, they are shaped by German reunification and its consequences. Global issues such as climate change have formed and are still forming this generation. At the same time, they have grown up in relatively stable family backgrounds and they are optimistic and willing to learn. Moreover, having grown up in times of rapid technological progress and globalisation, Oertel (2007: 168) describes them as communicative, tolerant, multicultural, and individualistic.

Another typology of German generations was developed by Bruch, Kunze and Boehm (2010). According to them, there exists no typical Swiss typology, but they assume that their German typology can be transferred to Switzerland (cf. Bruch/Kunze/Boehm 2010: 96). Here, the German counterpart of Gen Y is the Internet generation born since 1981. The name stems from the strong influence of the rapid technological progress on this generation. Nevertheless, this generation is still mostly named generation Y in Germany. This Internet generation or generation Y is the first generation to benefit from globalisation, worldwide mobility, and interconnectedness (cf. Kunze/Boehm/Bruch 2010: 94). At the same time, it is also the first to suffer from the negative impacts of globalisation such as increased competition among industrialised states (cf. Kunze/Boehm/Bruch 2010: 94). This generation has to rely on short-term planning, since clear and predictable career paths are no longer easy to obtain (cf. Bruch/Kunze/Boehm 2010: 109). Therefore, members are also often called "generation internship" because they complete several internships before actually getting a job (cf. Briedis/Minks 2007). Bruch, Kunze and Boehm (2010: 111) ascribe the following characteristics to the German-speaking generation Y: willingness to learn, affinity for technology, flexibility, mobility, and tolerance.

Generation Y in Russia

The post-Soviet generation (born since 1975) is often mentioned as a possible counterpart of generation Y in Russia (cf. Schewe/Meredith 2004: 59). The "defining moments" of this generation include privatisation and economic reforms, the Chechnya War, and the stock market collapse in 1998 (cf. Schewe/Meredith 2004: 59). Most literature on the current Russian youth refers to them as generation Y, indicating that despite the tense history between the US and Russia the theories about this special generation have been partially adopted.

Furthermore, the Russian generation Y is sometimes called the "abandoned generation" or "lost generation", because their parents were concerned with their own interests during the end of the Cold War (cf. Schewe/Meredith 2004: 59; Sokolov 2006: 43). This post-Soviet generation is often tainted with relatively negative characteristics, such as being self-sufficient, materialistic, and amoralistic[7] (cf. Schewe/Meredith 2004: 59; Sokolov 2006: 43 f.). The Russian generation Y has grown up in a turbulent period of Russian history with a lot of upheaval (cf. Mankoff 2010: 5 f.). A major proportion of the Russian population felt that their personal security was undermined by "hyperinflation, rampant criminality, and the disastrous first war in Chechnya" (Mankoff 2010: 6). Nevertheless, this young generation somehow managed to benefit from this insecurity; it has become much more entrepreneurial, more efficient, and self-sufficient. Members believe in their power to change their lives and society and are optimistic and self-confident (cf. Mankoff 2010: 6; Petro 2008: 23 f.; Sokolova 2010: 50 ff.). According to Mankoff (2010: 6), this generation is proud of successful Russians in business and members desire to join them. This may lead to the false conclusion that Russian generation

7 Since these statements are mostly made by older generations, they may also reflect the general generational differences in perceptions and conflicts, which are similar around the world (cf. Deal/Altman/Rogelberg 2010: 192).

Y individuals value money more than their western European counterparts may. But this is not the case in general, as studies have shown that the Russian youth does value other factors, such as training and development, much more than salary alone (cf. Sokolova 2010: 50 ff.).

It is often said that the Russian generation Y is highly nationalistic and nostalgic compared with their generational counterparts in other countries (cf. Petro 2008: 22; Hole/Zhong/Schwartz 2010: 94). This nationalism and nostalgia often carry negative connotations, especially in western countries. A survey of the Russian youth by the Fund for Public Opinion, the Yury Levada Analytical Centre, and the All-Russian Public Opinion Research Centre shows that what the young Russians admire about the past is not the regime or the ideology, but the sense of common purpose and the pride the citizens felt (cf. Petro 2008: 22). It is argued that the Russian generation Y views patriotism as a defence mechanism against the permanent criticism of Russia's past within Russia and by other countries (cf. Petro 2008: 23). Iadova (2007: 25 ff.) argues that in the period of active transformations in Russian society in the past several decades it has become extremely difficult to speak about any of the accepted standards of behaviour. This is because countries undergoing post-communist transformations are characterised by a big discrepancy between social norms that are codified in cultural roots and those that are actually practiced as new models of behaviour evolve. That is why it becomes especially important "to study the behavioural attitudes of young Russians whose worldview and behaviour have been formed under the influence of post-Soviet changes" (Iadova 2007: 25).

Most Russian generation Y individuals have grown up with the same technological advancements as their western European counterparts (at least in the big cities) (cf. Sokolova 2010: 50 ff.). Russian Gen Y individuals are increasingly willing to travel and to stay abroad (cf. Mankoff 2010: 6). These remarks about the Russian generation Y highlight that they are similar to the Gen Y in the western world. It will be discussed later in the book if this statement is perhaps too superficial since it is primarily supported by the popular literature on Gen Y in Russia. Iadova (2007: 33) provides evidence that well-educated respondents[8] are more ambitious,

8 The data in Iadova's study cover only Muscovites.

independent, tolerant, liberal, and politically literate. The results of her research indicate clearly that "the value rational archetype of goal setting and goal accomplishment that is prevalent in Russian culture has been replaced (or at least affected) by the Western goal rational archetype" (Iadova 2007: 35). "This supposed 'change in mentality' is the logical result of the Europeanization of Russia's young people [...]" (Iadova 2007: 36). In recent decades, the ideology of individualism, which is not usually characteristic of the Russian mentality, has become prevalent in Russia (cf. Iadova 2007: 40). Summarising the results of her study, Iadova (2007: 42) concludes,

> [...] that the consciousness of the groups of post-Soviet young people [..] is distinguished by an odd and paradoxical combination of modern and traditional behavioural attitudes. It seems clear that this dichotomy is a response to the contradictions of Russian reality (Iadova 2007: 42).

In another study carried out a year earlier, Beliaeva (2006: 30) provides evidence that almost 70% of young students who have not yet completed their higher education are oriented towards the market economy and corresponding values, while about 80% reported to be in favour of the greater differentiation of incomes depending on the results of personal achievements and hard work. Based on her analysis, she concludes that there is undoubtedly a good reason to say that a new culture of the younger generation is taking shape in Russia. Further,

> the content of this culture will make up a new way of self-determination and self-assertion of the generation under the changed conditions of the new institutional matrix, ways of correlating with traditional cultural values and acquiring progressive liberal values. [...] The individualization of consciousness and behavior, and the rejection of paternalism, constitute an important prerequisite for the modernization of society [...] (Beliaeva 2006: 43).

When reviewing the literature on Russia's generation Y, it becomes apparent that in Russia this generation has a greater relationship with politics than those seen elsewhere. A proportion of this generation is, for instance, called "Generation Putin" (cf. Petro 2008: 22 ff.). Generation Putin and generation Y are often mixed up even though not all generation Y members support Putin's political course[9] (cf. Mankoff 2010: 6 f.).

9 Especially in light of recent political events (e.g. the Duma elections in December 2011 and demonstrations followed by the presidential elections in March 2012 and youth demonstrations thereafter), the majority of young urban well-educated Russians are thought to be guided by western values and in no case belong to "Generation Putin".

Ramachandran and Artiuch (2007: 21) provide evidence that the cultural paradigm for Gen Y is changing dramatically in Russia (and Eastern Europe) more than in any other region of the world. They substantiate their claims by stating that Russia's Gen Y did not live under communist rule and thus that members have difficulty appreciating the suffocating circumstances endured by their parents and grandparents. The older generation sees the young as individualistic, materialistic, aggressive, and separated from their roots, since Gen Yers show a complete rejection of the old values and institutions.

In light of these changes at the generational level, i.e. that Gen Y tends to have much more in common across nations than did preceding generations, the generational paradigm becomes highly relevant for management research aimed at recruiting young Gen Yers. However, in order to avoid generalisations in respect to this new global generation and to substantiate the relevance of the research within the cross-national context, the place of national culture in the globalised world has to be discussed before the objectives of the present research are defined.

1.1.4 National culture in a globalised world

In the new millennium, "cross-cultural research is no doubt one of the most important subsections of marketing and international business research" (Orr/Hauser 2008: 2)[10]. In order to analyse a culture's influence on generation Y's expectations towards its employers, a common understanding of the concept of culture must be developed. Furthermore, a discussion of the two conflicting paradigms of cultural convergence and cultural divergence (see also chapter 2.3.4) should lead to the elaboration of the question of whether culturally induced differences persist between generation Y individuals or if this generation is the first in which culture no longer plays a role.

Geertz (1993: 89) suggests that culture is "a historically transmitted pattern of meanings embodied in symbols, a system of inherited conceptions expressed in symbolic forms by means of which men communicate, perpetuate, and develop their knowledge about attitudes towards life".

10 See also Hubschmid/Thom (2010: 115 ff.).

Kuper (1999: 227) provides a shorter definition of culture as "a matter of ideas and values, a collective cast of mind". Hofstede (1980: 25) defines national culture as "[...] the collective programming of the mind which distinguishes the members of one human group from another".

There exist different approaches to cultural influence on management theory, each of them providing diverging views on culture's effects. At the dynamic level of cultural research[11], the "convergence thesis" and "divergence thesis" have been represented by culture researchers. The "convergence thesis" states that cultural differences are becoming weaker and a "world culture" is emerging (cf. McGaughey/De Cieri 1999). By contrast, the "divergence thesis" argues that the value and norm systems of different cultures are gradually drifting apart or at least are not converging (Hofstede/Hofstede/Minkov 2010; Trompenaars/Hampden-Turner 2010).

> The wider convergence – divergence debate also tends to assume that the HRM system as a whole has to converge or remain divergent, rather than considering whether some parts of the overall HR-system might be converging, in some regions or geographies, while other parts might be diverging (Brewster/Sparrow/Harris 2005: 952).

However, Brewster, Sparrow and Harris (2005: 952) continue that even within a single HR function, e.g. recruitment marketing, there might be convergence at one level but divergence at another. "The culture-specific thesis [..] argues that economic change and technological development will not lead to a total convergence of managerial approaches" (Verhoeven/Chansarkar/Williams 2009: 88). Axelrod (1997: 203) mentions that people do indeed become more similar as they interact, but the tendency to converge almost always stops before it reaches completion.

In addition, Verhoeven, Chansarkar and Williams (2009: 89 f.) allege that the Internet culture can be characterised as collectivist and that this collectivistic culture group exceeds national boundaries. Members of this group are all part of an Internet culture, which has its own norms and values, and, therefore, its members are not subjected to national norms and values. "If cultures are changing, we can expect to find evidence of those changes

11 As opposed to the static level where national culture is viewed as a stable unchangeable construct. The present research is based on the assumption that national culture should be studied from a dynamic perspective.

among young people first" (Prašnikar/Pahor/Vidmar Svetlik 2008: 6)[12]. Because of the existence of different viewpoints on cultural development and its relevance for management, in particular for HR, it seems of significant scientific importance to prove which thesis can be applied to young university graduates.

To sum up, together with demographic changes, the increasing economic and cultural integration across nations because of globalisation processes with geographic-based economic barriers falling has a big impact on labour supply (cf. Beechler/Woodward 2009: 275). According to Brewster, Sparrow and Harris (2005: 949), companies are dealing with "competing demands of global integration and local differentiation". "But the increasing connection between countries does not mean that cultural differences are disappearing or diminishing" (Javidan/House 2001: 291). "To be successful in dealing with people from other cultures, managers need knowledge about cultural differences and similarities among countries" (Javidan/House 2001: 292).

1.2 Objectives of the research

This research aims to show that individuals – whereupon the focus is Gen Y university graduates in two different countries (Switzerland and Russia) – engage with the world of work differently because of their subjective frames of reference.

> Work is not purely a technical matter which individuals undertake: it is a personal matter which involves the location of self and identity in an ongoing social process of engagement with the labour process within which they operate (Tomlinson 2007: 287).

The overall practical objective of the research can be defined as follows: to develop recommendations for efficient recruitment marketing strategies to target Gen Y in a cross-national context. The focus of the study lies in assessing the influence that national differences, if any, exercise over the expectations of Gen Y individuals from the German-speaking part of

12 The results from the study of Prašnikar, Pahor and Vidmar Svetlik (2008: 1, 18, 22) confirm the strong influence of national cultures on international business. They further allege that globalisation, however, plays an important role, too. Their results confirm the presence of the influence of national cultures on both managers and students, although the students in the three countries investigated (Russia, Serbia, and Slovenia) are much more alike compared with older age groups.

Switzerland and Russia towards their potential employers. These recommendations will lead to the development of the explicit conceptual framework that will be expanded after the data analysis has been completed in order to illustrate the degree of national influence on generation Y's expectations towards their employers and to highlight the variables that increase this influence. In order to develop the explicit conceptual framework for recruitment marketing in an international context, several theoretical objectives have to be accomplished.

1.2.1 Theoretical objectives

The main purposes of this research are (i) to investigate the influence of national culture on Gen Y university graduates[13] of different nationalities[14] in order to trace how cultural differences (if any) affect the process of shaping Gen Y's initial employment expectations and (ii) to develop a theory-based research model that combines the dimensions of Gen Y, national culture, and employer brand (EB) based on the initial employment expectations of potential Gen Y employees.

The theoretical objectives of the research are defined as follows:

- Definition of the research strategy;
- Examination of the conceptual and contextual theoretical foundations of the concepts of culture, generation Y, and EB;
- Development of a theory-based research model that combines the dimensions of generation Y, nationality, and EB and operationalises the main constructs, i.e. generation Y and EB.
- Elaboration of the preliminary conceptual framework for recruitment marketing in an international context based on a thorough analysis of the scientific literature and secondary data.

1.2.2 Practical objectives

The main practical objective is to generate recommendations regarding how companies have to (re)organise and frame their recruitment marketing activities (recruiting and employer branding instruments and measures among others) to attract university graduates of different nationalities

13 In Economics and Business Administration.

14 Swiss and Russian.

with the right potential. In other words, how they can achieve a match between the initial employment expectations of graduates and their own expectations as employers and how they can ensure a better link between recruiting and employer branding strategies to make recruitment marketing more efficient. The research findings and the methodological tool developed during this research process can assist HR practitioners and employer branding specialists in planning graduate recruiting and employer branding strategies as well as in assessing their own EBs. This tool might be useful as a part of an EB template[15] used in formulating and executing recruitment marketing strategy[16].

The philosophy behind recruitment marketing should be used to develop efficient recruiting instruments. The empirical validation of the proposed hypotheses will serve as the focal point for generating recommendations for employer branding strategies with a specific focus on Gen Y university graduates. It is, therefore, important to consider how graduates' initial employment expectations can be aligned with the brand's desired values (cf. Harris/de Chernatony 2001: 444 ff.).

After the main objectives of the research have been set, a brief epistemological disposition that underlies the research philosophy behind this study will be presented in the next chapter.

1.3 Epistemological disposition

The theory of science as a meta-science is concerned with studying science itself (cf. Schanz 1988: 1) and therefore precedes all specific fields of science (cf. Schreyögg/Steinmann 1980: 2395). Scientific-theoretical considerations deliver the answer to the question of how science itself should be studied and deal with scientific objectives, assertions, and important methods as well as the conceptual extraction of the results of performed analyses (cf. Lattmann 1998: 104; Raffée/Abel 1979: 1). Scientific theory performs a critical and a constructive function. The former allows for the critical observation of the scientific practice, whereas the latter strives to ensure the development of new concepts that are

15 Which must be adapted to the specific situation.

16 The further modification of a particular brand template should be undertaken according to the framework requirements of a certain case (e.g. target group) and/or organisation.

able to deliver efficient solutions (cf. Raffée/Abel 1979: 1 f.)

Thus, the theoretical embedment[17] should take place before a researcher starts drafting a research project, through which the main research objectives as well as instruments to achieve these objectives are shown (cf. Scherer 2006: 22). According to Kromrey (2002: 60 f.), there exist different scientific theoretical directions, of which the analytic-nomological paradigm is of paramount importance for social scientists. The analytic-nomological paradigm includes such forms as empirism, logical empirism, positivism, neo-positivism, critical rationalism, and scientific realism. The basis of the analytic-nomological paradigm is the assumption that scientific assertions (independent of time and space) can be formulated as laws and can be reviewed in an intersubjective manner (cf. Wiswede 1998: 50). Therefore, the analytic-nomological paradigm forms the basis for this research project.

Management research has been predominantly coined within the framework of critical rationalism. Karl R. Popper (1976) developed this school of thought through the synthesis of classical rationalism and classical realism. Critical rationalism is based on the assumption that there exists an ordered reality independent of human consciousness; he sees experience as a relevant criterion for the validity of scientific assertions (cf. Kromrey 2002: 25, 35 ff.; Scherer 2006: 26). As a consequence, scientific assertions must stand the test of reality, whereupon scientific assumptions can be falsified but never verified through experience (cf. Wiswede 1998: 50 ff.). Therefore, the predominant goal of science is the continu-

17 Of the stages of theory development described by Grochla (1978: 68 ff.), the first three are conducted during the course of this research. The relevant concepts are described within the first stage of the cognition of conceptual statements (cf. Zaugg: 2002: 15). During the course of the second stage of the cognition of descriptive statements, interpretational-speculative statements are developed. These statements demonstrate the relevance of the concepts by indicating their previous literary treatment (cf. Grochla 1978: 73). Furthermore, the practical relevance of the concepts is demonstrated exemplarily. The third stage of the cognition of explanatory statements comprises the conceptual construction of interrelations and the related explanation of certain circumstances (cf. Grochla 1978: 73). The third stage of theory development aims to result in justified causal assumptions of a hypothetical nature (cf. Zaugg 2002: 15). These three stages of theory development as well as the subsequent development of the conceptual framework are conducted through a thorough and systematic analysis of the existing literature as well as empirical studies (cf. Zaugg 2002: 16).

ous growth and progress of knowledge through the research findings and not securing approved knowledge (cf. Suchanek 1999: 87). The scientific process starts according to Popper (1974: 344) by bringing together experiences and theoretical knowledge, since "[…] observation always presupposes the existence of some system of expectations" (Popper 1974: 344). Popper refuses to accept induction as a scientific research method and instead develops a deductive-empirical research model (cf. Gadenne 2006: 34). Scientific progress can therefore be attained if the following principles are taken into account (cf. Diekmann 2007: 175):

1. Informative scientific hypotheses should be formulated.
2. These hypotheses should be subjected to numerous empirical tests in various situations.
3. Hypotheses rich in content, which have survived attempts to falsify them, should be kept in the first place, whereas falsified hypotheses should be refuted.

Although many elements of critical rationalism make up the basics for this research project, there are certain limitations that must be taken into account and that are not supported by the author, e.g. the exceptional acceptance of the deductive method as well as the assumption that hypotheses can never be verified. Furthermore, there is a lack of differentiation between social and natural sciences in terms of the application of this methodology (cf. Raffée/Abel 1979: 4 f.).

Therefore, there is a need for an alternative scientific-theoretical fundamental disposition that should neutralise the limitations of critical rationalism. In this respect, the scientific project is based on the principles of scientific realism, which also belongs to the analytic-nomological school of thought and occupies an important place in the modern theory of science: "It appears that the majority of philosophers of science now profess to be scientific realists […]" (Causey 1979: 192). Scientific realism pursues a classical realistic orientation and assumes the existence of a reality that is situated outside consciousness (cf. Hunt 1990: 9). The goal of scientific work is therefore "[…] a literally true account of the physical world […]" (Leplin 1984: 2). The representatives of scientific realism deny the existence of complete scientific objectivity (cf. Hunt 1984: 33). Hence, subjective perceptions as an integral part of the scientific process are accepted. Scientific realism is further aware of the imperfection of measurement instruments (cf. Hunt 1984: 33; Hunt 1990: 9) and advocates the following perspective on science: "[…] to use its method to improve our perceptual (measurement) processes, separate illusion from reality, and thereby generate the most accurate possible description and understanding of the world" (Hunt 1990: 9). One of the relevant aspects of scientific realism that represents an important reference point for this study is that hypotheses according to this school of thought can be empirically tested and accepted.

To sum up, the school of scientific realism unites in it many principles of the school of critical rationalism, but through the acceptance of the inductive methodology and the possibility of the stepwise acceptance of hypotheses it is closer to reality. Therefore, this school of thought underlies the research process of this study.

1.4 Structure of the book

The book is divided into seven basic parts. In the introductory *Part I*, the relevance of the topic has been emphasised, objectives of the research clearly defined, and the research philosophy according to a chosen epistemological disposition presented.

In *Part II*, the conceptual background of the research including the concepts of EB, employer attractiveness, generation Y, and culture are explained. Further, the current state of research provides a basis for identifying the research gap and setting a precise research focus.

Building on the background of the concepts being scrupulously analysed, the preliminary conceptual framework for the research is developed in *Part III*. This represents the main building blocks for the empirical strategy by including the key variables and defining the relations between them, which lays the basis for the empirical study.

In *Part IV*, the development of the research model follows through the operationalisation of the constructs of generation Y and EB. The generation of hypotheses at three levels of reasoning based on the thorough literature analysis completes this part of the book.

The empirical verification of the research model is the focus of *Parts V* and *VI*. First, the empirical setting, sample description, and data collection methods are described and the quantitative research methodologies applied in this study elucidated. *Part VI* is dedicated to the presentation of the empirical results and the empirical validation of the research model.

Part VII comprises a discussion of the results and the possible practical implications for the employer branding strategies of organisations operating on a global scale in multicultural environments. The results are summarised in the explicit conceptual framework for recruitment marketing. In addition, the scientific appraisal of the research takes place followed by a discussion of the relevant limitations of the study and suggestions for future research in the area. *Fig. 2* provides an overview of the structure of this book.

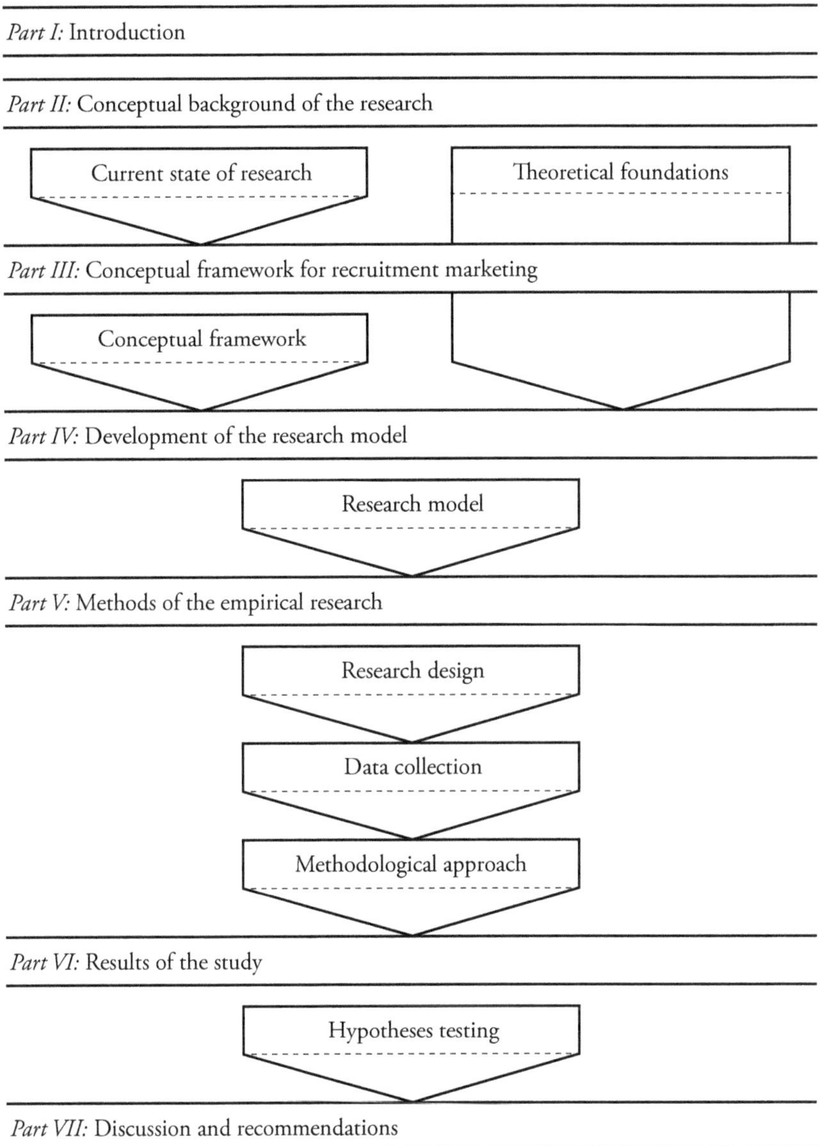

Fig. 2: Structure of the book (own representation)

2

CONCEPTUAL BACKGROUND AND THEORETICAL FOUNDATIONS OF THE RESEARCH MODEL

"There are always more smart people outside your company than within it."

Bill Joy

In the literature, recruitment marketing and employer branding are often used as synonyms. Within the scope of this book, there will be a distinction between the two: while recruitment marketing internalises all the different instruments of the recruitment marketing mix, employer branding mainly forms part of the communication mix[18].

2.1 Recruitment marketing as a cross-function of modern HRM

As previously indicated, many knowledge-intensive companies today are facing skill shortages. The need for value-adding employees will increase more drastically in the near future. Emerging countries such as China, India, and some countries in Eastern Europe are catching up technologically and, therefore, contributing to the increasing demand for skilled labour (cf. Mahroum 2000: 23; Moroko/Uncles 2008: 161). Traditional flows of talented people from emerging to industrialised states have shifted, and thus movements of "brain gain" and "brain drain" can be found in every direction. This change starts threatening those countries that have profited from the previous situation (cf. Mahroum 2000: 23). The situation is even more impaired because of the already mentioned ongoing demographic changes around the world (cf. Moroko/Uncles 2008: 161).

Therefore, attracting suitable employees has become similar to the traditional marketing problem of attracting customers (cf. Ewing *et al.* 2002: 15), whereas a sustainable supply of suitable employees is ensured by recruitment marketing (cf. Zaugg 2009: 349). The main objective of recruitment marketing is to analyse the needs of potential employees and to position the organisation as a desired place to work within the competitive environment (cf. Lindner-Lohmann/Lohmann/Schirmer 2008: 40;

18 Within the scope of recruitment marketing in the traditional sense, first of all, a thorough analysis of all relevant information regarding recruitment has to be performed, e.g. analysis of the labour market, potential employees, and competitors (cf. Lindner-Lohmann/Lohmann/Schirmer 2008: 45). This so-called situation analysis enables the organisation to position itself in the labour market (cf. Zaugg 2009: 351). Similar to the marketing mix, i.e. the sum of all marketing instruments ensuring the realisation of the marketing strategy (cf. Homburg/Krohmer 2006: 13), a recruitment marketing mix exists as well (cf. Zaugg 2009: 352). This mix includes the recruitment and communication mix (cf. Zaugg 2009: 349). The recruitment mix determines recruitment sources, while the communication mix entails the way of communicating job openings to potential employees.

Zaugg 2009: 349). Therefore, a thorough definition of the target individuals is essential since successful recruitment marketing ideally does not result in a large quantity of applications, but in few selected applications by preferred potential employees (cf. Hauer/Schüller/Strasmann 2002: 71). It becomes evident that recruitment marketing as a cross-function of HRM and recruitment as its process function are inseparable. When considering the whole recruitment process, recruitment marketing already plays a role in the first stage when determining the recruitment objectives[19].

Although the literature on the relationship between HR and marketing is limited in scope, it does support the idea that the responsibility for employer branding and employer attractiveness lies within the whole organisation and not just within the marketing department (cf. Roper/Davies 2007: 76).

> In the internal marketing and branding literature it has long been recognised that HR plays a potentially important role in embedding the desired brand ethos and culture; however, their role has often been restricted to communication support, rather than playing a more strategic role in shaping people management practices to reflect the desired brand experience (Mosley 2007: 129).

Alfes (2009: 168), in her recent research on the strategic roles of HR departments, proves that HR, as a strategic partner, adds to the economic effectiveness of HR activity in the organisation. Martin and Beaumont (2003: 5 ff.) state in their review of the relationship between branding and HRM that the marketing literature tends to restrict the role of HR to the communication of brand values; the point that HR in fact is the source of such values has often been ignored. Nonetheless, there is significant evidence to suggest that the attitude of HR to branding and brand management is beginning to change (cf. Barrow/Mosley 2005; Martin *et al.* 2005). "Job candidates today need to be approached in much the same way as prospective customers: carefully identified and targeted, attracted to the company and its brand" (Cappelli 2001: 140). Cappelli (2001: 140)

19 Observations in this chapter are geared towards external recruitment marketing, namely attracting potential employees. However, one should not neglect the internal function of recruitment marketing. Internal recruitment marketing ensures the motivation and retention of current employees and, therefore, ensures long-term competitive advantages (cf. Schmidtke/Backes-Gellner 2002: 322). Owing to the focus of this book, internal recruitment marketing will not be discussed in more detail.

further approves of this statement: "The hiring process [...] has become nearly indistinguishable from the marketing process"[20].

Grünig and Kühn (2005: 17 f.) show that strategic management comprises such activities as strategic planning, the implementation of strategies, and strategic control. In this respect, strategic HRM as a

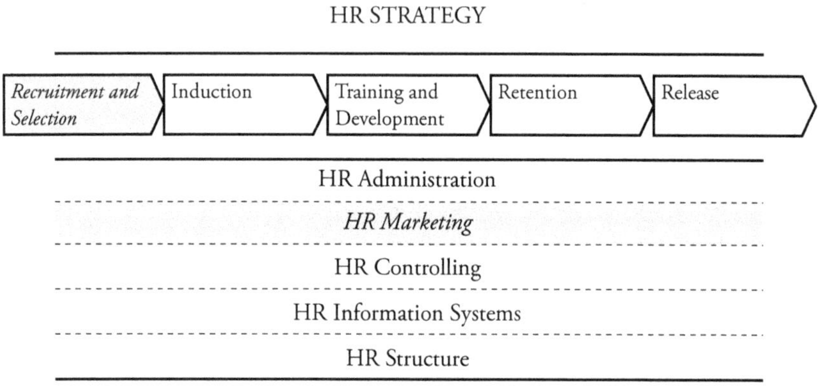

Fig. 3: Functions of HRM (based on Thom 2001: 118 and Thom 2001a: 156)

20 According to Kotler (2000: 85), during the marketing process, first it is necessary to segment the market, then select the appropriate market target, and finally develop the offer's value positioning. The essence of the strategic marketing process can be summarised as followed: segmentation, targeting, and positioning. "The marketing process consists of analyzing marketing opportunities, researching and selecting target markets, designing marketing strategies, planning marketing programs, and organizing, implementing, and controlling the marketing effort" (Kotler 2000: 86). Grünig and Morschett (2012: 290) further continue: "Markets consist of many different customers and even in the domestic market these customers are not homogeneous but differ in their needs, income levels, buying attitudes, etc. This heterogeneity is usually drastically increased in international marketing contexts. With customers from different countries, it is difficult or impossible to find a marketing approach that wil [sic] appeal to all. On the other hand, it is very expensive to target the marketing to individual customer needs. One solution to this problem is to divide the entire, heterogeneous market in which a company is active into a number of smaller, distinct segments which are characterized by homogeneous demand. Market segmentation allows the company to approach each segment in a rather standardized way while the different segments are targeted with a different market offer. This is a hybrid strategy combining the advantages of standardization (within segments) with the advantages of differentiation" (Grünig/Morschett 2012: 290). "A company that wants to use the same market offer internationally should first identify cross-country customer segments and decide whether the heterogeneity between the segments requires a segment-specific adaptation of the market offer" (Grünig/Morschett 2012: 296).

meta-function of HRM stresses the necessity of integrating personnel strategies when formulating the business strategy (cf. Thom 2001). *Fig. 3* shows the functions of modern HRM, whereas the focus of this book lies in the process function of recruitment and the cross-section function (or cross-function) of HR marketing.

The primary aim of recruitment is to remove personnel shortages and provide an organisation with the necessary HR. To succeed in this area and be able to quickly recognise the opportunities offered by the external and internal job markets (cf. Felser 2010: 13 ff.), companies should perform thorough labour market research, which can include a more in-depth look at the demographic development. Apart from this, companies will have to increasingly pay attention to their corporate images: the alignment between corporate image and EB has proven to be a decisive factor in making a company attractive for potential employees and improving a company's chances of gaining new personnel. These chances largely depend on the way a company manages to integrate the initial employment expectations of potential employees into its EB (cf. Thom 2001a: 158). According to Zaugg (1996: 20 ff.) and Felser (2010: 3), when it comes to HR recruitment, companies should strictly differentiate according to target groups (e.g. managers, specialists, university graduates, older employees) and design recruiting instruments for their employer branding strategies accordingly.

The cross-function of HR marketing is aimed at creating favourable conditions to increase employer attractiveness on both the external and the internal labour markets. The analogy to marketing lies in the fact that a potential employee is seen as a customer and the workplace is viewed as an aspect of the customer-oriented product (cf. Thom 2001a: 166 f.). Therefore, the integration of the initial employment expectations of Gen Y university graduates into the employer's branding strategy becomes of vital importance for organisations if they want to succeed in this hard competition for young Gen Y talent. A solid information base is a prerequisite for efficient employer branding, and this is when a connection to the process function of recruitment becomes apparent. It is here when insights from the research into the initial employment expectations (information side of HR marketing) of Gen Y become relevant for shaping efficient employer branding strategies (action side of HR marketing).

There is, however, no uniform definition of HR marketing in the scientific German-speaking literature. Different authors have tried to classify existing approaches to HR marketing. The following are the most essential approaches that show the important stages in the development of the concept in the German-speaking scientific world even before the term *employer brand* was coined by Ambler and Barrow (1996).

Classification according to Bleis (1992)

Bleis (1992) differentiates between the "classical" understanding in 1968–1975 and the "new" understanding of HR marketing, which started to dominate the literature from 1987. According to the "classical" definition, the function of HR marketing has been to organise a workplace in a way that makes employees content without stressing economic goals. The "new" understanding of HR marketing, on the contrary, stresses the necessity of achieving economic goals and thus it is defined as a long-term systematic strategy that aims at recruiting and retaining new employees.

Classification according to Bartscher and Fritsch (1992)

Bartscher and Fritsch (1992) define four main perspectives on HR marketing. In the late 1960s and early 1970s, workplace marketing was at the centre of HR marketing, i.e. workplace attractiveness was promoted through commercial activities with the goal of reaching a large pool of potential and actual employees. In the mid-1970s, HR marketing stood for managing all organisational divisions in a labour market-oriented way. The underlying idea was that any organisation had to fulfil a service function towards its employees that reflected the primacy of strong employee orientation. Later in the 1970s, HR marketing was viewed as an overall framework for managing HR tasks, followed again by an internal marketing perspective that was understood as a strategic instrument for recruiting the required personnel.

Classification according to Dietmann (1993)

Dietmann (1993) distinguishes between seven definitions of HR marketing. The first concept dominated the literature in the early 1970s and used HR marketing to solve HR problems, i.e. it considered the needs of employees. The next widespread concept in the early 1970s saw HR marketing as an overall management function in a modern enterprise. At the same time, a much narrower understanding of HR marketing as primarily a recruiting function was also popular. In the mid-1980s, the main goal of HR marketing was the attainment of employee and organisational objectives. Along with this perspective on HR marketing, another perspective of internal marketing was dominating the literature. Internal marketing was viewed as the instrument for acquiring information and controlling employee behaviour. In the late 1980s, the main goal of HR marketing was to achieve the highest level of employer attractiveness among potential and actual employees and ensure the achievement of corporate objectives. During the same period, proponents such as Fröhlich (1987) argued that the main purpose of HR marketing was to foster employee retention.

Classification according to Scholz (1995)

Scholz (1995) also developed a systematic classification of existing HR marketing concepts. In the early 1970s, HR marketing was seen as a comprehensive function that combined personnel-related research and profiling in both the internal and the external labour markets. Later, the focus moved to external HR marketing with the main goal of accessing external labour markets. In the late 1980s, a rather philosophical view of HR marketing, called heuristic HR marketing, dominated the literature (see also Staffelbach 1995). The concept of heuristic HR marketing was seen as the main goal of HR marketing in understanding the determinants of behaviour at work as well as during the process of entering an organisation. Scholz concludes his classification by defining HR marketing as a general principle of management orientation that implies the purposeful application of HR instruments with the goal of creating positive attitudes among current and future employees.

Classification according to Staffelbach (1995)

Staffelbach's (1995) HR marketing concept consists of three main approaches. The first sees the primary goal of HR marketing in advertising with a focus on recruitment activities. The second (HR marketing mix, see also Wunderer 1991) sees HR marketing as a systematic configuration of the "mix of measures" towards the satisfaction of employee needs. The third views HR marketing as a driver for competitive position in the labour market with a specific focus on attractive employment conditions.

2.1.1 Current state of research on recruitment marketing

Recruitment plays a crucial part in winning "the war for talent" (see Chambers *et al.* 1998) because of its function of drawing probably the most important resource into an organisation – the necessary HR (cf. Barber 1998: 1). Barber and Roehling (1993: 845) describe the effect of insufficient recruitment very drastically. According to them, "the ultimate cost of failure to attract applicants may be organizational failure" (Barber/Roehling 1993: 845).

Recruitment can be defined as searching for and acquiring appropriate potential job candidates in sufficient quantity and quality in order to facilitate the efficient and effective selection of the most competent candidates to fulfil job requirements (cf. Pilbeam/Corbridge 2006: 143; Dowling/Festing/Engle 2008: 109). The quality and quantity of the potential job candidates attracted through the recruitment process serve as a basis for the success of other HRM efforts, e.g. selection as well as training and compensation (cf. Barber 1998: 1). A more precise definition of recruitment is given by Breaugh, Macan and Grambow (2008: 45 f.). The authors define recruitment based on the intentions of several organisational actions. They state that recruitment involves all organisational actions that are intended:

- to draw potential job candidates' attention to current job offerings;
- to influence the possibility of these individuals actually applying for the job;
- to maintain interest in the position; and
- to influence whether a job offer is actually accepted.

This definition of recruitment is applicable to internal recruitment, i.e. attracting candidates within the organisation, as well as external recruitment, i.e. attracting candidates outside the organisation (cf. Breaugh/Macan/Grambow 2008: 46; Mathis/Jackson 2007: 204).

As stated above, recruitment serves as a basis for successful selection. These two HRM functions are carried out simultaneously. They are a "matching activity between applicant and job [...] utilizing appropriate recruitment methods and selection methods effectively [...]" (Pilbeam/Corbridge 2006: 142). Selection in this context is defined as the process of gathering information to appropriately and successfully evaluate and decide who should be employed in a particular situation (cf. Pilbeam/Corbridge 2006: 143; Dowling/Festing/Engle 2008: 109). This definition and the aforementioned definition of recruitment highlight the important but often neglected difference between recruitment and selection. "Selection [...] pares down the number of applicants, [whereas] recruitment [...] make[s] this paring down possible by expanding the pool of firm-specific candidates from whom new employees will be selected" (cf. Orlitzky 2007: 273).

Recruitment process

In recalling the detailed definition of recruitment given above, it becomes obvious that the recruitment process is complex in nature. According to Breaugh and Starke (2000), this process can be split into five stages[21] (see *Fig. 4*).

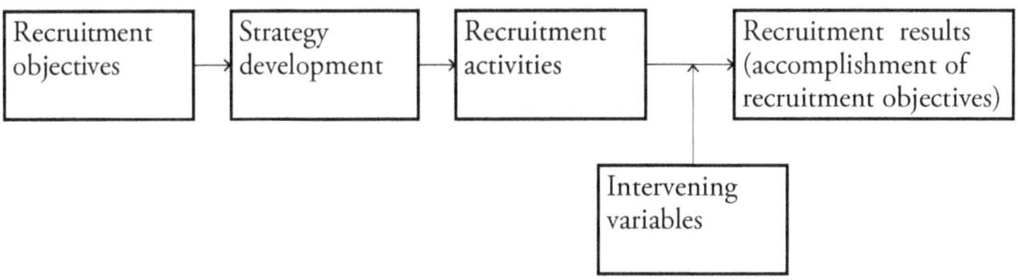

Fig. 4: Five stages of the recruitment process (cf. Breaugh/Starke 2000: 408)

21 Breaugh and Starke (2000: 406) indicate that not all employers progress sequentially through the stages of the recruitment process. The proposed sequence of stages within this chapter represents an idealised scheme. However, this simplification of reality is necessary in order to understand the fundamental principles of the recruitment process. Further, regardless of some stages of the recruitment process, the process itself often requires adapting to certain changes within the recruiting environment. For instance, realising that advertisements in local newspapers do not result in the attraction of targeted candidates will force a company to explore other channels of recruitment, thus partially changing or adapting its recruitment strategy. Another important factor within the recruitment process is time. The recruitment process stretches over a certain period, beginning with the announcement of the job opening and ending with the acceptance of the job offer by the preferred candidate. Naturally, the recruitment objectives and activities may change during the course of the recruitment process.

The first stage consists of the determination of the recruitment objectives (cf. Breaugh/Starke 2000: 409). These provide a basis for the development of the recruitment strategy, which in turn serves as a foundation to decide on certain recruitment activities (cf. Breaugh/Macan/Grambow 2008: 45). Obviously, the major objective of recruitment is the identification and attraction of potential job candidates (cf. Barber 1998: 10). Organisations are interested in attracting a certain quantity of potential employees with certain characteristics, knowledge, and skills. More detailed recruitment objectives than the mere attraction of potential candidates are necessary to secure a certain standard for the next stages of the recruitment process and the actual selection of appropriate potential employees. There is a multitude of recruitment objectives, which can be classified in terms of aspirational recruitment outcomes – pre-hire, post-hire, and post-hiring outcomes (cf. Breaugh/Starke 2000: 409). For instance, the quantity and quality of applicants are typical pre-hire outcomes, whereas job satisfaction of new employees and their initial job performances represent post-hire outcomes (cf. Breaugh/Starke 2000: 409). Post-hiring outcomes can be measured the day the employee starts working, e.g. recruitment costs and time needed to fill the job (cf. Breaugh/Starke 2000: 409).

Once the recruitment objectives have been defined, the recruitment strategy can be derived (cf. Breaugh/Macan/Grambow 2008: 46). In this respect, several questions have to be answered as a basis for formulating and elaborating on a sound recruitment strategy (cf. Orlitzky 2007: 274; Breaugh/Macan/Grambow 2008: 48 f.). The most important question to be answered is "who should be recruited" (cf. Breaugh/Macan/Grambow 2008: 48). Once the profile of individuals that an organisation wants to target has been defined, further questions can be addressed, e.g. (cf. Breaugh/Macan/Grambow 2008: 48):

- Where to recruit? (e.g. on campus);
- When to recruit? (e.g. immediately, at the end of the next term);
- What recruitment sources should be used? (e.g. Internet job boards, employee referrals);
- What message should be communicated? (e.g. job characteristics, organisational characteristics);
- Who should carry out the recruitment process? (e.g. headhunter, HR team).

Besides determining an answer to these questions, budget limitations also have to be taken into account when developing the recruitment strategy (cf. Breaugh/Macan/Grambow 2008: 48).

The development of the recruitment strategy allows an organisation to launch particular recruitment activities (cf. Breaugh/Starke 2000: 409). These recruitment activities are determined within the strategy development phase and they may include the recruitment sources, message to be conveyed, and recruiters (cf. Breaugh/Starke 2000: 412 ff.). Combining and accomplishing these recruitment activities leads, at best, to the attraction of targeted individuals and, in combination with selection, to the actual job choice of the preferred candidates and thus the achievement of the desired pre-hire and post-hire outcomes.

Certain variables influence the relationship between recruitment activities and recruitment results. To capture this relationship Breaugh and Starke (cf. 2000: 409 ff.) created the class of intervening variables, which explain the relationship between recruitment activities and outcomes. For example, perceived[22] organisational and job attractiveness can influence the success of recruitment activities. Both recruitment activities and intervening variables play a crucial part in the recruitment process by determining its success.

According to Barber (1998: 12 f.), the recruitment process can be divided into three time-selected phases (see *Fig. 5*). Describing the recruitment process using these phases helps examine the motivations and goals of both applicants and organisations over the course of the recruitment process (cf. Ma/Allen 2009: 335). These three phases serve to meet different recruitment objectives. Therefore, the recruitment methods and conveyed information differ during the course of the recruitment process. The classification of potential employees as they move through the recruitment process – applicant population, applicant pool, and selectees – serves as a basis for the characterisation of these phases (cf. Barber 1998: 12 f.). Moving from one category to another indicates the onset of a new recruitment phase (cf. Barber 1998: 13).

22 Perceptions may vary because of the different cultural backgrounds of potential employees.

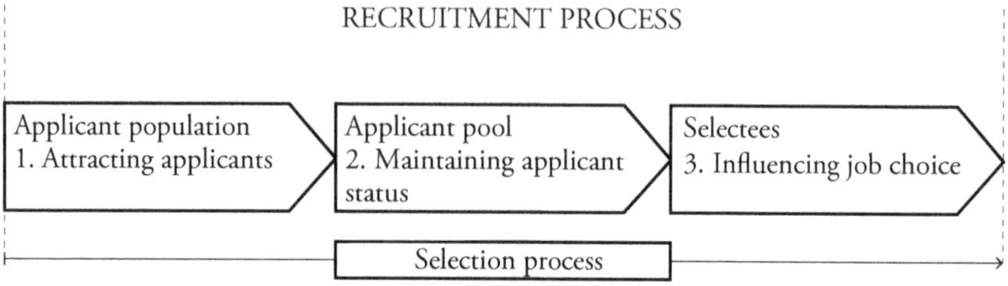

Fig. 5: Phases of the recruitment process and the classification of potential employees as they move through this process (based on Barber 1998: 12 f.)

In the first phase – attracting applicants – the employer intends to attract a sufficient number of job candidates to be able to choose from a sufficient pool. The employer defines which individuals should be targeted and which should thereby constitute the applicant population. After being attracted to the organisation, some individuals will decide to apply for the job, thereby becoming members of the applicant pool (cf. Barber 1998: 13). The second phase – maintaining applicant status – consists of attempts to maintain the interests of the potential candidates within the applicant pool, e.g. by gaining a more in-depth knowledge of the company (cf. Barber 1998: 13; Ma/Allen 2009: 340). As previously indicated, the selection and recruitment processes progress simultaneously. When candidates from the applicant pool have been offered a particular job, they become selectees (cf. Barber 1998: 13). In the third phase – influencing job choice – the main goal is the actual job choice by these selectees (cf. Barber 1998: 13; Ma/Allen 2009: 341), meaning that the company reaps the fruits of its employer branding activities, thereby confirming its employer of choice (EOC) status.

Recruitment activities, as already described, as well as intervening variables represent factors that influence the outcomes of the recruitment process. Several researchers have studied these influences (cf. Chapman *et al.* 2005; Carless/Imber 2007; Breaugh 2008; Schreurs *et al.* 2009). A variety of factors has been examined within these studies and some of the most prevalent factors will be discussed briefly within the course of this chapter. Owing to the high numbers of factors studied, this brief overview does not intend to be complete. Rather, it focuses on the factors that an organisation can influence in order to successfully recruit Gen Y individuals.

Job and organisational attributes – instrumental vs. symbolic

Applicants' initial impressions of an organisation as a potential employer highly affect their decisions during the whole recruitment process – from the first attraction to the actual job choice (cf. Barber 1998: 12 ff.; Carless/Imber 2007: 328). Studies indicate that organisational attraction is influenced by applicants' perceptions of the job and the organisational characteristics (cf. Carless/Imber 2007: 328). Collins and Stevens (2002: 1125 ff.) suggest that recruitment activities are indirectly related to intentions and decisions through two dimensions of EB image: general attitudes towards the company and perceived job attributes. Job characteristics (attributes) are those specific to the job, e.g. salary, fringe benefits, and type of work, whereas organisational characteristics refer to the characteristics reflecting the organisation as a whole, e.g. organisational image, size, and work environment (cf. Chapman *et al.* 2005: 929). Job and organisational characteristics are referred to as instrumental attributes describing the job or organisation in terms of objective, concrete, and factual attributes (cf. Lievens/Highhouse 2003: 80). These instrumental attributes trigger the individual's interest by connecting a particular utility to the acceptance of a certain job (cf. Lievens/Highhouse 2003: 80). Several studies have investigated which job and organisational characteristics are rated as most important. For instance, Boswell *et al.* (2003: 28) stated that company culture, advancement opportunities, nature of work, provided training, work/life balance, and benefits and compensation are of importance among graduate students. This study gives the first hint of the EB attributes to consider when planning recruitment activities for Gen Y individuals.

When considering organisational attraction as a result of certain job and organisational characteristics, another concept is of great importance – perceived person–job (PJ) and person–organisation (PO) fit. This concept explains the attraction of individuals to organisations based on the person–environment fit theory (cf. Carless 2005: 441). With regard to recruitment and selection, PJ fit describes the perceived match between an individual and the requirements of a particular job, whereas PO fit refers to the perceived match between an individual and the broader organisational characteristics (cf. Carless 2005: 411 f.). Individuals interpret job and organisational characteristics in light of their own needs and values and thus subjectively determine the degree of fit (cf. Chapman *et al.* 2005: 929). A study performed by Carless (2005) demonstrates that during the course of the recruitment and selection process, perceived PJ and PO fit significantly predict the extent to which an organisation and the associated job are perceived as beneficial and attractive. By contrast, the intention to actually accept a job offer is primarily related to PJ fit (cf. Carless 2005: 422). This change in focus is induced by the progress of time and by the undergone steps during the recruitment process, as indicated by Barber (1998: 13 f.). A meta-analytic review by Chapman *et al.* (2005: 938) shows that these described perceptions of fit are one of the strongest influences on organisational attraction. The authors, however, argue that even though perceptions of fit result in increased organisational attraction, influencing perceived fit is considerably more complex and resource-intensive (i.e. time-consuming and cost-intensive) than attracting candidates based on broader job and organisational characteristics. Therefore, the option to maximise perceived fit may be reserved for the staffing of certain key positions (cf. Chapman *et al.* 2005: 938).

Along with instrumental attributes, other researchers claim that symbolic attributes also influence organisational attraction (cf. Lievens/Highhouse 2003; Schreurs *et al.* 2009). Similar to brand personality in the marketing literature, individuals ascribe symbolic meanings in terms of personality traits to organisations, e.g. an organisation is perceived as being innovative and exciting (cf. Schreurs *et al.* 2009: 35 f.; Slaughter/Greguras 2009: 1). Again, the PO fit theory plays a crucial role here. Schreurs *et al.* (2009: 37) argue that the perceived match between the ascribed traits and an individual's personality significantly influences organisational attraction. Several studies have demonstrated this relationship (cf. Lievens/Highhouse 2003; Schreurs *et al.* 2009; Slaughter/Greguras 2009). Therefore, it is necessary to consider perceived organisational personalities in addition to instrumental attributes when planning the recruitment process (cf. Slaughter/Greguras 2009: 13). Lievens and Highhouse (2003: 76) even argue that especially in the initial stages of the recruitment process, where the individual does not possess much information about the job and the organisation, his/her perceived organisational personality can play a crucial role in differentiating an organisation from its competitors in the labour market.

The perceptions of instrumental as well as symbolic job and organisational attributes differ fundamentally across individuals, explaining why different individuals are attracted to different organisations (cf. Schreurs *et al.* 2009: 42). In order to attract favoured individuals, organisations have to be aware of these complex relationships. The initial attraction of individuals to an organisation with the help of instrumental as well as symbolic attributes can be achieved through elaborate employer branding.

Recruitment practices – sources, recruiters, realistic job previews (RJPs), and perceptions of the process

Other factors that have been emphasised as influencing the outcomes of recruitment are recruitment sources, the recruiter, RJPs, and the perceptions of the recruitment process. The following part of this chapter will cover these aspects briefly.

Recruitment sources refer to the ways of making targeted individuals aware of job openings (cf. Breaugh/Macan/Grambow 2008: 57). According to Wanous (1992), the multitude of recruitment sources can be divided into three distinctive groups (see also Moser 2005: 189):

- Internal recruitment sources (e.g. referrals, rehires, internships, and in-house notices);
- External recruitment sources (e.g. job advertisements, employment agencies, job fairs, and Internet job boards); and
- Walk-ins (e.g. direct applications).

Considerable attention has been attached to studying the effectiveness of various recruitment sources since they affect pre- and post-hire outcomes (cf. Moser 2005: 188; Breaugh 2008: 108). Electronic and Internet-based recruitment sources such as employer websites and professional social communities have gained particular importance recently (cf. Breaugh/Macan/Grambow 2008). Most studies focus on measuring their impact on post-hire outcomes, e.g. job satisfaction/performance and commitment, rather than studying the effects on pre-hire outcomes such as the number of qualified applicants (cf. Breaugh/Macan/Grambow 2008: 58).

There are two theoretical explanations why different recruitment sources lead to different recruitment outcomes – the realistic information hypothesis and individual difference hypothesis (cf. Breaugh/Starke 2000: 412).

The realistic information hypothesis states that individuals attracted by certain recruitment sources possess a more accurate understanding of the requirements of the job and organisation (cf. Zottoli/Wanous 2000: 368 f.; Breaugh 2008: 108). For instance, new employees recruited with the help of internal recruitment sources tend to have more realistic information about the job and organisation (cf. Moser 2005: 195). More accurate information enables an individual to make more precise and realistic decisions about whether to accept a job and, therefore, in the long run yields better post-hire outcomes (cf. Breaugh/Starke 2000: 412). The individual difference hypothesis suggests that different recruitment sources address different types of potential applicants and this in turn leads to different recruitment outcomes (cf. Zottoli/Wanous 2000: 370 f.; Breaugh 2008: 10)[23]. Research has shown that employee referrals and direct applications to an organisation result in better employees than those employees recruited with the help of other sources (cf. Breaugh/Macan/Grambow 2008: 57). Breaugh and Starke (2000: 413) also set an example based on Ullman (1996), stating that individuals recruited with the help of employee referrals may be more capable than the ones recruited with the help of advertisements.

A different aspect referred to in research concerns the outcome effects due to differences in recruiters' behaviour, demographics, and functions (cf. Breaugh/Macan/Grambow 2008: 67 f.). It is assumed that the applicant's perception of the recruiter influences the individual's attraction to the employer (cf. Chapman *et al.* 2005: 929). Even though research in this area has decreased recently based on the assumption that recruiter effects are weaker than the effects of organisational and job characteristics, one should not neglect the question as a whole (cf. Rynes/Bretz/Gehart 1991: 20). Breaugh, Macan and Grambow (2008: 68) provide three reasons why recruiters may influence the outcomes of the recruitment process. First, some recruiters possess more knowledge about the job than others do. Hence, they are able to provide the applicant with better information. Second, some recruiters are perceived to be more trustworthy and, therefore, the information provided by them is perceived as more credible as well. Both aspects are in line with the realistic information

23 Breaugh, Macan and Grambow (2008: 58) criticise this approach, since pre-hire outcomes are often of major importance to employers.

hypothesis – enhanced information leading to better recruitment outcomes. Third, the influence of recruiters depends on the extent to which they are perceived to be representatives of the company, indicating what it would be like to work for the company (cf. Rynes/Bretz/Gehart 1991: 20 f.). Recruiter training, experience, or function have been found to play no measurable role in the recruitment process (cf. Breaugh 2008: 111). The study conducted by Boswell *et al.* (2003: 30) indicates that poor interviewer (recruiter) behaviour and attitude have a significant negative impact on Gen Y's perceptions of organisational attractiveness.

A further aspect that has been emphasised is RJPs, which provide potential employees with both positive and negative information about a particular job (cf. Werner/DeSimone 2009: 259). These previews are based on the assumption that most applicants have incorrect perceptions of the job and organisation they apply for (cf. Breaugh 2008: 106). If the individuals are then hired, these incorrect perceptions lead to dissatisfaction and an increased probability of quitting (cf. Breaugh/Starke 2000: 415 f.). With the adjustment of perception prior to the actual hiring, RJPs foster a kind of self-selection (cf. Werner/DeSimone 2009: 259). Furthermore, RJPs result in role clarity and the perception of the organisation being honest (cf. Breaugh/Starke 2000: 415). RJPs can be delivered by a variety of media, e.g. printed information materials, presentations, discussions, and interviews (cf. Werner/DeSimone 2009: 261). It is assumed that RJPs communicated via face-to-face contact attract more attention, are more understandable, and are more credible (cf. Breaugh/Starke 2000: 416 f.) The content of RJPs seems to be essential as well. In particular, the extent of negative information included in them is crucial to their success (cf. Werner/DeSimone 2009: 262). For instance, some individuals place a more negative weight on the information provided by organisations and this leads to less organisational attraction (cf. Bretz/Judge 1998: 336). In general, research shows that RJPs reduce incorrect information and have a beneficial effect on turnover, satisfaction, and commitment (cf. Werner/DeSimone 2009: 263).

The final important factor to recruitment and its outcomes to be discussed is the general treatment during the recruitment process. Again, treatment during the recruitment process has a signalling effect. It can indicate to candidates how they would be treated later on if they were to work for the organisation (cf. Rynes/Bretz/Gehart 1991: 20 f.). Therefore, organisations have to keep this signalling aspect in mind when structuring their recruitment processes or instructing the employees in charge of recruitment. The already mentioned study by Boswell at al. (2003: 29 f.) indicates that opportunities to meet with multiple people, site visit arrangements, and a follow-up by the company positively influence actual job choice if properly handled, whereas problems with the site visit, no follow-up, and slow getting back and other delays negatively influence the attitudes of Gen Yers towards the organisation. One factor worth mentioning in this context are time delays, which have a strong signalling effect (cf. Rynes/Bretz/Gehart 1991: 23 f.). Some individuals may perceive delays as an inference about themselves and, accordingly, about their chances of getting the job. Other individuals may interpret delays as a sign of poor organisational quality.

To sum up, the importance of employees is emphasised within the corporate brand literature (Balmer/Gray 2003; Harris/de Chernatony 2001; Wilson 2001). Hart and Murphy (1998: 30 ff.) and Ind (1998: 325) state that strong corporate brands are able to recruit the best talent. However, to develop a strong corporate and employer brand the brand's identity needs to be understood by stakeholders, and each stakeholder's perspective of these expectations needs to be measured (cf. Balmer 1998: 970).

> As Gen Y enters the workforce, […] industries have to better understand their needs in order to effectively address human resource management issues. […] This emerging demographic segment will dominate the job market and provide service industries with new challenges to consider as they enter the workforce (Josiam *et al.* 2009: 5 ff.).

Consistently attracting new graduates of different nationalities and meeting their employment expectations may require new recruiting strategies and a long-term commitment (cf. Stevens-Huffman 2006: 42).

2.1.2 Current state of research on employer branding

One method to fight the lack of qualified personnel is to implement a thoroughly planned employer branding strategy (cf. Thom/Hubschmid 2011: 171). The main purpose of creating an employer branding strategy is to attract and recruit the right potentials[24]. Recruiting the right people requires ensuring that the company is attractive to the right people (cf. Mosley 2007: 130).

By providing a common platform for marketing and HR, managing employer reputation represents a significant evolution in the quest for corporate brand integrity (cf. Mosley 2007: 123). "The employer branding philosophy [..] requires the application of marketing principles, to the company's recruitment [...] strategy. [...] Employer branding uses aspects of corporate identity and reputation specifically to achieve the multiple objectives of human resource management" (Sutherland/Torricelli/Karg 2002: 13 f.). Employer branding is the internal as well as external positioning of an organisation as a credible and attractive employer (cf. DEBA 2007: online). "Employer branding and recruiting activities can be regarded as the central segments of a broader funnel that starts with general awareness of a company's characteristics and progresses to questions about recruiting and on-boarding new hires" (Strack *et al.* 2011: 21).

24 Previous research has focused on so-called high potentials, whereas other graduate potentials that most probably can perform well on the job were not viewed as an important target group. "High Potentials, as they have come to be referred to, are a massive asset [...]. It is crucial for companies world-wide to think about how to care for their High Potentials in proper ways" (Thom/Luethi 2006: n/a). According to Eggers and Ahlers (1999: 39), the notion high potentials describes the latent skills and achievement potential of students and graduates that will allow them to take up leadership positions in the future. Factors that can help identify high potential graduates include the following: good grades, internships, staying abroad, engagement outside the university, ability to work under pressure, multilingualism, and social competences (cf. Bauer 2003: 5 ff.). The following description of high potentials is common in the literature. Potential is "operationally defined as the ability to move up into specific managerial positions to which the corporation attaches value" (Derr/Jones/Toomey 1988: 275). High potentials tend to "attend and change roles faster than their peers"; "their careers are carefully monitored and managed by senior line executives, human resource professionals and management review committees"; they "are a small and elite group"; and "the company can count on their stamina and their willingness to make the necessary personal sacrifices to continue in their fast-paced career paths" (Derr/Jones/Toomey 1988: 275). This small group of people, according to the definition above, cannot cover the labour shortage forecasted for the years to come. Schamberger (2006: 79) argues that only 5% to 10% of graduates of the same age group can be characterised as high potentials. Since almost all organisations today want to recruit the same high potentials, the differentiation between high and normal potentials is blurred (cf. Schmidt 2007: 22). The relevant literature offers neither uniform definitions nor generally valid defining criteria. The Staufenbiel Institute (Cologne) characterises *high potentials simultaneously* as *right potentials*. Their profile: top junior employees with above average university degrees, fast completion of studies, qualified traineeships, professional experience and periods of working/studying abroad, fluent in at least two foreign languages, and convincing manner. "[...] Due to heterogeneous requirements on High Potentials depending on branch and position within the company, it appears sensible to refrain from a general definition. [...] each company should elaborate its own definition of the High Potential personality. [...] In order to speak of a High Potential, certain key parameters should arguably be fulfilled:

"Employer branding has gained favour as a management tool over the last decade" (Moroko/Uncles 2009: 181). Part of employer branding is building an image as an employer, whereas turning that image into a positive working relationship with potential employees is a process, which includes the *consideration of different employees' characteristics* (cf. IOMA's Human Resource Department Management Report 2004: 7). Herman and Gioia (2000: 3 ff.) argue that because knowledge workers determine what they want they will look for employers that offer the special and unique combination that suits their particular needs. Moroko and Uncles (2009: 181 ff.) allege that market segmentation[25] is crucial for the success of employer branding strategies, and that employer branding segmentation is a strategic lever of employer branding specialists. Market segmentation has been discussed in terms of final consumers, who differ from one another according to their geography, purchase and usage behaviour, decision-making processes, demographics, lifestyles, psychographics, personality, and motivation. Similar logic is applicable in the context of employer branding (cf. Moroko/Uncles 2009: 181). Branham (2000: 18) defines employer branding as "applying traditional marketing principles to achieving the status of Employer of Choice [...]. The process of placing an image of being a great place to work, in the mind of the targeted candidate pool".

higher education (university, college, or higher special education), very strong motivation and pleasure in challenging tasks, socially competent manners with colleagues and superiors, constant urge for personal and professional development" (Thom/Moser 2006: 597 f.). Dries and Pepermans (2008: 85 ff.) also note that the differentiation between high potentials and other groups of employees is not always clear. They indicate that the further clarification of terms across nations and economic environments is needed. Thus, focusing on the right potentials as suggested by Schmidt (2007: 22) represents a more viable approach. Smith and Krüger (2005: 25) support this statement, asserting that the question of how to attract graduates with the right potential will be a key issue of future human capital marketing and recruitment strategies. Therefore, throughout this thesis, the author refers to the *right* instead of *high potentials* since the definition of high potentials is industry- and company-dependent. Each organisation defines and strives to recruit high potentials according to its specific needs. Further, the author uses the notion *potentials,* since the target group of the research is represented by university graduates, i.e. potential employees who have not yet been assessed with regard to their job performances.

25 According to Kotler (2000: 85 ff.), there are three phases in the classical marketing process: the segmentation of the market, the selection of the appropriate target market, and the development of the offer's value positioning to appeal to that target market. The development of the offer's value positioning means integrating the initial employment expectations of the target group into the organisation's branding strategy and shaping the strategic recruitment marketing function with the specific focus on Gen Y university graduates.

Acquiring value-adding employees makes firms work harder on their own positioning and promotion as desirable employers for potential co-workers (cf. Moroko/Uncles 2009: 182). A job must attract and motivate employees to apply, thereby satisfying their needs and wants as those of internal customers, while addressing the overall objectives of the organisation (cf. Berry/Parasuraman 1991: 27 ff.). Thus, employer branding seems to be more complex than product or service branding since the management of *stakeholder perceptions* requires a longer-term and a more holistic approach (cf. Sutherland/Torricelli/Karg 2002: 14).

The concept of employer branding[26] is a three-step process (cf. Backhaus/Tikoo 2004: 502). First, an organisation has to develop an EVP, i.e. an unambiguous package of benefits offered by a company to its current and potential employees (cf. Moroko/Uncles 2008: 164). This EVP is related to the unique selling proposition (USP) concept in marketing and constitutes the core of an EB. It contains everything a person experiences and obtains while he/she works for the company. It answers the question of why a motivated and well-qualified candidate should prefer a certain employer over another (cf. Michaels/Handfield-Jones/Axelrod 2001: 44). Following the creation of an EVP, the organisation needs to market and communicate its value proposition to the targeted potential employees in order to attract them (cf. Backhaus/Tikoo 2004: 502). As previously indicated, the aim of employer branding is to position the company as a great place to work. Very successful employer branding can even lead to the establishment of being an EOC. EOCs are not only great places to work, they "outperform their competition to attract, develop, and retain people

26 A recent study by Hewitt Associates "Arbeitgeber Attraktivität – Employer Branding und Talent Supply 2010" (Employer Attractiveness – Employer Branding and Talent Supply 2010) emphasises the relevance of employer branding. A total of 76 medium-sized and large organisations predominantly from Germany and Austria were surveyed. The majority of organisations appreciated the advantages created by a successful EB, for instance increased employee retention as well as faster staffing. Further-more, the study found that the majority of organisations believed that the scarcity of appropriate employees is a function of general labour shortages as well as of the lack of awareness/attraction level of the organisation and insufficient differentiation from the competition. These issues could be solved, as already mentioned, by appropriate and thorough employer branding. Although organisations invest into their employer branding, they are not tapping its full potential to solve the aforementioned problems in attracting and selecting employees with the right potential and thus creating a sustainable competitive advantage (cf. Hewitt Associates 2010: online).

with business-required talent" (Sutherland *et al.* 2002: 14). An EOC is defined as "an organisation which top talent aspires to work for as a result of its reputation and employer brand message, both of which are tailored to appeal to the target audience" (Sutherland/Torricelli/Karg 2002: 14). This external marketing of the EB is also carried out to support the product and corporate brands (cf. Backhaus/Tikoo 2004: 502). Parallel to the external marketing of the EB, internal marketing has to take place as well, which enhances the commitment of the workforce to the organisation as such and the values and goals established by it. This enhanced commitment generates a workforce that is hard to imitate (cf. Backhaus/Tikoo 2004: 503).

2.1.2.1 Employer brand

A brand name is "essentially a seller's promise to deliver a specific set of features, benefits, and services consistently to the buyers" (Kotler 2000: 404). It needs to deal with the requirements of employees as stakeholders. The first recorded paper on the EB concept, originated by Simon Barrow and researched in partnership with Tim Ambler of the London Business School, was published in the *Journal of Brand Management* in 1996 (cf. Ambler/Barrow 1996: 185 ff.; Mosley 2007: 123). As first defined by Ambler and Barrow (1996: 186), the *EB concept* includes "the package of functional, economic and psychological benefits provided by employment and identifies with employing company", with the primary role of the EB being "to provide a coherent framework for management to simplify and focus priorities, increase productivity and improve recruitment, retention and commitment" (Ambler/Barrow 1996: 186).

By establishing a unique EB, a company defines its identity as an employer, delivers promises to current and potential employees, and differentiates itself from its competitors (cf. Backhaus/Tikoo 2004: 502; Trost 2009: 16). Hence, the overall goal of an EB is to attract, motivate, and retain the company's current and potential employees that match the company's beliefs and job requirements (cf. Backhaus/Tikoo 2004: 502). A strong EB thus helps differentiate a company within a more and more competitive environment from an employee perspective (cf. Hunt/Landry n/a.: 35)[27]. Compared with employer image, the EB follows a strategic alignment with the objectives to influence and shape the image in a certain way among the target group (cf. Trost 2009: 16). Taking into consideration the growing competition between companies for the most talented employees, a decisive part for the company's success as an employer is the better fulfilment of the most important demands of candidates than its competitors. If an employer reaches this goal, competitive advantage can be secured (cf. Simon *et al.* 1995: 16, see *Fig. 6*).

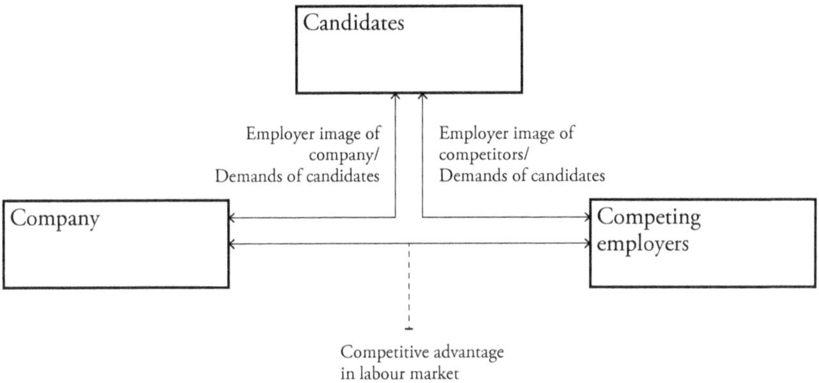

Fig. 6: Strategic triangle of HR marketing (cf. Simon *et al.* 1995: 16)

Further, the EB pursues the goal of increasing society's awareness of the company as an attractive employer (cf. Trost 2009: 16). Or as Backhaus and Tikoo (2004: 502) state, "the employer brand establishes the identity of the firm as an employer. It encompasses the firm's value system, policies and behaviours towards the objectives of attracting, motivating, and retaining the firm's current and potential employees".

27 When speaking of an EB, it is important to point out the difference to the image as an employer. Employer image equals the uniform perception of a company as an employer in society. It is grown historically through bulletins in various media, events, achievements, products, and direct experiences. Further, it is necessary to differentiate between employer image and company image. Company image significantly exceeds employer image. It is defined as the way a company as a whole is perceived in society compared with the employer image, which represents the perception of the company within potential, current, and previous employees and therefore can be seen as a part of company image (cf. Trost 2009: 16).

To become an attractive employer in the eyes of graduates, an organisation should build and sustain an EVP that is compelling and different according to the expectations of Gen Y (cf. Sherry 2000: 66). Employer branding, therefore, is concerned with building an image in the minds of the potential labour market of university graduates that the company is a place to work where the expectations of employees as the first customers of the company are met. Therefore, a company needs to provide a strong EVP, a compelling answer to the question "Why should a talented, well-qualified, and motivated person prefer this company over all others as an employer?" (cf. Michaels/Handfield-Jones/Axelrod 2001: 44). The EVP builds the core of the EB and sends out promises to current as well as potential employees (cf. Trost 2009: 16). According to Michaels, Handfield-Jones and Axelrod (2001: 43), the EVP is "the holistic sum of everything people experience and receive while they are part of a company – everything from the intrinsic satisfaction of the work to the environment, leadership, colleagues, compensation and more". When defining the EVP, a company has to think of where compared with its competitors it is superior and where inferior. In other words, companies need to think strategically about their current and potential employees (cf. Michaels/Handfield-Jones/Axelrod 2001: 44).

The EVP needs to clarify what prospective employees can expect from the organisation in terms of rational and emotional benefits. The definition of an EVP and implementation of an employer branding strategy follows a closed cycle. The starting point is the segmentation and definition of critical target groups, which afterwards are thoroughly analysed (cf. Hubschmid 2011). In particular, current employer image, preferences of the target groups, employer characteristics, and the facing competition are examined (cf. Homburg/Kuester/Krohmer 2009: 3 f.). The results give the company hints of what makes it distinctive from others and how to best define its EVP. Defining the EVP is crucial since it marks out the core of an employer branding strategy. Following that, implementation – compiling communication material and establishing rules and processes to induce the employer branding campaign – takes place (cf. Trost 2009: 18).

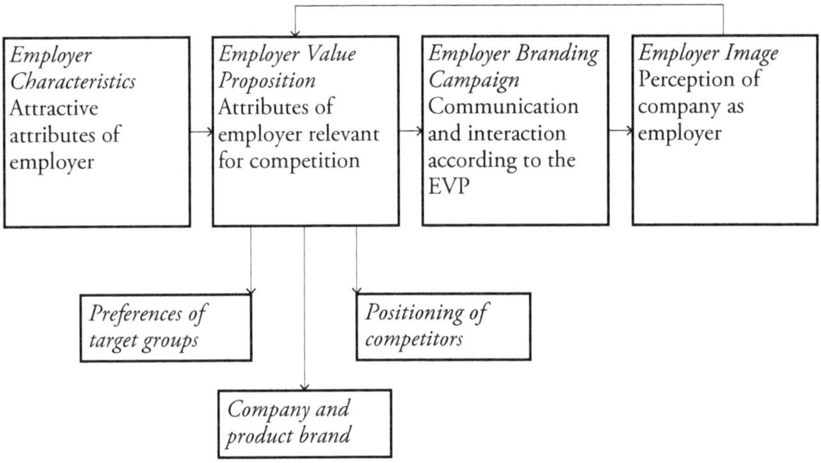

Fig. 7: Relationship between employer characteristics, EVP, and employer image (cf. Trost 2009: 19)

Fig. 7 shows the relationship between employer characteristics, EVP, and employer image and points out that the definition of the EVP is influenced by the following factors: employer characteristics, preferences of the target groups, company's brand strategy, positioning of competitors, and current employer image (cf. Trost 2009: 18 f.).

The function of a brand depends on the beholder's perspective and varies accordingly (cf. Homburg/Kuester/Krohmer 2009: 68 ff.). In terms of employer branding, the function can be evaluated either from an employer's or from an employee's perspective (cf. Petkovic 2008: 59 f.). The difference between the two is highlighted further.

Perspective of an employer

One of the primary functions of the EB from an employer's perspective is setting up preferences in terms of the particular target groups (cf. Esch 2003: 10). The objective is to reach the status of being the EOC (cf. Andratschke/Regier/Huber 2009: 13). In other words, this means that when university graduates as jobseekers decide on which company to apply to, the company is "top of mind" and first choice (cf. Petkovic 2008: 61). The preference function can also be applied to the current employees of a company. In this sense, preference represents the confirmation of a prior decision concerning the EOC. It can be viewed as the degree of success in employee retention and/or satisfaction and loyalty to the employer (cf. Petkovic 2008: 61). It is obvious that with increasing loyalty, the fluctuation rate decreases and recruitment costs for attracting new personnel go down (cf. Andratschke/Regier/Huber 2009: 14; Petkovic 2008: 61).

Another important function of a brand is differentiation from competitors. In the sense of employer branding, a company wants to differentiate itself to the extent of being perceived as the EOC (cf. Andratschke/Regier/Huber 2009: 14). If the services (or products) offered by a company are not distinguishable from others on the market, the differentiation function of an EB becomes crucial (cf. Esch 2003: 155). Through the EB, a company has the chance to express its individuality as an employer that is only observable from an internal point of view. As a consequence, a company is able to reach a unique positioning in the labour market (cf. Andratschke/Regier/Huber 2009: 14; cf. Petkovic 2008: 62 f.).

A further function of employer branding lies in establishing emotionality with the goal to rouse sympathy in the eyes of attractive candidates for the company as an employer (cf. Petkovic 2008: 63). A positive and emotionally charged EB raises the consideration of the company as an employer and increases current as well as potential employees' satisfaction levels (cf. Koppelmann 2001: 43).

These three functions explained are tightly interconnected. Through the adaption of an EB that enhances "preference", "differentiation", and "emotionality", a company is likely to reach the two main goals of employer branding. First, a company is able to rouse the attention of its target group and consequently recruit new employees. Second, a company is able to augment the retention of current employees and therefore secure its human capital in the long run (cf. Andratschke/Regier/Huber 2009: 15 f.).

Perspective of an employee

By contrast, brands fulfil the purpose of an orientation anchor within a complex, information-overloaded world. They help customers reduce complexity and speed up their searches and decision-making processes (cf. Andratschke/Regier/Huber 2009: 16). In terms of a company as an employer, a candidate has difficulties finding information in advance because of a lack of transparency (cf. Kroeber-Riel/Weinberg 2003: 248 ff.). In the early stages of an application process, candidates only have limited knowledge of the specific working conditions. Therefore, a candidate turns to the company's EB as an orientation and rationalisation anchor (cf. Simon *et al.* 1995: 56 f.). In addition, an EB should generate trust in the company. As already mentioned, candidates are lacking information and experience about the company as an employer. In this condition of uncertainty, the EB reduces the risk and builds trust (cf. Petkovic 2008: 65).

The choice of and loyalty to an employer does not solely depend on certain company or workplace criteria. Subjective emotional feelings also have a great impact on choice and loyalty (cf. Petkovic 2008: 65). Candidates identify themselves with a company the more its communicated values equal the candidates' ones (cf. Stuart 2001: 49). The better the match between employer and employee values, the greater are the benefits on both sides (cf. Petkovic 2008: 66). The costs and time intensity of the recruitment process can be significantly reduced when these values are communicated through the right channels. Additionally, the satisfaction of potential employees increases because they know what to expect from the employer (cf. Andratschke/Regier/Huber 2009: 18 f.).

2.1.2.2 Employer attractiveness and employment expectations

Employer branding, therefore, can only be carried out effectively once organisations understand the factors contributing towards *employer attractiveness.* These factors include the *initial employment expectations*[28] *of potential employees towards an employer.*

28 Employment expectation is a relational phenomenon that is emergent and influenced largely by graduates' "lived experiences" (cf. Tomlinson 2007: 287). Individuals' experiences of work are subjective, and this is likely to influence their actual perceptions of an employer and shape further their propensities for employment. Expectation in this sense may be seen to be value- and identity-driven, relating to graduates' own dispositions, biographies, and cultural backgrounds (cf. Tomlinson 2007: 287). The term *employment expectation* has been chosen instead of work or job expectation because in the sociological and psychological literature there has been an inconsistent use of the terms *job* and *work* and this has complicated the understanding of both constructs. These concepts differ significantly in their scope. Job is considered to be more of a component of a specific occupational experience, whereas work is viewed as a general and complex concept that involves the consideration of specific intrinsic and extrinsic components, such as involvement and motivation (cf. Blood 1969; Dubin 1956; Lodahl/Kejner 1965; Wollack *et al.* 1971). Employment expectation is a multidimensional construct that has to be segmented into several composite categories of consideration. The process of clarifying the components of employment expectation is necessary because of the common misuse of variables (cf. Josiam 2009: 8).

The concept of employee attractiveness has been broadly discussed in the areas of vocational behaviour (cf. Soutar/Clarke 1983: 12 ff.), management (cf. Lievens/Highhouse 2003: 75 ff.), applied psychology (cf. Jurgensen 1978: 267 ff.; Collins/Stevens 2002: 1121 ff.), communication (Bergstrom/Blumenthal/Crothers 2002: 133 ff.), and marketing (cf. Ambler/Barrow 1996: 185 ff.; Gilly/Wolfinbarger 1998: 69 ff.; Ewing *et al.* 2002: 3 ff.). Berthon, Ewing and Hah (2005: 156) define employer attractiveness as

> the envisioned benefits that a potential employee sees in working for a specific organisation. […] The construct may be thought of as an antecedent of the more general concept of employer brand equity. In other words, the more attractive an employer is perceived to be by potential employees, the stronger that particular organisation's employer brand equity (Berthon/Ewing/Hah 2005: 156).

According to Beechler and Woodward (2009: 277), "'employee consumerism' is rising, especially for those with in-demand skills and experience". Thus, as already mentioned in the thesis, the first step towards creating an attractive external reputation requires understanding what potential employees indeed value and whether different demographic groups making up the talent pool perceive job attributes differently (cf. Sutherland/Torricelli/Karg 2002: 15). It should always be kept in mind (while exploring the employment expectations of different groups of potential co-workers) that there will not only be differences based on factors such as age, sex, and educational background. There are also likely to be cross-national differences in employment expectations and, as a result, in the perception of employer attractiveness (cf. Thom/Hubschmid 2011a: 19). As Berthon, Ewing and Hah (2005: 169) put it, employer attractiveness "cannot easily be extended cross-nationally without further psychometric testing. Organisations need to understand the impact of different cultures and nationalities on the perceptions of potential employees with regard to their employer brand".

Franke (2000: 75 ff.) systematises scientific empirical surveys on employer attractiveness among university graduates that were conducted between 1980 and 1996[29] (cf. *Table 1*). In Switzerland, separate surveys provide information on the preferences of Swiss graduates in economics[30] (cf. Thom 2009: 187; Thom/Friedli 2008: 32 ff.).

29 Before Ambler and Barrow drove the attention of the scientific community to the term *employer brand* through their publication in 1996.

30 Work content rates first on the list of employment expectations.

AUTHORS	EMPIRICAL STUDY	RESEARCH QUESTION
Bergmann/Taylor (1984)	n=1286 college students in business and engineering, questionnaires, survey in one company; Frequency rows, no differentiation of target groups	What criteria are important for students in their decision to apply for a position in the company?
Simon (1984)	n=613 students in economics and business administration, questionnaires, survey in 20 companies; Preference measurement, differentiation of target groups according to few demographic criteria	Perceptions and preferences of the students regarding big corporations
Bokranz/Stein (1989)	n=27 firms, questionnaires; Utility value analysis and cluster analysis	How intensive do big corporations apply HR-marketing instruments in relation to students?
Von Rosenstiel/Nerdinger/ Spiess/Stengel (1989)	n=497/365/382/253 students in social sciences, interviews; Frequency rows, factor analysis, difference tests, detailed differentiation into sub-groups	How does the career entry of the students happen (selection), what happens after the entry (socialisation, career growth, leave)?
Boeckenholt/ Homburg (1990)	n=91, students in industrial engineering sciences, questionnaires, survey in 12 big corporations; LISREL, no differentiation of target groups	What kinds of perceptive organisational dimensions exist, how are they intertwined, and how do students perceive these big corporations?
Schwaab (1991)	n=364, students in banking management, questionnaires, survey in 9 banks, 109 bank officers; Frequency rows, correlation analysis, no differentiation of target groups	How attractive do students find big banks, and how do big banks assess their image among students?
Kolter (1991)	n=770 students in technical disciplines in Germany, Spain and Great Britain, questionnaires in 15 companies; Frequency rows, no differentiation of target groups	Qualities and plans of the students, perceptions and preferences regarding big companies
Moll (1992)	n=151 students in engineering, questionnaires; Frequency rows, no differentiation of target groups	How do students assess the suitability (appropriateness) of certain HR-marketing instruments?
Lieber (1995)	n=110 students in economics, questionnaires, survey in 15 companies; Frequency rows, factor analysis, difference tests, correlation analysis etc., differentiation of target groups according to few demographic criteria	What goals do students pursue when applying for a job, how attractive do they perceive companies, how strong is the influence of employer branding strategies?
Werbel/Landau (1996)	n=242 newly employed marketing personnel in a big company, differentiation according to various criteria; ANOVA	Which employees are more efficient on the job: the ones recruited through the university contacts or the ones recruited through employment advertisements?
Suess (1996)	n=293 students in economics, questionnaires, survey across 25 industries; Frequency rows, factor analysis, no differentiation of target groups	What employer image do certain industries have, what criteria are important for employer attractiveness, what should the unpopular industries do to improve their image?

Table 1: Selected scientific empirical surveys on employer attractiveness among university graduates (cited in Franke 2000: 75 ff.)

Table 1 shows that except for Simon (1984 and 1984a) and Lieber (1995), there has been no systematic segmentation (according to cultural criterion) of university graduates into target groups, which is a huge gap in the research designs of the majority of studies. Little attention has also been paid to the *comparative cultural paradigm* underlying student expectations with regard to first employers. If available, this kind of information could help organisations become more effective and efficient during the various stages of recruitment (cf. Hieronimus/Schaefer/Schröder 2005: 12).

Recently, different companies around the globe have carried out surveys among student with the goal of eliciting their expectations towards potential employers. Most employer attractiveness surveys that rank favourite employers by industry as well as surveys based on graduates' academic focuses, such as business, engineering, or science, are carried out on a regular basis. A number of studies (e.g. Accenture "Net Generation Survey", "European Student Barometer" (cf. Viel 2007: 5 ff.), Universum Graduate Survey, Universum Student Survey (cf. Gonzales 2008: 6 ff.), Top-100 Employers (e.g. Swiss 100), Russia's Ideal Employers, Best Employers, Favourite Employers (of MBA, engineering students, etc.), Survey of Leipzig Hochschule and E-Fellows.net, and Study of the Madrid Business School Instituto de Empressa among others) throughout different countries have attempted to identify student expectations related to their first EOCs. Nonetheless, the primary goal of these surveys has been to find out what company was rated as the favourite employer.

Through popular "best employer" annual surveys, organisations have the opportunity to approach the media and to disseminate brand-related messages to the public. These "best employer" surveys are widely distributed since they target thousands of employers and are carried out in almost every country in the world. The problem with these surveys is that despite the fact that they cover fairly exhaustive "best HR practices", and present results that receive top media and press attention, there is little relevance for a particular organisation as a participant. The sponsoring organisations usually define criteria that are used to judge and rate employers. The use of a tag "best employer" has been around for many years. One disadvantage of this approach over time is saturation, since many organisations position themselves as "best employers". The Swiss Employer Award, for example, is given on an annual basis. Both in Switzerland and Russia surveys that choose "the best companies to work for" are common. There even exists "The World's Most Attractive Employers" survey. In this respect, it seems that the "best employer" brand is losing its status to a certain degree and is no longer appealing and being perceived as one-of-a-kind; a lot of organisations are rated as "best employers" or "EOCs". The question arises of how much longer this "EOC tag" will be able to promote an organisation's strategy to build and sustain its image as well as distinguish itself from other organisations in order to attract the right young potentials (cf. Love/Singh 2011: 177 ff.)

At the same time, different consulting companies continue to conduct surveys that deliver insights into the importance of EB attributes among graduates. The "StepStone Employer Branding Report 2011", for instance, is based on the online survey that was carried out in April 2011 in eight European countries: Belgium, Denmark, Germany, France, the Netherlands, Norway, Austria, and Sweden. The goal of the survey (sample consisted of 6,800 candidates and 830 firms) was to find out the most important priorities in shaping the communication and positioning strategy of the EB. The results of the study support the majority of the findings on the importance of EB attributes such as a good reputation, work environment, performance-related bonus, secure employment, good possibilities for promotion, and career growth. In addition, authentic communication and relevant communication channels, an efficient EB public relations system, and internal EB initiatives should make up the focus of employer attractiveness (cf. Rottländer 2012: 53; StepStone 2011).

In the survey carried out by PricewaterhouseCoopers in 2011 among 2,894 graduates across 75 countries, respondents marked the top three benefits that they would most value from an employer as training and development, flexible working hours, and cash bonuses.

The Trendence Graduate Barometer 2011 gained responses from 96,431 business students. This survey looks at graduates' preferences and priorities when selecting a first employer after graduation and examines their strategies when looking for information about potential employers. Further, graduates were asked to select the employers they consider to be attractive first employers from a list of 120 companies (cf. Heyne 2011: 2).

The Trendence operating range included both Switzerland and Russia. Interestingly, job search optimism per country (overall 24 countries surveyed) equalled 83.2 for Russia (fourth place in Europe) and 78.7 for Switzerland (seventh place in Europe)[31].

In 2010, Johnson Controls (2010: 12) conducted a worldwide survey on generation Y's expectations towards the workplace. Furthermore, they provided detailed country reports. They showed that the most important factor influencing the job choices of German Gen Yers is salary closely followed by colleagues and meaningful work. These findings are particularly interesting since one of the most important factors in other participating countries was opportunities for learning (this was only sixth position in Germany) (cf. Johnson Controls 2010: 15). In reference to what triggers the productivity and creativity of Gen Y, the German sample did not show any differences compared with the worldwide sample: people, ambiance, atmosphere, and technology were regarded as most important (cf. Johnson Controls 2010: 15). These findings indicate that the prevalent characteristics of Gen Y in the German-speaking world are similar to the proclaimed characteristics in the American literature. Further, the German Gen Y desires to work flexible hours, although only a minority expects employers to react to this desire (cf. Wang 2010: online). A fixed and personal workplace (e.g. desk etc.) is also of high importance (cf. Johnson Controls 2010: 16).

Another survey conducted by Kienbaum Management Consultants (2010) supports the abovementioned findings. It showed that the factors most important to organisational attractiveness are challenging work, salary, and a cooperative working environment (cf. Kienbaum 2010: 6). Development and training as well as career advancement are also important factors. Interestingly, work/life balance is only ranked sixth, while even location is rated more important than work/life balance (cf. Kienbaum 2010: 7)[32].

31 The Trendence Optimism Index is an indicator of graduate confidence in relation to job prospects. It is calculated from two parameters, which are chosen on an annual basis as part of the evaluation of the job application process (in 2011 these were the number of anticipated applications and length of time it takes to get a job) (cf. Heyne 2011: 19).

32 In this study, managers were also asked how they perceive Gen Y in the workplace. It was frequently mentioned that Gen Yers are ambitious and motivated, want to learn, and demand advancement and support. Further, they are team-oriented and individualistic. Besides these mostly positive aspects, managers stated that they perceive this generation as having a sense of entitlement (cf. Kienbaum 2010: 11).

A study that surveyed generation Y's expectations in the whole German-speaking world (Switzerland, Germany, and Austria) was conducted by the DEGW (2008) and several scientific institutes. The results of this study are partially different compared with the aforementioned studies. They state that organisational attractiveness is no longer determined by a high salary, but by a cooperative working atmosphere and opportunities for development and advancement (cf. DEGW 2008: 19 f.). The study shows, furthermore, that this generation demands a fixed and personal workplace in a creative working environment. Moreover, the image of an organisation is important for Gen Y individuals (cf. DEGW 2008: 21 f.).

Mercer's latest *What's Working* survey 2011 gathered data from nearly 30,000 employees worldwide, and the results suggest that there is a change at a global level – at least among the youngest members of the workforce – in respect to cultural norms in the job search process. The research suggests that cultural norms no longer have a powerful influence on the views and attitudes of potential employees and have stopped being country-specific. The young age group of graduates from a specific country is more likely to think and act like their peers around the world. This emerging pattern is consistent across the elements that make up the total work experience, including engagement, benefits, retirement, pay, career, organisational leadership, teamwork, and work/life balance. The views of younger workers are most strongly aligned globally around issues related to careers, benefits, and leadership opportunities (cf. Mercer 2011: 7 f.).

2.2 Concept of generation Y

Concept of generation

The concept of generation refers to a widely used term in a variety of sciences and fields of reference (cf. Oertel 2007: 17 f.). Tremmel (2008: 149) even states that there is a so-called "definition mist". To handle the various and sometimes blurred definitions of generation, the sociological classification of three concepts of generation seems appropriate (cf. Hoepflinger 1999: 6).

The genealogical concept of generation refers to the succession of generations within a family (cf. Hoepflinger 1999: 6). This concept of generation can be directly derived from its etymological roots (cf. Tremmel 2008: 153). Generation originates from the Latin *generatio*, which refers to conception and fertility (cf. Tremmel 2008: 153). Hence, the smallest entity of a society – the family – is the focus of this concept (cf. Franz 2009: 24). Generational relationships within families are determined by social, cultural, and demographic changes. The demographic change that, for example, the western world faces today leads to a shifted ratio between grandchildren and grandparents (cf. Hoepflinger 1999: 6).

The pedagogic concept of generation refers to the transfer of norms, knowledge, and skills from one generation to another (cf. Hoepflinger 1999: 8). Only two generations are involved in this transmission process – the transferring and the learning generations (cf. Franz 2009: 25). This transfer of norms, knowledge, and skills is in most societies closely linked to age – the "older" generation teaches the younger generation the principles of life (cf. Hoepflinger 1999: 8). However, in the fast changing environment most of us encounter nowadays, the younger generation has to acquire knowledge and skills that are fundamentally different to those of the older generation (cf. Hoepflinger 1999: 8). Therefore, the age-related pedagogical relationship can change – the younger teaches the older generation (cf. Franz 2009: 25).

The third concept, *the historic-societal concept of generation*, traces back to the classical theory of Karl Mannheim (1963: 380 ff.). His understanding of generation implies that members of a generation are held together by having experienced the same historical events from the same perspectives and thereby developing a generational consciousness (cf. Edmunds/Turner 2005: 560). Thus, generations can be described as groups of individuals who are born roughly around the same time and experience similar external events, which constitute their values, attitudes, and preferences (cf. Hoepflinger 1999: 10; Oertel 2007: 18). The external events forming a generation can be referred to as "defining moments" (cf. Schewe/Meredith 2004: 51). The power of "defining moments" is most intense during adolescence and early adulthood (cf. Franz 2009: 25).

In the scientific literature, there is an ongoing debate about the synonymous use and definition of *cohort* and *generation*. Cohorts are defined as groups of individuals sharing specific characteristics that have experienced certain individual events (e.g. birth, adolescence) or societal/historical events (e.g. economic crisis, war) during the same period of time (cf. Schewe/Meredith 2004: 52). "A *generational cohort* is a society-wide peer group born over a period roughly the same length of time as passage from youth to adulthood (about 20 years), who collectively possesses a common persona" (Lindquist 2008: 56). This group is identified by three attributes: perceived membership of a common generation, common beliefs and behaviours, and a common location in history. A generational cohort is, therefore, a product of its times and tastes: music that is heard, heroes shared, passions agreed upon, channels used for communications, and defining moments experienced[33] (cf. Lindquist 2008: 56). It becomes obvious that the definition of *cohort* and the aforementioned *historic-societal concept of generation* are virtually identical. Therefore, the discussion about the synonymous use of cohort and generation shall not be examined and elaborated on, but the synonymous use will be adopted.

The interest of business scholars as well as practitioners in the concept of generation has grown only recently. Both marketing scholars and professionals have recognised its value as a possibility to segment customer markets (cf. Schewe/Meredith 2004: 52). In line with this approach, there exist generationally determined lifestyles, preferences, and buying behaviour and thus generations are an appropriate classification to apply targeted marketing activities to (cf. Kupperschmidt 2000; Chen/Choi 2008; Gursoy/Maier/Chi 2008). Parry and Urwin (2011: 80) continue by saying that each generation brings different changes to the cultural landscape, leaves a lasting impact, and defines its own cultural narrative.

Especially in the field of HRM, the concept of generation has become enormously important (cf. Parry/Urwin 2011: 79 f.), since practitioners and scholars have become aware of the fact that there are several different generations participating in today's working environment (cf. Rump/Eilers 2006: 15). *Fig. 8* represents these different generations for

33 Behrens (2009: 20) and Kalinina (2010: online) allege that Gen Yers both in Russia and in western countries have little if any memory of the Soviet Union and the Cold War.

the USA, Germany, and Russia[34]. This generational diversity within an organisation can have positive and negative impacts. On one hand, it may lead to creativity and enhanced problem solving because of the co-operation of individuals with different perspectives, ideas, and experiences (cf. Gursoy/Maier/Chi 2008: 449). On the other hand, there are several intergenerational problems caused by different values, attitudes, and behaviours, which may have a negative influence (cf. Wong *et al.* 2008: 878). In this context, e.g. leadership styles (cf. Arsenault 2004) as well as interaction and communication (cf. Myers/Sadaghiani 2010: 226 ff.) represent important issues.

	1950 – 2000				
USA	*	Baby Boomers (1946–1964)	Generation X (1965–1981)	Generation Y (1982–1999)	
GERMANY	**	Economic Miracle Generation (1946–1955)	Baby Boomers Generation (1946–1955)	Generation Golf (1966–1980)	Internet Generation (1981 and after)
RUSSIA	The Thaw (1937–1952)	Stagnation (1953–1968)	***	Post-Soviet (1991–after)	

* Silent Generation (1925–1945)
** Post-War Generation (1935–1945)
*** Perestroika (1986–1991)

Fig. 8: Generational types in today's working environment (own representation)

Recalling the definition of a generation previously in the thesis, generations can be described as groups of individuals who are born roughly around the same time and experience similar external events, which constitute their values, attitudes, and preferences (cf. Hoepflinger 1999: 10; Oertel 2007: 18.). As indicated earlier, these external events can be referred to as "defining moments" (cf. Schewe/Meredith 2004: 51). These "defining moments" differ significantly across differ ent cultures. For instance, Baby Boomers (1946–1964) in the US are formed by the assassination of

34 The US generation typology is based on Twenge *et al.* (2010), the German typology is based on Bruch, Kunze and Boehm (2010), and the Russian typology is based on Schewe and Meredith (2004).

John F. Kennedy and the Vietnam War, whereas their Russian counterparts, the Thaw (1937–1952) and Stagnation generations (1953–1968), have been influenced by the "Prague Spring" and the rise of Gorbachev (cf. Schewe/Meredith 2004: 54, 57; Beliaeva 2006: 24).

One of the biggest challenges in generational research is the three different time effects that may cause differences in attitudes, values, and beliefs across generations – generational, age, and life-stage effects (cf. Bruch/Kunze/Boehm 2010: 93). In order to truly investigate generational differences and characteristics, one has to control for the influence of age and life-stage effects (cf. Levenson 2010: 258; Parry/Urwin 2010: 7 f.).

The concept of generation has further gained importance since much attention has been paid to generation Y as a generation revolutionising the working environment (cf. De Hauw/De Vos 2010: 293; Hershatter/Epstein 2010: 211). A lot of practitioners and scholars have emphasised the importance of recruiting and retaining this generation. This issue is even more fostered by the demographic development ongoing in industrialised countries as well as in the emerging world (cf. Bruch/Kunze/Boehm 2010: 25).

Generation Y

The historic-societal concept of generation is the underlying construct of concepts such as generation Y. Numerous events around the world have shaped or are shaping this generation, partly at a global level and partly at a national level, and thus shaping similar values, norms, and attitudes as well as expectations towards employers. As already emphasised, the concept of generation is a very broad one and acts merely as a framework to capture the complexity and diversity of reality. When ascribing particular characteristics, values, and attitudes to individuals based on their belonging to a specified generation, one should always keep in mind that the individuals within a generational group are to some extent still heterogeneous and, therefore, individual differences can appear. However, if recommendations are to be made, such generalisations are necessary and appropriate. "Although it is important for employers to recognize the uniqueness of each individual employee, it is also important to understand generational distinctiveness, which can explain differences among workers that at first seem confusing and sometimes disruptive" (Lindquist 2008: 56).

The best-educated representatives of Gen Y are those currently entering the working world after having recently graduated from university. By taking on their first jobs and gaining initial practical experience, they challenge companies with their different attitudes, behaviours, and expectations (cf. Bernauer *et al.* 2011: 37). Gen Yers are said to have a huge social and economic impact (cf. Schnorbach 2009: 34). "They are racially and culturally diverse; extremely independent [...]; more egalitarian in their social views than older generations; highly connected to their peers; and feel a true sense of empowerment [...]" (Schnorbach 2009: 34).

Several scientific studies have been conducted to analyse Gen Y characteristics, attitudes, behaviours, worldviews, and expectations towards their employers (cf. Macky/Gardner/Forsyth 2008; Twenge *et al.* 2010; Twenge 2010 among others). However, most such research has been conducted in the United States, and little research on the Gen Y phenomenon has taken place in other countries (cf. Covri/Bigi/Ng 2007: 2 f.). The results of US studies have often been adapted for European or other countries in order to describe Gen Y and its influence on the business world without questioning. In addition, many characteristics ascribed to Gen Y have not been scientifically substantiated; they are often the products of personal observations and experiences and thus highly subjective (cf. Hubschmid 2011: 11).

This cohort has been described in many terms such as Gen Y, the Internet (Bruch/Kunze/Boehm 2010) or Net Generation, Millennials, Nexters (Marshall 2004: 18), Echo Boomers (Behrens 2009: 19), Generation Facebook, Generation Me (Twenge *et al.* 2010), and Generation Internship (Briedis/Minks 2007). "Demographers, unable to agree on a defining label for this generation, have called them the Millenniums, Generation www, the Digital Generation, Generation E, Echo Boomers, N-Gens, and, most often, Generation Y"[35] (Tulgan/Martin 2001: xi) (see also Shih/Allen 2006: 90; Motley 2005). Despite some variations in the way the literature names this generation and classifies start and end dates, there is general descriptive consensus among academics and practitioners regarding Gen Y

35 Based on a thorough analysis of secondary sources, the author decided to refer to this generational cohort throughout the book as generation Y (Gen Y) and its representatives as Gen Yers, since this term is most frequently used in the scientific literature.

(cf. Eisner 2005: 4). "Generation Y is variously defined, but is usually taken to mean people born between 1978 and 1994" (Macleod 2008: 3). Clare (2009: 42) and Howe and Strauss (2000) refer to Gen Y as Millennials and argue that they were born between 1985 and 2003. According to Marshall (2004: 18), Nexters are those born since 1980. The oldest of this generation are already integrated into the workforce and many are still on internship. While definitive dates vary among researchers regarding the boundaries of generational cohorts, there seems to be clear agreement that the oldest representatives of Gen Y were born around 1975.

Generally, Gen Yers are the most educated[36] generation to enter the workforce (cf. Herbison/Bosemann 2009: 33). They are defined by the intensive use of technology and are culturally resistant to any form of centralised control. Gen Y is particularly important to this study not only because it is considered to be the workforce of the future but also because it represents the largest demographic segment of consumers in most developed societies (cf. Rugimbana 2007: 304). If companies are efficient at recruiting Gen Yers, they are most likely to be efficient at selling their products and services to them, enabling connection between employees and consumers. However, most workplaces are not designed to integrate the needs and expectations of this successive generation, neither nationally nor internationally (cf. Behrens 2009: 21).

It is important to emphasise that apart from the difference in national background, some researchers (Tapscott 2009; Tulgan 2009; Parment 2009; Cheese 2007; Kopf 2008; Müller 2007; Schamberger 2006) allege that today's graduates all belong to the same new generation and therefore possess similar qualities. According to Cheese (2007: 33), "today's graduates, born after 1980, have grown up with new technology; they network, collaborate and respond instinctively to the demands of business in the Internet age". Only recently have more scientific studies on generational differences, in particular on Gen Y, been conducted. These studies have showed that Gen Yers and their expectations towards their employers are different compared with other generations in today's working environment. However, these differences seem to be less fundamental

36 Considering formal levels of education.

than proclaimed by the popular literature and media. Gen Yers differ from previous generations primarily in their relationships with technology. It is, after all, not by chance that they have often been dubbed "digital natives" (cf. Tapscott 2009[37]). The use of digital technologies has removed communication barriers and paved the way for a truly global generation of youth to emerge. Research suggests (Tapscott 2009; Tulgan 2009; Parment 2009; Cheese 2007; Kopf 2008; Müller 2007; Schamberger 2006) that young people's lifelong exposure to digital technologies has given rise to unique generational attributes that makes Gen Y very different from previous generations in their role as citizens, consumers, and employees. The important fact is that Gen Y is characterised by its "common fate" and the tendencies of the modern time (cf. Accenture 2009: online). Gen Y handles most technologies with ease and technological achievements such as the Internet and computers are taken for granted (also within an organisation). "Internet penetration has reached more than 2 billion people and continues to increase worldwide" (Strack *et al.* 2011: 19). Furthermore, Gen Yers are deeply concerned about their personal and career development as well as the social relationships in their lives including in the workplace. A supportive and cooperative working atmosphere is of the utmost importance to this generation. They demand continuous recognition and feedback. Herbison and Bosemann (2009: 33) characterise generation Y as a "[…] conundrum: educated and smart but needing guidance; more connected than any previous generation but challenged by face-to-face conflict; outwardly confident but possessing a delicate sense of self; high performing but irritatingly high maintenance". The aforementioned factors and their special manifestations may be summarised as being typical for Gen Y[38] (cf. Tapscott 2009; Tulgan 2009).

As Gen Yers are the first generation to grow up with high-speed digital technology, they are used to continuous and constant access to computers,

37 The terms "digital native" and "digital immigrant" were invented and popularised by Marc Prensky.

38 Some researchers (e.g. Tomlinson 2007: 286) continue to depict Gen Y graduates as being a performance-oriented social and occupational group that will access a wage premium and fulfil their potential through careers as "knowledge workers". However, in the author's opinion, graduates should not be viewed as a homogeneous group independent of their national backgrounds. This means that further differentiation is required.

the Internet, and mobile phones. To them, the usage of social networks is a common way to stay in touch and share experience with friends across geographical borders (cf. Bernauer *et al.* 2011: 37). As a result, it is not surprising that with the overall rising usage, increasing spread, and consequently growing significance of social media, the recruitment process for companies also needs to be adapted dramatically. It is no longer the employee who applies for a position in a firm, but rather companies have to present themselves to potential candidates (cf. Bernauer *et al.* 2011: 31). Kopf (2008: 14) further alleges that this generation brings change into the perception of national differences. Drawing on their experience of the World Wide Web, Gen Y increasingly employs new tools in the workplace to form ad hoc communities that transcend national boundaries. These new communities are changing the very nature of work and blurring the lines of demarcation between cultures (cf. Adachi *et al.* 2012: 20 ff.).

Tapscott (2009: 160 ff.) identifies eight characteristics that best describe members of Gen Y: freedom[39], customisation, scrutiny, integrity[40], collaboration[41], entertainment[42], speed[43], and innovation. If companies want to hire and keep Gen Y employees, they need to understand Gen Y's norms (cf. Tapscott 2009: 160)[44].

Freedom refers to the fact that Gen Y employees like to choose when and where they work. Most of them reject "nine to five" working hours heavily and want to be able to work outside the office. In this way, they

39 Excerpt from the contribution of a Gen Yer from India aged 23: "I would be more loyal to a company that shows respect for my efforts and time, and acknowledges any sacrifices made vis-à-vis personal life" (Tapscott 2009: 160).

40 Excerpt from the contribution of a Gen Yer from the USA aged 27: "The most attractive companies offer a chance to do volunteer work as part of the job" (Tapscott 2009: 162).

41 Excerpt from the contribution of Tapscott's son Alex Tapscott: "There shouldn't be team work just for the sake of teamwork. Rather, you bring together teams when you need different types of minds to come together with certain skill sets." (Tapscott 2009: 163).

42 Excerpt from the contribution of a Gen Yer from the USA aged 27: "One day at work they took away our tools, like Facebook, Pandora, Bebo, NPR. Work is slow, cold and boring." (Tapscott 2009: 165).

43 Excerpt from the contribution of a Gen Yer from Hong Kong aged 26: "Having an opportunity to fast-track up the career ladder has to be in the foreseeable future, not 5 years down the road but 1 or 2 years." (Tapscott 2009: 168).

44 The team of The Grown Up Digital Book Project conducted qualitative research through the creation of a community on Facebook of over 200 people to solicit views and stories from Gen Yers. Additionally, a global network of 140,000 Gen Yers hosted a series of discussions over several months on behalf of the research team (cf. Tapscott 2009: xiii).

can be more creative and productive. Gen Y has also a high need for good work/life balance. They work so that they can lead a decent life. In addition, they feel free to mix work with their personal lives, seeing work as an indispensable part of life. Another important aspect is that Gen Y members expect to be judged on their performances rather than on physical presence or time spent at the office. Therefore, a good way for companies to attract them is to offer contracts that e.g. include flexible working hours, job sharing, on-call, and shift work. Companies also have to keep in mind that Gen Yers are only loyal to their career paths, tasks that challenge them, and their peers. Consequently, they desire structure and internal mobility. As long as the company invests in them and shows its loyalty to Gen Yers, they will stay loyal in return. The offered wage is also a decisive criterion for a student to choose a company (cf. Tapscott 2009: 160 f.), since Gen Yers view salary as direct feedback on the results they achieve.

Gen Y attaches great importance to customisation. Gen Yers appreciate having the things their way and they want to be perceived as individuals instead of a big group. For companies, this implies that they need to offer individualised learning and development opportunities or adaptable, project-based role descriptions. If firms are able to create highly customised job descriptions, work systems, or compensation plans among other things, they are more likely to keep Gen Y employees in the company (cf. Tapscott 2009: 161).

Another specific characteristic of Gen Yers is the fact that they are very sceptical and check out many company-related details before they accept a job offer. Owing to the transparency also supported by the Internet, information is easy to access and spreads faster. In return, the company is also able to find out many private details about the candidate, especially on social network platforms (cf. Tapscott 2009: 161 f.).

Scrutiny is inseparable from integrity. Since information is easier to come across, it is essential to be honest and tell the truth. Gen Y defines integrity as being honest, considerate, and transparent. Therefore, Gen Y employees appreciate companies that communicate openly and act transparently (cf. Tapscott 2009: 161 f.). The status, hierarchy, or power within a company is not of importance to Gen Yers. What counts for them is interesting challenging work and team effort. Collaboration is part of their digital upbringing and the way they want to get things done (cf. Tapscott 2009: 162 f.). In this respect, for Gen Y work should contain fun and take place in a friendly work environment. This implies that the work itself should be fun. For example, if companies let employees compensate for stressful situations by surfing online, they will be encouraged to work effectively. Gen Y likes to have ways to cool off, take a break, and then go back to work and achieve results (cf. Tapscott 2009: 165 f.).

Instant responses, fast recruiting cycles, immediate feedback, fast promotion – Gen Yers need speed in almost every aspect of their lives. Gen Y employees thrive on information to improve their performances on a daily basis. Speed can also increase their loyalty. If bureaucracy rules the organisation and it takes a long time until a recruitment decision or a job offer is made, Gen Y employees are likely to leave the company sooner (cf. Tapscott 2009: 166 f.). Innovation is the hallmark of Gen Y culture. What Gen Yers strive for in a job is adding value, making a difference, constantly challenging the status quo, and knowing how they can contribute to the company's success (cf. Tapscott 2009: 167 f.).

When reviewing the scarce scientific literature on Gen Y it becomes apparent that most characteristics ascribed to this generation either by the media or by the popular literature cannot be substantiated with empirical findings. Rather, they are often even rejected (cf. Deal/Altman/Rogelberg 2010: 194; Real/Mitnick/Maloney 2010: 310). However, some expectations[45] and personality traits are discussed frequently in this context, e.g. work/life balance, social connections, career advancement, training and development, meaningful and interesting work, and salary (cf. De Hauw/De Vos 2010: 294). These findings will be discussed briefly in the remainder of this chapter.

45 Herman and Gioia (2000: 9 ff.) identify eight factors that knowledge workers look for in evaluating their decisions to apply for a position in a company: company reputation, company culture, enlightened leadership, treatment of people, opportunity for career growth, meaningful work, compensation, and benefits. Further criteria were suggested by Branham (2000: 19 ff.): the offer of opportunities for rapid advancement, a high risk–reward profile, an exciting challenge, and improved lifestyle benefits. The literature overwhelmingly suggests that the key characteristic of the company that attracts knowledge workers is that it provides personal and career growth opportunities (cf. Sutherland/Torricelli/Karg 2002: 15). Intergenerational expert Bruce Tulgan (2009: 153 ff.) also shows in his research that people are preoccupied mainly with growth opportunities. Herman and Gioia (2000: 93 ff.) further indicate that an organisation that provides plenty of opportunities for people to learn, grow, and reach their full potential is highly viewed by prospective employees as an EOC.

Personality traits

As described earlier in the chapter, it is assumed that individuals within a generation share the same values, attitudes, and beliefs and to some extent the same general personality traits as well (cf. Twenge/Campbell 2008: 863). Howe and Strauss (2000) – who first coined the term Millennials – ascribed the following personality traits to Gen Yers: special, sheltered, confident, team-oriented, conventional, pressured, and achieving (cf. Shih/Allen 2006: 90). According to Shih and Allen (2006: 90), the first three personality traits are caused by their protected childhoods. Their parents made them feel special and they taught them that they could achieve anything they set their minds to. The parents of Gen Y invest a lot of effort, time, and money into their children, they are deeply concerned about their children's futures, and they do their best to pave the way for their children into a happy and successful future (cf. Hershatter/Epstein 2010: 215). At the same time, this implies that tremendous pressure is being put on Gen Y, which older generations, especially Gen X, are often not aware of (cf. Hershatter/Epstein 2010: 215).

In their review of personality traits across different generations, Twenge and Campbell (2008: 864) show that three major personality traits differentiate Gen Y from previous generations – higher individualism, self-esteem, and narcissism. Gen Yers tend to be individualistic. Because of this individualism, they tend to perceive other people as individuals and do not judge them based on racial or gender groups (cf. Twenge 2010: 206). Furthermore, they have higher self-esteem and narcissism compared with Gen X and Baby Boomers (cf. Twenge/Campbell 2008: 865). This higher narcissism may cause difficulties when interacting with other people and lead to inconsistent behaviour. High self-esteem can be accompanied with better performance but also with the inability to accept criticism. Both higher narcissism and higher self-esteem may lead to higher expectations towards employers (cf. Twenge/Campbell 2008: 865). Moreover, Gen Yers tend to have a more external locus of control, i.e. they perceive the outcomes of an event as being controlled by the environment (cf. Twenge *et al.* 2010: 869). An external locus of control can result in blaming others or fortune when things go wrong and, therefore, Gen Yers tend to be less willing to take responsibility for failure. At the same time, it increases the sensitivity of an employee towards support by the organisation, leading to higher satisfaction and commitment (cf. Twenge/Campbell 2008: 870).

Many scholars argue that Gen Yers have a feeling of entitlement, which may represent serious challenges for organisations (cf. Lindquist 2008: 57). This feeling of entitlement arises when individualism and the feeling of being something special crosses into narcissism (cf. Lindquist 2008: 57; Twenge 2010: 206). Entitlement can be translated into "expecting something for nothing" (Twenge 2010: 206). A study by Twenge *et al.* (2010: 18) supports the idea of entitlement showing the combination of Gen Yers wanting to work less and putting more value on leisure but still wanting more money and status.

Work/life balance

One of the most discussed items in connection with Gen Y's expectations is work/life balance or the centrality of work (cf. Twenge *et al.* 2010; Ng/Schweitzer/Lyons 2010). The increased importance of reasonable work/life balance is caused by Gen Yers' personal observations and a common social shift of the importance of work in society (cf. Hershatter/Epstein 2010: 219). Gen Yers are considered to emphasise the concept of work/life balance, because they have seen their Baby Boomer parents work hard and spend more time working than enjoying life, only to be laid off by the organisation at the next best occasion (cf. Ng/Schweitzer/Lyons 2010: 282; Hershatter/Epstein 2010: 219). Of course, phrasing it that way is an exaggeration, but it reflects a particular prevailing mood within this generation, which is closely connected to their parents (cf. Shih/Allen 2006: 90).

A study by Twenge *et al.* (2010: 17) shows that Gen Yers place more value on leisure than Gen X individuals and Baby Boomers. The increased valuation of leisure is associated with a greater demand for a reasonable work/life balance and a decrease in work centrality. Other studies by Ng, Schweitzer and Lyons (2010: 289) and by Cennamo and Gardner (2008: 898) support the notion that a reasonable work/life balance is important to Gen Yers. Moreover, the focus on work/life balance is accompanied by a greater orientation towards family. Even though most Gen Yers have not yet started their own families, their family orientation can be observed in terms of their close relationships with their parents (cf. Hershatter/Epstein 2010: 219).

However, there is also scepticism among scholars concerning the increased importance of work/life balance as a Gen Y characteristic. First, it is argued that the shift towards a higher emphasis on work/life balance can be alternatively attributed to a common social shift from work centrality to the higher importance of leisure and family orientation (cf. Twenge *et al.* 2010: 18). Second, work/life balance is a highly individual concept, which is also positively loaded (cf. Koc 2008: 3). Therefore, individuals tend to state that they value good work/life balance, even though this balance is accompanied with 50-hour weeks that others would not perceive as balanced at all. Furthermore, Gen Yers are currently in their mid-twenties, which implies, for instance, that in most cases they have no family or care-taking commitments and, therefore, value work/life balance differently to experienced employees (cf. Koc 2008: 3).

Social aspects of work

Another topic recently discussed with respect to Gen Y is the social aspects of work (cf. Ng/Schweitzer/Lyons 2010: 283). These are, for example, reflected by the amicable and affiliative environment within a company and are manifested in enjoyable interaction and communication. This social environment can serve as a source of motivation for Gen Yers (cf. Twenge *et al.* 2010: 205). It is often assumed that Gen Yers have a high demand for collaboration (cf. Martin 2005: 40). This desire for collaboration is fostered during their kindergarten and school years, where great emphasis is placed on the early development of social and soft skills (cf. Ng/Schweitzer/Lyons 2010: 283).

A study by Lyons, Duxbury and Higgins (2005: 68) shows that Gen Yers value the social aspects of work more compared with Gen Xers, Baby Boomers, or the Silent Generation. They even attach the highest importance to these social aspects. Another study by Wong *et al.* (2008: 6) supports these findings. They also point out that Gen Yers are more affiliative than both Baby Boomers and Gen X individuals.

Contradictory findings are provided by Twenge *et al.* (2010). They argue that the desire to belong or be connected to a group is lower for Gen Yers compared with Gen X individuals and Baby Boomers (cf. Twenge *et al.* 2010: 19). The authors attribute these findings, on one hand, to the increased focus of Gen Y individuals on themselves (narcissism) (cf. Twenge *et al.* 2010: 19) and, on the other hand, to the fact that this generation no longer relies on the working environment to make friends, since technological developments allow them to cultivate friendships at any given time and place (cf. Twenge *et al.* 2010: 19).

These different findings may be because of the type of study conducted. Wong *et al.* (2008) and Lyons, Duxbury and Higgins (2005) performed a cross-sectional study, whereas Twenge *et al.* (2010: 205 f.) conducted a time-lag study. For instance, cross-sectional studies could have measured age effects rather than true generational effects (cf. Parry/Urwin 2010: 8 f.).

Career advancement, recognition, and feedback

The desire or requirement for rapid advancement opportunities, recognition, and continuous feedback as a key factor to Gen Yers is mentioned frequently (cf. Martin 2005; Wong *et al.* 2008; Ng/Schweitzer/Lyons 2010; Twenge 2010). These desires are already rooted in their childhood. Some argue (see also Hershatter/Epstein 2010) that Gen Yers have been overwhelmed with gold stars and medals in their childhood for almost everything and that this has resulted in a strong demand for continuous approval and affirmation. Because of this constant need for approval and affirmation, Gen Yers tend to be in need of guidance and direction (cf. Hershatter/Epstein 2010: 217), although they are considered to be self-confident and independent (cf. Martin 2005: 40). They seek managerial support and plain instructions, but at the same time they want a certain degree of flexibility in accomplishing the task (cf. Martin 2005: 40).

Opportunity for advancement is identified as most important to Gen Y individuals in a study by Ng, Schweitzer and Lyons (2010: 288 f.). Moreover, the study points out that there is no direct relationship between the academic performances of the surveyed students and their expectations of advancement. This further supports the opinion that Gen Yers have a sense of entitlement (cf. Ng/Schweitzer/Lyons 2010: 289). The findings of Wong *et al.* (2008: 7) also show that Gen Yers attach greater importance to advancement opportunities compared with Baby Boomers and Gen X individuals. They do, however, admit that these differences could be a result of the different life stages of the surveyed individuals. To older and experienced employees that have often been promoted during the courses of their careers, advancement may no longer be as important compared with someone in the early stages of his or her working life (cf. Wong *et al.* 2008: 7).

Advancement is also associated with prestige and status, which are relatively important to Gen Yers compared with older generations (cf. Lyons/Duxbury/Higgins 2005: 67). A study by Cennamo and Gardner (2008: 902) also indicates that status is of more value to the younger generation. Again, these differences may be because of the just described life-stage effects.

Meaningful work and professional development

It is often ascribed to Gen Yers that they seek meaningful and interesting work and, therefore, place great importance on the intrinsic values of a particular job (cf. Martin 2005: 40). However, empirical studies have shown that this assertion does not hold when comparing Gen Yers with Baby Boomers and Gen Xers. A study by Twenge *et al.* (2010: 17) shows that the value of the intrinsic attributes of a particular job has declined. Cennamo and Gardner (2008: 902) support this finding; in their study, no significant differences in the importance placed on intrinsic values could be demonstrated between generations. Lyons, Duxbury and Higgins (2005: 69) show that intrinsic values are even more important to Gen X than to Gen Y individuals.

It is often argued that Gen Yers attach great importance to training and development opportunities within an organisation. Two qualitative studies by Broadbridge, Maxwell and Ogden (2009: 412 f.) and Terjesen, Vinnicombe and Freeman (2007: 517) support this idea.

Pay and benefits

Some researchers (Twenge/Campbell 2008: 866; De Hauw/De Vos 2010: 294) have pointed out that Gen Yers place greater importance on the intrinsic values of a job than on extrinsic values such as salary. Yet others (cf. Lindquist 2008: 57) argue that Gen Yers have extremely high expectations regarding salary. These high expectations towards salary may be associated with the notion of entitlement.

The empirical study by Twenge *et al.* (2010: 16) shows that Gen Yers value extrinsic job values less than Gen X individuals, but more than Baby Boomers. Therefore, it can be assumed that extrinsic work values such as salary still play a role, because feedback is tremendously important to Gen Yers and salary may be perceived as a type of feedback (cf. Ng/Schweitzer/Lyons 2010: 282). Further, a study by Ng, Schweitzer and Lyons (2010: 288) disproves the notion that Gen Yers have enormous expectations towards their salaries. They show that the majority of their surveyed Gen Yers have rather realistic expectations towards their initial salaries in their first jobs after graduation.

Loyalty

Gen Yers are often said to be less loyal towards their employers and have no qualms about changing workplaces if they do not feel satisfied with their current situations (cf. Parment 2009: 73; Ng/Schweitzer/Lyons 2010: 282 f.). This willingness to change employers is comparable to their consumer behaviour. They know their power as a consumer and easily switch to another brand that better fits their needs (cf. Shih/Allen 2006: 91). In today's world, increased alternatives present themselves in all areas of life and Gen Yers have been advised of these alternatives while growing up (cf. Parment 2009: 35 ff.) This abundance of alternatives is not, however, to imply that Gen Yers do not have the capacity to be loyal. For instance, "[...] they are loyal to organizations that are loyal to them" (Hershatter/Epstein 2010: 220). Organisations have, therefore, to engage in activities that strengthen the connection between Gen Y employees and the organisation in terms of employee satisfaction, e.g. by providing adequate working hours as well as training and development (cf. Hershatter/Epstein 2010: 220 f.). Gen Yers require organisations to be authentic; they have to fulfil any previously made promises. If an organisation does not keep its promises, Gen Yers will most likely leave the company (cf. Twenge/Campbell 2008: 866).

Another example of a factor that may influence Gen Y loyalty is corporate social responsibility (CSR). For instance, the survey of Gen Y expectations by PricewaterhouseCoopers (2008: online) shows that 82% of respondents across Europe would leave an organisation because of underperforming CSR efforts. Social responsibility and commitment to diversity are of major importance to Gen Y individuals and, therefore, as also implied by the PricewaterhouseCoopers study, organisations should consider their social responsibilities in order to strengthen Gen Y's loyalty towards them (cf. Ng/Schweitzer/Lyons 2010: 289).

This emphasis on CSR should not be confused with the increased importance of altruistic work values. Altruistic work values describe the desire to do good (while working), e.g. by helping underprivileged people (cf. Lyons/Duxbury/Higgins 2005: 63). Many companies believe that the younger generation attaches more importance to altruistic work values, as suggested by the degree of voluntary work among high school seniors. Based on this belief, organisations apply these values to their recruitment strategies (cf. Twenge 2010: 204). However, they may be misjudging the motivations of youths, since the increase in volunteering may be connected to the amount of social commitment required for college applications[46] (cf. Twenge 2010: 204). This would then have nothing to do with increased altruistic work values. This view is also supported by empirical findings showing that there are no significant differences between Gen Y and previous generations with regard to altruistic work values (cf. Twenge *et al.* 2010: 17).

Technological requirements

Besides the aforementioned personality traits and expectations towards employers, another major difference between Gen Y and previous generations is its particular relationship with technology (cf. Hershatter/Epstein 2010: 212). Gen Yers grew up during a period of accelerated technological progress (cf. Hershatter/Epstein 2010: 212; Deal/Altman/Rogelberg 2010: 192). The world is steadily becoming flat and borderless. Social media has revolutionised the world from broadcast, one-way communications to greater interactivity in the sense of web 2.0. Therefore, Gen Yers are

46 Relates here to English-speaking countries.

often referred to as "digital natives" and "techno-savvy", having completely internalised these new technologies (cf. Shaw/Fairhurst 2008: 368). "The most valuable and talented people are likely to already be using a range of social networking technologies, including Facebook, Twitter, Xing, Plaxo, LinkedIn, YouTube, Vimeo, the new Google+, etc., via computer and/or smart phone" (Clayton 2012: 2). The Internet itself is, based on its year of birth, a member of generation Y (cf. Hershatter/Epstein 2010: 212). In recent years, milestones in technological progress have been attained, such as the rise of social networking platforms such as Facebook, influencing the way in which people interact and communicate, especially Gen Y (cf. Deal/Altman/Rogelberg 2010: 192). Technologies such as the computer are taken for granted by Gen Yers. They use these new technologies in every imaginable sphere of life in a completely natural way. Gen Y teaches us to value social networking for sharing and collaboration, for developing creative solutions with peers, and for enhancing personal networks (cf. Clayton 2012: 8).

According to the study carried out by the Russian HR website hrm.ru, LinkedIn and Facebook represent the most popular online networks for graduates in search of information about their potential employers (hrm.ru. 2011: online). "'Social' is the word that is transforming almost every talent practice. [...] Employees now post comments and feedback on Facebook, LinkedIn, Glassdoor, Twitter and almost any website in the world" (Bersin 2011: 6 f.). The strong affinity with the Internet is doubtless because academic studies today are impossible to imagine without a mastery of new media: for example, 87% of Swiss people aged between 16 and 25 are members of Facebook (cf. Kuhn-Spogat 2011: n/a).

Moreover, it is not only the popularity of these social networks that matters. According to the Achievers survey (cf. Ruettimann 2011: 6), the majority of HR respondents (527 HR professionals) believe that, first and foremost, social networking tools can have a hugely positive impact on reducing the costs of recruiting and communication. Strack *et al.* (2011: 5, 20) postulate that the rise of online social media will change how HR interacts with potentials employees of all generations, not just young ones. Further, they allege that the top opportunities that online social networks offer include employer branding, attracting young professionals, knowledge sharing, and attracting graduates as well as skilled workers. Davison, Maraist and Bing (2011: 155) suggest that Gen Yers may be less concerned about privacy issues than prior generations and, therefore, they are more accepting of the use of social media sites for the purposes of recruitment. Moreover, being results-oriented they are aware of the cost-effectiveness of using these sites to establish contact compared with more traditional recruitment channels and approaches.

Table 2 summarises the main findings about the job attributes that are important to Gen Y. All studies have either a quantitative or a qualitative empirical basis, and the samples were derived from different nationalities. They are classified according to the main research topic and provide solid ground to consider these aspects when choosing the EB attributes that are relevant for Gen Y and for the current study.

TOPIC	FINDINGS	AUTHORS
Personality traits	Gen Y individuals are *special, sheltered, confident, team-oriented, conventional, pressured, and achieving.*	Howe/Strauss (2003)
	Their parents did everything for this generation, providing them with a sheltered childhood, but putting high pressure on them at the same time.	Hershatter/Epstein (2010)
	Compared with previous generations, Gen Y is defined by higher *individualism, self-esteem, and narcissism.*	Twenge/Campbell (2008)
	Gen Y's high *self-esteem* and *narcissism* may lead to high expectations towards employers.	Twenge/Campbell (2008)
	Gen Y individuals have an *external locus of control.*	Twenge *et al.* (2010)
	Their *individualism* and feeling of being something *special* leads to higher *entitlement.*	Lindquist (2008), Twenge (2010)
	Gen Y individuals' sense of *entitlement* can be described as wanting to work less and *value leisure* but still wanting *money* and *status.*	Twenge *et al.* (2010)
Work/life balance	Gen Y individuals attach more importance to *work/life balance.* This might be a result of a common shift in society.	Twenge *et al.* (2010) Ng *et al.* (2010) Hershatter/Epstein (2010)
	Gen Y individuals *value leisure* more than previous generations, which also leads to the importance of *work/life balance.*	Twenge *et al.* (2010) Ng *et al.* (2010) Cennamo/Gardner (2008)
	Work/life balance is also accompanied by greater orientation towards *family.*	Hershatter/Epstein (2010)
Social aspects of work	For Gen Y individuals, the *social aspects of work* such as an amicable and affiliative environment and enjoyable interaction and communication are important and serve as a source of motivation.	Twenge *et al.* (2010) Ng *et al.* (2010)

	Gen Y individuals have a high demand for *collaboration*, among other things because of their kindergarten and early school years.	Martin (2005) Ng *et al.* (2010)
	Gen Y individuals value the *social aspects of work* more than previous generations.	Lyons *et al.* (2007) Wong *et al.* (2008)
	By contrast, some studies show that Gen Y individuals put less value on *collaboration* than previous generations because of their *narcissism* and expertise in *technological developments*.	Twenge *et al.* (2010)
Career advancement, recognition, and feedback	The desire or requirement for rapid *advancement opportunities, recognition, and constructive feedback* of Gen Y is mentioned frequently.	Martin (2005) Wong *et al.* (2009) Ng *et al.* (2010) Twenge (2010)
	Gen Y individuals have been overwhelmed with awards in their childhood, resulting in a strong demand for *continuous approval and affirmation*.	Hershatter/Epstein (2010)
	Gen Y individuals tend to need *guidance and direction*.	Hershatter/Epstein (2010)
	Gen Y individuals are considered to be *self-confident and independent*, they *need managerial support* and *plain instructions* but want to stay *flexible* in accomplishing their tasks.	Martin *et al.* (2005)
	The opportunity for advancement has been identified as most important to Gen Y individuals.	Ng *et al.* (2010)
	Gen Y individuals place greater value on *advancement opportunities, status,* and *prestige* than previous generations.	Wong *et al.* (2008) Lyons *et al.* (2007) Cennamo/Gardner (2008)
Meaningful work and professional development	Owing to their preferences for *meaningful* and *interesting work*, it is often mentioned that Gen Y individuals put greater importance on the *intrinsic values* of a particular job.	Martin (2005)
	However, empirical studies show controversial results concerning the importance of *intrinsic values* to Gen Y compared with Gen X or Baby Boomers.	Twenge *et al.* (2010) Cennamo/Gardner (2008) Lyons *et al.* (2007)
	Gen Y individuals attach great importance to *training and development opportunities* within an organisation.	Broadbridge *et al.* (2007) Terjesen *et al.* (2007)
Salary	For Gen Y individuals, the *intrinsic values* of a job are more important than *extrinsic values* such as *salary*.	Twenge/Campbell (2008) De Hauw/de Vos (2010)
	Others say that Gen Y individuals have extremely high expectations regarding *salary* because of their sense of *entitlement*.	Lindquist (2008)
	Gen Y values *extrinsic job characteristics* less than Gen X individuals but more than Baby Boomers. Therefore, *extrinsic work values* are important, especially when *salary* serves as some kind of feedback.	Twenge *et al.* (2010) Ng *et al.* (2010)
Loyalty	Gen Y individuals are often perceived to be less loyal towards their employers and open to changing workplaces, particularly if organisations do not keep their promises.	Parment (2009) Ng *et al.* (2010) Twenge/Campbell (2008
	Gen Y individuals are less *loyal* in their role as a customer.	Shih/Allen (2006)
	Gen Y individuals have the capacity to be *loyal*, especially if organisations are loyal to them.	Hershatter/Epstein (2010)

Technological requirements	Their particular relationship with *technology* is one major difference between Gen Y and previous generations, because Gen Y individuals have grown up parallel to accelerated *technological* progress.	Hershatter/Epstein (2010) Deal *et al.* (2010)
	Therefore, Gen Y individuals are often referred to as *"digital natives"* and *"techno-savvy"*, having completely internalised these new technologies.	Shaw/Fairhurst (2008)

Table 2: Summary of the scientific findings on generation Y (own representation)

To conclude, great emphasis is put on Gen Y and on the interrelated challenges to the working environment. Therefore, a variety of researchers has investigated this generation from both an empirical and a non-empirical perspective, e.g. their attitudes towards work (e.g. Howe/Strauss 2000; Kowske/Rasch/Wiley 2010). However, the respective findings are also subject to generalisations. To date, as previously mentioned, very little research has been conducted on the differences of Gen Yers around the world due to culture. Covri, Bigi and Ng (2007: 2 ff.) investigate the differences and similarities between European and US Millennials and conclude that there are crucial differences owing to social, cultural, and environmental factors (cf. Covri/Bigi/Ng 2007: 17 f.). The study by Egri and Ralston (2004: 215 f.) compares different generations in the US and China and finds significant differences between them. Their study supports the importance of cultural influences on the formation of generations as well as on generational characteristics. Another study that showed the differences across generations due to culture despite a common language was conducted by Zhang, Straub and Kusyk (2007)[47]. A more popular scientific work by Hole, Zhong and Schwartz (2010) comes to similar conclusions. It is argued that believing "[...] millennials are millennials wherever they are in the world is tantamount to blithely saying that customers are customers the world over" (Hole/Zhong/Schwartz 2010: 87).

2.3 Comparative culture studies

Robbins, Odendaal and Roodt (1998: 24 ff.) report that cultural values play an important role in influencing one's perceptions of the work envi-

47 The comparison of 33 work/life values among business students was performed in two regions: Paris (France) and Quebec (Canada).

ronment. Schamberger (2006: 42), on the contrary, argues that globalisation tendencies contribute to more globalised thinking and to cultural assimilation in the behaviour of students of different nationalities.

There are different approaches to cultural influences in management theory, each of them providing diverging views on culture's effects. Comparative culture studies and the models derived thereof enable researchers to compare different cultures based on cultural dimensions or certain categories (cf. Mead 2005: 28). These models are widespread in various scientific fields as well as in the business world. They are common in intercultural and international management, marketing and communication research (cf. Chiang 2005; De Mooij 2010). Within these models, interpretable dimensions or categories are used to describe different cultures. These dimensions or categories represent answers to the problems all human societies face (cf. De Mooij 2010: 68). They are either based on the analysis of empirical data (cf. Hofstede 2001; Hofstede/Hofstede/Minkov 2010; Trompenaars/Hampden-Turner 2010; House *et al.* 2004) or on anecdotal events, experience, and qualitative research (cf. Lewis 2010).

Regardless of the wide diffusion of these models, they do have certain weaknesses. Therefore, in order to use these models beneficially it is necessary to keep their limitations in mind (cf. Osland/Bird 2000: 66). According to some anthropologists, they may lack the descriptive depth required to characterise a particular culture or nation in detail (cf. Mead 2005: 28). These models draw on "sophisticated stereotypes" by reducing a complex culture to a comprehensive description based on theoretical concepts (cf. Osland/Bird 2000: 66), which, consequently, can lead to descriptive breadth (cf. Mead 2005: 28). Describing an entire nature based on dimensions or categories involves the danger of neglecting differences within a certain society's culture which, in turn, may lead to an overvaluation of the developed "stereotypes" (cf. Mead 2005: 28).

In the following section, after the presented definition of culture and its characteristics, four comparative culture models on which a substantial part of the theoretical assumptions in this book is based will be discussed in detail, while keeping in mind the weaknesses mentioned before. "Theoretical frameworks to account for observed between-country differences in many psychological processes may be developed using dimensions other than individualism versus collectivism" (Matsumoto/Hee Yoo 2006: 239). That is why there is a need to rely on several models that exist in cultural research, thus ensuring a variety of assumptions.

Definition and characteristics of culture

Culture has been widely discussed and analysed in various disciplines (cf. Kutschker/Schmid 2006: 666) and it is used in far broader terms than implicated by its original meaning. In anthropology as well as sociology, culture refers to the "[...] complex [..] which includes knowledge, belief, art, morals, law, custom, and any other capabilities and habits acquired by a man as a member of society" (Tylor 1871: 1).

In this book, the anthropological and sociological concept of culture will be applied. In these scientific domains, a remarkable number of different definitions exist. By 1952, anthropologists Alfred Kroeber and Clyde Kluckhohn (1952) have already identified and categorised 164 separate definitions of culture. Regardless of the multitude of definitions, they all assign similar characteristics to the concept of culture. Kroeber and Kluckhohn (1952: 86) define culture as

> [...] patterned ways of thinking, feeling and reacting, acquired and transmitted mainly by symbols, constituting the distinctive achievements of human groups, including their embodiments in artifacts; the essential core of culture consists of traditional [...] ideas and especially their attached values (Kroeber/Kluckhohn 1952: 86).

Hofstede, a Dutch cultural research expert, shortened this definition by stating that culture is "the collective programming of the mind that distinguishes the members of one group or category of people from another" (Hofstede 2001: 9). Hoecklin (1995: 24) describes culture as a shared system of meanings which "[...] guides how the world is perceived, how the self is experienced and how life itself is organized", thus creating a feeling of togetherness (cf. Hoecklin 1995: 24). Another definition of culture is provided by Kutschker and Schmid (2006) as a synthesis of the gathered definitions of Kluckhohn and Kroeber (1952). They define culture as the basic assumptions, values, norms, attitudes, and beliefs of a social entity, which are expressed by a multitude of behaviours and artefacts that have developed over time because of the various challenges the social entity faces (cf. Kutschker/Schmid 2006: 666).

The concept of culture has been analysed and defined at different levels of culture: the national level (cf. Hofstede 2001; Trompenaars/Hampden-Turner 2010), the organisational level (cf. Deal/Kennedy 2000; Schein 2004), and the level of sub-cultures (cf. Hall/Jefferson 1993). Within the scope of this book, the national level of culture will be examined[48]. This perception of culture can be difficult, because culture does not stop at national borders. Even within one country, several cultures may exist (cf. Kutschker/Schmid 2006: 725). Using countries as a symbol of different cultures is a simplification that is necessary in order to manage the complexity of cultural and cross-national research. However, it is elementary to be aware of the generalisation caused by these simplifications and of the fact that all statements made to differentiate between countries and cultures can only be seen as exemplary and by no means as universal.

Hofstede (2001: 2) distinguishes three levels of mental programming, which refers to the way an individual acts, feels, and thinks in a certain situation. The mental programming of an individual is partly unique, partly shared, and partly universal. *Fig. 9* provides an overview of the different levels of mental programming. The first level, the universal level, is shared by almost all humans. It originates from our biological fundamentals. Along with the biological operating systems of the human body, this level includes the basic expressive behaviours of individuals, which can also be found in more highly developed animals, e.g. squinting eyes as a sign of aggravation. This level is mostly covered by ethnological research. At the second level of the pyramid, the collective level, mental programming is shared among individuals belonging to a group. Moreover, the shared mental programming distinguishes the individuals belonging to this group from other individuals. Therefore, this level can be referred to as culture. The topmost level of the pyramid, the individual level, represents the truly unique part of mental programming – an individual's personality. It is both learned and inherited and leads to differences in behaviour within the same cultural entity.

48 Therefore, within the context of this thesis, "culture" refers to national culture unless otherwise stated. The terms nationality factor or nationality will be used in the research (especially in its empirical part) to mean the national level of culture.

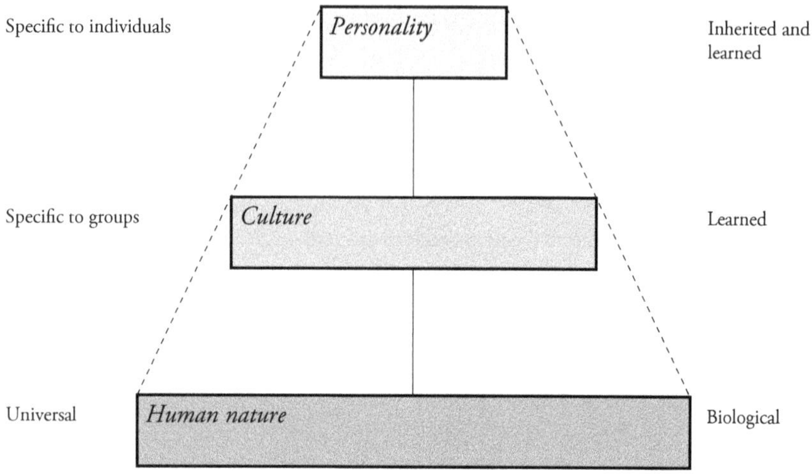

Fig. 9: Three levels of human mental programming (own representation, cf. Hofstede 2001: 3; Hoecklin 1995: 25).

As can be derived from the distinction of mental programming by Hofstede, one characteristic of culture most cultural researchers agree on is that culture is learned (cf. Hoecklin 1995: 24 f.; Kutschker/Schmid 2006: 666 ff.). Already in their childhoods, individuals are socialised by the rules and norms of their culture (cf. Mendenhall/Punnett/Ricks 1995: 70 f.). Therefore, culture stems from an individual's social environment and does not originate from an individual's genes (cf. Hoecklin 1995: 25). The process of growing into a culture is referred to as "enculturation" (cf. Kutschker/Schmid 2006: 668). Nevertheless, the learnability of a culture is limited with respect to the adaption of a new culture (cf. Kutschker/Schmid 2006: 668). Obviously, the ability to adapt to another culture depends on the individual's personality and the perceived cultural proximity of the new culture.

Furthermore, Hofstede's distinction indicates that members of a social entity share its culture; hence, culture is not an individual phenomenon but a collective one (cf. Hoecklin 1995: 25; Mendenhall/Punnett/Ricks 1995: 71). Moreover, culture, on one hand, is the result of certain individual behaviour patterns, i.e. culture reflects the past of a social identity. On the other hand, culture constrains and influences behaviour in the present and future (cf. Kutschker/Schmid 2006: 667 f.). This determination of behaviours is often subconscious; therefore, it is important to understand culture in order to understand individual behaviour (cf. Mendenhall/Punnett/Ricks 1995: 71).

Another important characteristic of culture is that it is of implicit and of explicit nature (cf. Kutschker/Schmid 2006: 667). The deeper values in life incorporated within a culture can only be observed based on the behaviour of individuals and the practices (symbols, heroes, and rituals) embedded in a culture (cf. Hofstede 2001: 5 ff.). Furthermore, as the various characteristics already indicate, a culture performs a wide range of functions. First, culture acts as guidance for individuals. It indicates what is right and what is wrong, and, therefore, determines how individuals belonging to a certain group should react in various situations (cf. Kutschker/Schmid 2006: 669; Mendenhall/Punnett/Ricks 1995: 7). Moreover, culture provides a group with an identity by creating inner unity and external differentiation. Culture also has a legitimating function; it justifies behaviour within and outside a certain culture (cf. Kutschker/Schmid 2006: 669).

2.3.1 Cultural dimensions according to Hofstede

Geert Hofstede developed perhaps the most popular and most cited classification of cultural dimensions. Even though his work has been and is still criticised heavily, it has become fundamental when thinking about culture in both academia and the business world (cf. Fang 2010: 156). "Geert Hofstede's dimensional model of national culture has been applied to various areas of global branding and advertising, and the underlying theories of consumer behaviour" (De Mooij/Hofstede 2010: 85). "A reason for the widespread adoption of Hofstede's classification of culture lies in the large number of countries measured and the simplicity of his dimensions, which are straightforward and appealing to both academic researchers and business people" (De Mooij/Hofstede 2010: 87 f.).

The data serving as a basis for the development of Hofstede's first four dimensions of culture were collected within IBM. IBM, as a multinational company, launched an international employee survey programme. Two rounds, 1967 and 1973, were carried out. The survey produced 116,000 answered questionnaires from 72 countries in 20 languages. A statistical analysis of the answers showed four common problem areas similar in all countries, whereas the solutions to these problems differed across countries (cf. Hofstede 1983: 46 ff. and Hofstede 2001: 28 f.). These four problem areas led to the identification of the first four cultural dimensions named power distance (large vs. small), uncertainty avoidance (strong vs. weak), individualism vs. collectivism, and masculinity vs. femininity (cf. Hofstede 2001: 28 f.). Every country represented in the study was assigned to a position between the extreme poles of the dimensions (cf. Hofstede 2001: 28 f.). In the following, the four dimensions are briefly described.

Power distance (small vs. large) (PD): Hofstede's first dimension deals with how human inequality is handled within a society. Inequality can emerge in different domains, e.g. prestige, wealth, and power. The evaluation of the importance of equality in these domains va-ries across societies. Power distance, therefore, expresses the extent to which individuals within a certain culture are willing to accept power inequality (cf. Hofstede 2001: 79 ff.).

Individualism vs. collectivism (IDV): The second dimension refers to the predominant relationship between the individual and the collective within a society. This way of living together influences values and norms. Therefore, in some cultures individualism is seen as the way of life to aspire to and as elementary to an individual's well-being, whereas in other cultures it is seen as preposterous and plaintive. Therefore, this dimension measures the extent to which individuals are oriented towards themselves rather than towards a group (cf. Hofstede 2001: 209).

Masculinity vs. femininity (MAS): The third dimension deals with the social implications of different genders (cf. Hofstede 2001: 28). Studies of the importance of work goals have shown that women emphasise social goals, e.g. relationships, cooperativeness, and the physical environment, whereas men accentuate ego-related goals, such as money and their careers. Therefore, this dimension expresses the degree to which a culture is more oriented towards socially attributed "women" or "men" characteristics (cf. Hofstede 2001: 279 ff.).

Uncertainty avoidance (strong vs. weak) (UA): The fourth dimension measures the level of stress an uncertain situation creates within a society. Uncertainty is a characteristic of nature and human life and individuals try to cope with it by reverting to technology, law, and religion. Uncertainty avoidance, therefore, demonstrates the degree to which individuals within a certain culture feel at ease when facing uncertain situations (cf. Hofstede 2001: 145 ff.). In cultures with strong UA, there is a strong emotional need for both written and unwritten rules and formalities to structure life, which translates into the belief in experts and formal structures while ignoring reality (cf. De Mooij/Hofstede 2010: 89; Naumov/Puffer 2000: 711).

As Orr and Hauser (2008: 1) put it: "[..] Hofstede's initial four [..] fundamental dimensions of culture still serve today as basic, fundamental criteria in most interdisciplinary, cross-cultural comparative research". *Fig. 10* represents the scores that were assigned to Switzerland and Russia in Hofstede's research on the four classical dimensions of culture.

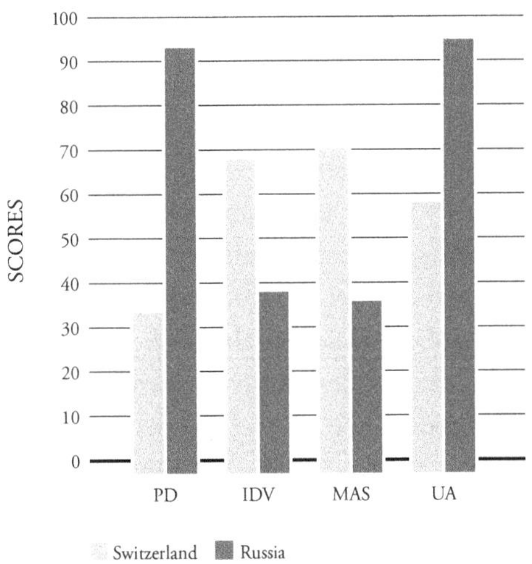

Fig. 10: Rankings of Switzerland and Russia on Hofstede's four classical cultural dimensions (own representation)

Russian respondents scored relatively high on UA (95 points), which might present an aberration during the period of economic and political stagnation in the 1980s when Russian citizens were guaranteed a job and a modest standard of living if they did not question the status quo. However, the transformation processes in Russian society during the 1990s and its turn towards a market-oriented economy gave rise to greater uncertainty and diverted decision-making processes to individuals. Therefore, the UA was declining compared with its high level prior to perestroika (cf. Naumov/Puffer 2000: 712 f.). The study of Prašnikar, Pahor and Vidmar Svetlik (2008: 20) also shows that the younger generation of students have a lower UA score than managers, i.e. the older generation. Students in post-Soviet economies are more willing to take risks and they have less emotional resistance to change compared with the representatives of the older generation.

Further, the lower score for Russia on the IDV dimension can be explained by the suppression of individualism during times of socialism, when official egalitarian values were promoted at the expense of personal freedom and freedom of expression. However, young managers and students are already much more characterised by the individualism brought about by modern times (cf. Prašnikar/Pahor/Vidmar Svetlik 2008: 6, 22).

In 1985, a fifth dimension, long- vs. short-term orientation, was developed based on different data. This dimension added the previously missing *attitude towards time* to the set of dimensions (cf. Kutschker/Schmid 2006: 721). New data were gathered from student samples derived from the Chinese Value Survey conducted within 23 countries by Michael Bond and colleagues. This survey, first and foremost influenced by "eastern minds", showed existing differences in the importance attached to several topics within the eastern cultural area compared with the western-shaped IBM dataset (cf. Hofstede 2001: 351). It seems as though both poles of this fifth dimension are influenced by the teachings of Confucius (cf. Hofstede 2001: 351).

Long- vs. short-term orientation (LTO): This fifth dimension describes whether effort within a society is oriented towards the present (short-term-oriented) or the future (long-term-oriented) (cf. Hofstede 2001: 351 ff.). In 2010, another entirely new dimension, based on Minkov's World Values Survey data analysis covering 93 countries, was added to the set of the already existing dimensions – *indulgence vs. restraint* (cf. Hofstede/Hofstede/Minkov 2010: 280 ff.).

Indulgence vs. restraint: This new dimension refers to the extent to which the gratification of needs, leading to enjoying life and having fun, is approved of within a certain culture. A culture oriented towards indulgence allows its members to satisfy these needs, whereas a culture oriented towards restraint limits and controls this satisfaction with the help of strict social norms (cf. Hofstede/Hofstede/Minkov 2010: 280 ff.)[49].

As mentioned, Hofstede and his work have been heavily criticised. This criticism refers to different aspects of his work, such as the sample pool and the method. A short overview of the most contentious arguments is given below.

Numerous researchers have questioned Hofstede's methodology. Because Hofstede's cultural dimensions are based on the international employee survey programme within IBM, the data he collected focus on a single company within which he discerns national samples (cf. McSweeney 2002: 95; Kutschker/Schmid 2006: 724; Orr/Hauser 2008: 6, 14). Another common criticism of this piece of work is based on the fact that Hofstede assumed that cultures equate with nations and that cultural borders match national borders – an illegitimate assumption according to several authors and studies (cf. Kutschker/Schmid 2006: 725; Baskerville 2003: 1 ff.). Other concerns with regard to his work touch on the fact that Hofstede seems to have ignored the existence of different cultures within organisations along with succumbing to the notion that all individuals have the same national culture (cf. McSweeney 2002: 96, 100). It has further been criticised that most of his research was conducted with a western mindset and his survey, therefore, at least partly focuses on questions that may be irrelevant for other cultures (cf. Kutschker/Schmid 2006: 704; Orr/Hauser 2008: 6). Baskerville (2003: 1 f.) mentions the general lack of confidence in the assumption of the stability of cultural differences as well as the lack of theoretical basis for research using Hofstede's indices.

> The weak theoretical basis makes it unclear what Hofstede was theorizing; he might not have studies culture at all. The connections between his dimensions and socio-economic aspects such as Gross Domestic Product suggest that he was measuring socio-economic factors (Baskerville 2003: 2).

49 Since the LTO dimension is more relevant to the Asian cultural paradigm, the hypothesised direction and level of importance of different EB attributes for different national groups of graduates are explained by referring to the four classical dimensions only; the applicability of Minkov's dimension has not yet been sufficiently tested because of its novelty.

The question of time relevancy has also often been raised (cf. Orr/Hauser 2008: 6). Trompenaars and Hampden-Turner (2010) allege that cultural categories are not mutually exclusive as Hofstede postulates: being individualistic does not necessarily have to mean that one cannot be a collectivist. Javidan *et al.* (2006a: 898, 909) as well as Orr and Hauser (2008: 8) criticise the consulting nature of Hofstede's research project; it lacks many of the critical steps required for a rigorous cross-cultural scientific research project.

Orr and Hauser (2008: 1 ff.) suggest in this respect the need to re-examine the cultural dimensions within the global-based context of the early 21st century:

> [...] it appears that Hofstede's theoretical constructs need to be thoroughly re-examined within the context of early 21st century cross-cultural attitudes and patterns of behavior. Cross-cultural relationships [...] have changes dramatically over the past quarter of a century, be they political, economic, or from a business perspective. Worldwide political systems, such as communism, have dramatically lost their influence since Hofstede first posited his cultural dimensions. Free market economies have taken a foothold [...] in many cultures while businesses have become more global in their reach and influence. [...] As political and economic systems decayed, long constrained cultural and sub-cultural differences have re-emerged [...]. With this in mind, Hofstede's original dimensions may be inaccurate, or at the least, outdated in defining contemporary cultural differences be they within or across different countries. [...] The study of cross-cultural values is simply too important in this time of globalization. [...]. We recommend that additional research be undertaken to build on Hofstede's cross-cultural dimensions to better adapt them to the 21st century global environment. [...] Hofstede's work has contributed significantly to the foundations of cross-cultural analysis and understanding. But like any good model, it needs to constantly be re-examined, re-defined, and adapted to the current environment (Orr/Hauser 2008: 16).

2.3.2 Cultural dimensions according to the GLOBE study

The GLOBE (Global Leadership and Organisational Behaviour Effectiveness) project is a global research programme concerned with leadership and organisational practices. Its meta-goal "[...] is to develop an empirically based theory to describe, understand, and predict the impact of specific cultural variables on leadership and organizational processes and the effectiveness of these processes" (House *et al.* 2001: 492). According to the GLOBE research team, this theory development is needed because of changes in the business environment as well as ongoing globalisation and the increasing interdependencies among nations (cf. House *et al.* 2001: 489; House *et al.* 2002: 3; Javidan/House 2002: 1; Brodbeck 2006: 16 ff.; Javidan *et al.* 2006: 84; House/Quigley/Sully de Luque 2010: 112).

The idea to create a global research programme was conceived in 1991 by Robert J. House (cf. House *et al.* 2004: 11). "An initial goal of Project GLOBE was to develop societal and organizational measures of culture and leader attributes that would be appropriate to employ across all cultures" (Chhokar/Brodbeck/House 2007: 6). The GLOBE project had started its research in 1993, while 170 scientists and management scholars all over the world are now currently engaged in the project. The GLOBE project database comprises over 17,000 questionnaires from 951 organisations in 62 societies (cf. House *et al.* 2004: 41). According to Chhokar, Brodbeck and House (2007: 2), the GLOBE study represents "[...] a rich source of information for anyone interested in understanding the culture and leadership of countries and organizations across the world".

On the basis of middle managers' responses to 735 questionnaire items based on the previous literature and independent theorisation in two pilot studies, nine dimensions of organisational as well as national culture[50] and six dimensions of effective leadership have been identified (cf. House *et al.* 2004: 11 f.). In the following, a brief description of these nine cultural dimensions is presented.

Uncertainty avoidance conveys the extent to which members of an organisation or society try to evade uncertainty by relying on social norms, rituals, and bureaucratic procedures (cf. House *et al.* 2001: 495). Individuals of high UA cultures actively look for opportunities to decrease the probability of unexpected events occurring (cf. House *et al.* 2004: 12).

Power distance is defined as the extent to which the members of an organisation or society expect and accept power being unequally divided (cf. House *et al.* 2001: 495).

Collectivism I: societal collectivism represents the degree to which collective action and the distribution of resources is encouraged and rewarded by organisational and institutional practices (cf. House *et al.* 2004: 12).

Collectivism II: in-group collectivism conveys the extent to which pride, loyalty, and cohesiveness is expressed within a group (cf. House *et al.* 2004: 12).

50 In the GLOBE project, culture is defined as: "[...] shared motives, values, beliefs, identities, and interpretations or meanings of significant events that result from common experiences of members of collectives that are transmitted across generations" (House *et al.* 2004: 15).

Gender egalitarianism represents the extent to which an organisation or society boosts gender equality (cf. House *et al.* 2004: 12).

Assertiveness refers to the degree to which social relationships within an organisation or society are characterised by assertiveness, confrontation, and aggressiveness (cf. House *et al.* 2004: 12).

Future orientation represents the prevalence of future-oriented beha-vi-our, e.g. planning, investing etc., within an organisation or society (cf. House *et al.* 2004: 12).

Performance orientation refers to the degree of encouragement and gratification of performance improvement and excellence within an organisation or society (cf. House *et al.* 2004: 12).

Humane orientation represents the degree to which fair, altruistic, friendly, generous, and caring behaviour is encouraged and rewarded within an organisation or society (cf. House *et al.* 2004: 12).

The data collected from these 62 societies have been further consolidated into 10 cultural clusters to allow for inter-cluster as well as cross-cluster comparison. Such cultural clusters also help summarise intercultural similarities and differences (cf. Gupta *et al.* 2002: 11). These clusters were composed based on the results of previous empirical studies and factors such as common language, geography, religion, and historical accounts (cf. Gupta et al. 2002: 12). Austria, Germany (former East and former West), the Netherlands, and the German-speaking part of Switzerland form the Germanic cluster. Russia is part of the Eastern Europe cluster together with Hungary, Kazakhstan, Albania, Poland, Greece, Slovenia, and Georgia[51]. Researchers involved in the GLOBE project tend to assume that national samples obtained in such an extensive cross-cultural research project mirror typical country characteristics (cf. Javidan *et al.* 2006a: 910).

The countries within the Eastern Europe cluster have different characteristics with regard to language, ethnicity, religious traditions, and economic backgrounds but, for the most part, share a feeling of unity rooted in the construct of the former Soviet Union that comprised elements such as a centrally planned economy (cf. Bakacsi *et al.* 2002: 70). The GLOBE

51 In the author's opinion, the Eastern Europe cluster has a vast bundle of completely different countries from a cultural perspective. Further differentiation between these countries is desirable.

study's description of this cluster includes the observation that "[...] its social culture is highly group oriented and dominated by hierarchical managerial practices [... and that] countries in this cluster tolerate more uncertainty and practice more gender egalitarianism than the GLOBE countries as a whole" (Bakacsi *et al.* 2002: 75).

By contrast, the countries within the Germanic cluster share most characteristics such as language (except for the Netherlands), ethnicity, religious traditions, and economic backgrounds to a certain degree. According to the GLOBE study, this cluster is defined by "[...] high practices of performance orientation, uncertainty avoidance, future orientation, and assertiveness [... and] this cluster is also characterized by relatively low values of institutional collectivism, in-group collectivism, gender egalitarianism, and humane orientation" (Gupta *et al.* 2002: 14).

Fig. 11 compares the values of the Eastern Europe and Germanic clusters based on the nine cultural dimensions according to the GLOBE study.

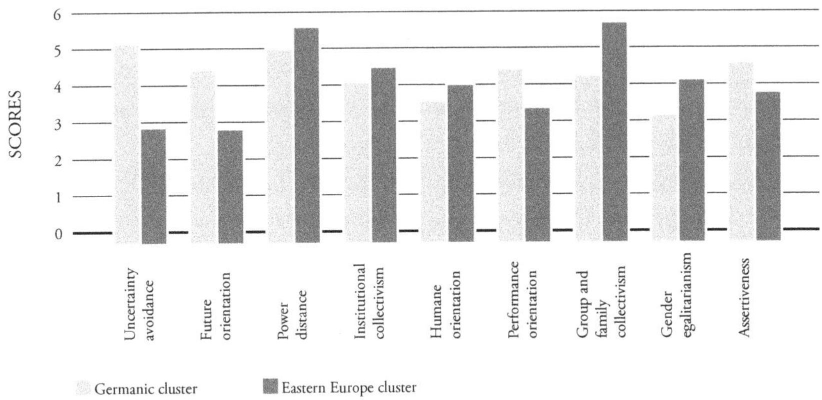

Fig. 11: The GLOBE's cultural dimensions for the Germanic and Eastern Europe clusters (own representation)

Fig. 11 illustrates that the biggest discrepancies can be observed with regard to the value of uncertainty avoidance and future orientation, with a higher score in UA or future orientation within the Germanic cluster, and a higher score in in-group and family collectivism within the Eastern Europe cluster. Contrariwise, the differences within the other cultural dimensions are relatively small.

Owing to its broad setup and composition on the basis of already existing and well-known cultural studies, the GLOBE study has been less criticised than, for example, Hofstede's or Trompenaars's studies. Never-theless, it has also been subject to intense criticism, mainly by Geert Hofstede himself. One of the two important aspects of Hofstede's critique worth mentioning is the fact that the GLOBE study focuses only on answers given by managers, not including employees from different levels. Second, Hofstede criticised that the design and analysis of the GLOBE study strongly reflects US hegemony and, therefore, suffers from a US national bias (cf. Hofstede 2006: 884).

2.3.3 Cultural dimensions according to Trompenaars and Hampden-Turner

Fons Trompenaars, a Dutch research expert in the area of intercultural communication, provides another set of cultural dimensions in order to describe cultural differences and show how they affect business life and management. Trompenaars's dataset consists of 30,000 questionnaires from 55 countries (cf. Kutschker/Schmid 2006: 727). In contrast to Hofstede's research, Trompenaars' final dataset (about 15,000 respondents[52]) came from different companies, such as Heineken, Volvo, and Eastman Kodak (cf. Rothlauf 2009: 45).

According to Trompenaars and Hampden-Turner (2010: 6), cultures can be distinguished by how certain problems are solved and existing dilemmas reconciled. Therefore, in their opinion, it is convenient to investigate these problem-solving mechanisms in order to analyse differences between cultures (cf. Trompenaars/Hampden-Turner 2010: 7). The underlying problems can be described by three problem categories: problems that arise from relationships with other people, problems that come from the passage of time, and problems that relate to the environment (cf. Trompenaars/Hampden-Turner 2010: 8). Trompenaars's research examined cultures using these categories. A survey was conducted asking several questions related to how different problems are solved across countries. Based on this survey, seven fundamental dimensions of culture were developed (cf. Kutschker/Schmid 2006: 730). In the following, the dimensions and problem categories they relate to are described briefly.

52 For more details, consult Hofstede (1996: 190).

Relationships with people: This category contains five dimensions concerned with the ways in which individuals deal with each other (cf. Trompenaars/Hampden-Turner 2010: 8 f.). Most cultures internalise each pole of the following dimensions. However, which pole happens to be prevalent depends on the specific situation. Nevertheless, Trompenaars's research allows for a general statement about the tendency of a culture towards one pole.

Universalism vs. particularism: This first dimension describes how other people's behaviour is judged. There are two alternative types of judgments. Universalists attach great importance to strict compliance with rules. For them, rules are more important than relationships. By contrast, proponents of particularism evaluate a specific situation based on personal relationships (cf. Trompenaars/Hampden-Turner 2010: 8, 35, 39). In Switzerland, individuals tend to be more universalistic in most instances, whereas Russians tend to be particularistic.

Individualism vs. communitarianism: The second dimension is similar to the dimension of "individualism vs. collectivism" in Hofstede's model. It answers the question: "Do people regard themselves primarily as individuals or primarily as part of a group?" (Trompenaars/Hampden-Turner 2010: 8). Individualists are primarily oriented towards themselves and base decisions on their own interests. Communitarianists, on the other hand, are oriented towards the common goals and objectives of the community and make decisions based on these common interests (cf. Trompenaars/Hampden-Turner 2010: 57 ff.). In contrast to Hofstede's categorisation, Russia tends to be individualistic despite its communist past according to Trompenaars and Hampden-Turner (2010: 56) and thus it has a common ground with Switzerland in terms of individualism.

Neutral vs. emotional: Relationships between people are characterised by emotion and reason. Individuals from highly affective countries freely display their feelings and emotions while communicating or interacting with others. By contrast, individuals belonging to neutral cultures do not show their feelings and emotions, but rather control them and limit their display (cf. Trompenaars/Hampden-Turner 2010: 9, 69 ff.). Switzerland and Russia tend to be affectively neutral cultures, although the percentage of Swiss respondents who would not show their emotions openly was 10%

higher compared with the percentage of Russian respondents (cf. Trompenaars/Hampden-Turner 2010: 70).

Specific vs. diffuse: This dimension represents the degree to which an individual's areas of life, e.g. family and profession, are separated. In diffuse cultures, different areas of life are indistinguishable, whereas in specific cultures they are strictly separated (cf. Trompenaars/Hampden-Turner 2010: 9, 87 f.). Swiss respondents seemed to be much more specific in this regard than their Russian counterparts.

Achievement vs. ascription: This dimension describes whether status is achieved or ascribed within a culture. Some cultures accord status to individuals based on their achievements. In these cultures, status depends on doing something, whereas other cultures accord status based on being something. Status in these cultures depends on age, gender, class, or education (cf. Trompenaars/Hampden-Turner 2010: 9). Switzerland tends to be achievement-oriented, whereas Russia is positioned somewhere in-between with a tendency towards ascription (cf. Trompenaars/Hampden-Turner 2010: 105 f.).

Attitudes to time: The perception and valuation of time in different cultures vary to a great extent, which entails certain consequences. Trompenaars and Hampden-Turner (2010: 10, 122 ff.) distinguish between cultures that view time as sequential and cultures that view time as synchronic. The sequential perception of time indicates that the past, present, and future are ordered successively. The synchronic perception views the past, present, and future as interrelated, i.e. the ideas of the future and memories of the past influence present actions. Trompenaars and Hampden-Turner (2010: 126) further classify cultures as future-oriented, present-oriented, or past-oriented. The Swiss culture tends to be more future-oriented, whereas the Russian culture seems to be more oriented towards the past. Furthermore, it can be deduced that in Russia a sequential view of time is prevalent, while in Switzerland a synchronic view of time is dominant[53].

Attitudes to the environment: The last dimension describes the role people assign to their natural environments. Representatives of different

53 Hofstede harshly criticises this dimension since it was evaluated in a completely different way and did not comprise a series of freestanding items (such as with the other dimensions) (cf. Hofstede 1996: 191).

cultures either believe that they can and should control nature being masters of their own fate or that they are part of nature and that they have to live with it and by its rules. In Switzerland, for instance, people tend to believe that what happens to them is their own doing (77% vs. 49% in Russia) (cf. Trompenaars/Hampden-Turner 2010: 10, 144).

In *Fig. 12,* these seven dimensions for both countries in question are represented. The scores are provided for six of them, since the dimension *attitudes to time* requires a specific graphical depiction.

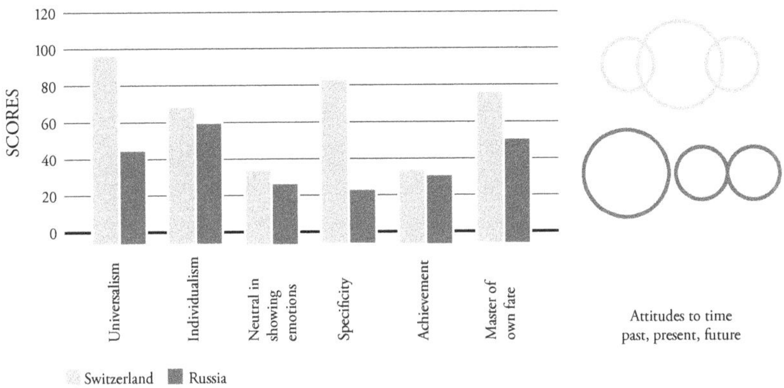

Fig. 12: Cultural dimensions of Trompenaars and Hampden-Turner for Switzerland and Russia (own representation)

As shown in *Fig.12,* the biggest differences between the two countries are on the dimension of universalism vs. particularism with Russia being more particularistic, on the dimension of specificity vs. diffusion with Russia being more diffuse, and on the dimension of attitudes to environment with Russians being more superstitious and Swiss being the masters of their own fate. Finally, the different attitudes to time should be highlighted, with Russians showing a tendency to view time as a sequence of separate periods of life as opposed to their Swiss counterparts who view their lives as a synchronic pattern of interrelated periods of the past, present, and future.

Trompenaars's work has been criticised comparatively heavily as well. One of the major points of this criticism is the probable bias inherent to the specific sample of respondents. Trompenaars's research was based on a sample of management training participants who most likely already have a high degree of intercultural skills (cf. Kutschker/Schmid 2006: 732). Another aspect that is often subjected to criticism is the fact that the mere data published by Trompenaars and the marginal explanations of the methodology provide only insufficient support for his dimensional model (cf. Kutschker/Schmid 2006: 734). Furthermore, it is hard, merely based on his published book, to examine the detailed positions of single countries on these dimensions. One of the fiercest critics was Geert Hofstede. He argues that the theory of Trompenaars is not supported by the data. He further mentions the evident lack of content validity of the instrument (cf. Hofstede 1996: 189) and alleges that the empirical analysis of Trompenaars's data provides only limited support for the seven-dimensional model, as respondents distinguished a maximum of four separate issues that were then recombined with the original categories existing in the intercultural research (cf. Hofstede 1996: 193). Hofstede claims that Trompenaars confuses conceptual categories that are present in the mind of any researcher with dimensions. In this respect, he criticises that Trompenaars relies heavily on the conceptual categories of American sociologists and anthropologists of the 1950s and 1960s. In so doing, his research remains guided by the American literature of the middle of the 20th century, which was unavoidably ethnocentric (cf. Hofstede 1996: 195, 197). "He did not change his concepts on the basis of his own findings either, nor did he follow the development of the state-of-the-art in comparative culture research since 1961" (Hofstede 1996: 197 f.).

2.3.4 Lewis's categories of culture

Richard D. Lewis, a British cross-cultural communication expert, does not characterise different cultures with the help of individual dimensions, but rather assigns them to predefined culture categories.

Lewis's categories are aimed at business life and employees confronted with various cultural settings, e.g. expatriates. Owing to his linguistic background, Lewis emphasises that the ability to interact and communicate successfully with foreign partners has become essential in a world of globalised business, IT-caused proximity, and politico-economic associations (cf. Lewis 2010: 27 f.). Therefore, cross-cultural training followed by international experience, which enables individuals to appropriately and thus successfully interact and communicate in any cultural setting, has to be undertaken (cf. Lewis 2010: 28). The insights gained within the training and the actual experiences create a stance of an individual towards a certain country. Hence, the individual internalises behaviour and thought patterns, enabling him/her to deal with the challenges presented by this particular culture (cf. Lewis 2010: 28). Unfortunately, one cannot internalise innumerable behaviour and thought patterns to deal perfectly with every culture in the world (cf. Lewis 2010: 28). Therefore, a certain level of standardisation is needed to sum up cultures into broader categories. This categorisation enables us "[...] to predict a culture's behavior, clarify why people did what they did, avoid giving offense, search for some kind of unity, standardize policies, and perceive neatness and *Ordnung* [sic]" (Lewis 2010: 29).

Lewis's categorisation of cultures is based on the prevalent attitudes towards time, communication, and information gathering. He developed three broad categories: linear-active, multi-active, and reactive cultures. Lewis assigns to each category several distinct characteristics and behaviours and describes how they influence the communication and interaction between the cultures of different categories. Lewis himself admits, however, that this broad categorisation of cultures and assignment of characteristics may lead to stereotyping (cf. Lewis 2010: XVII f.). Therefore, he underlines that the characterisation of cultures based on these categories should be taken as a very general one and that there are a lot of individual variation within cultures (cf. Lewis 2010: XVII f., 28 ff.). Nevertheless, the categorisation, say, provides managers with a broad overview of what to expect and how to adapt while doing business abroad and, therefore, can reduce prejudice, misunderstanding, and offense, thereby enhancing communicational and interactional success (cf. Lewis 2010 28 ff.).

Fig. 13 provides a diagrammatic disposition of the culture categories and variations among major cultures. The assignment of cultures to the categories is based on thorough observations and numerous assessments of cultural profiles[54]. The position of a country within this figure does

54 Lewis (2010) covers more than 60 countries and every major region in the world. However, it has no clear scientific research method behind it and no peer reviews. Therefore, certain cultural descriptions may appear as insightful cultural generalisations. Nevertheless, Lewis's model has been accepted as one of the most important in intercultural research.

not indicate the cultural distance between each nationality, but its relative positioning in terms of its linear-active, multi-active, and reactive nature (cf. Lewis 2010: 41). Hence, the closeness of Russia and Italy in the figure does not imply that they share similar core beliefs or values, it rather indicates that they are linear-active/multi-active to a similar degree (cf. Lewis 2010: 41).

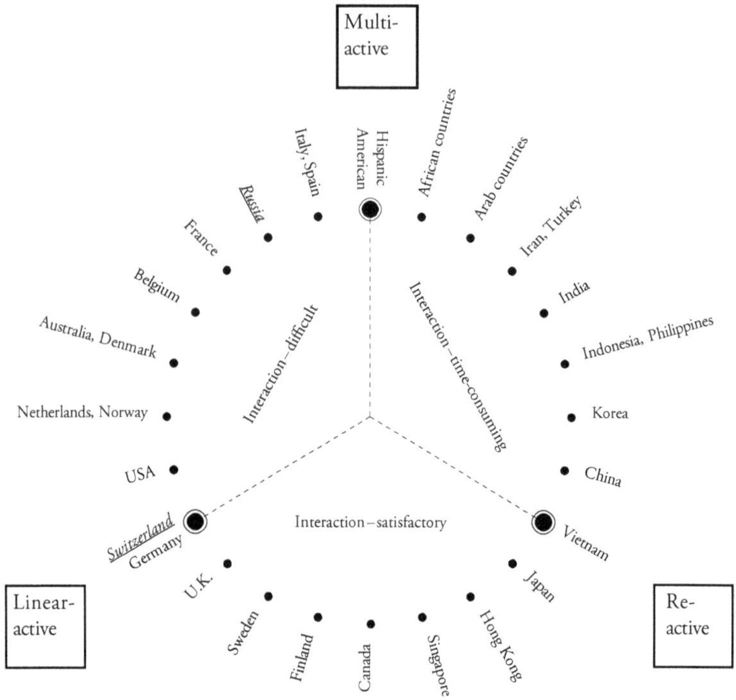

Fig. 13: Lewis's cultural categories and their interactions (based on Lewis 2010: 39, 42)

Lewis presents an extensive list of features assigned to each category (cf. Lewis 2010: 27 ff.). Hereafter, the different categories are described briefly and only the most obvious features are stated.

Linear-active cultures: The individuals of this culture category follow a linear-active time system, i.e. they do one thing at a time, concentrate hard on this one thing, and complete it within given schedules. Sequential steps of action are organised and planned and, therefore, schedules and punctuality are very important. Individuals from these cultures separate their social and professional lives and, therefore, they are job-oriented while working. Interactions and communication in business life are processed in an unemotional way. They confront negotiation partners with logic. The use of body language is limited and while someone else is talking they are patient instead of promptly interrupting. Information is gathered from statistics, reference books, and databases (cf. Lewis 2010: 29 ff.). As can be seen in *Fig. 13*, Switzerland tends to be linear-active.

Multi-active cultures: Members of this culture category pursue a multi-active time system – doing many things at once often in an unplanned order. They are highly flexible. Schedules and punctuality are not rated highly. They are highly extroverted, talkative, and use body language constantly. Their social and professional lives are interwoven because of their high people-orientation. They confront their counterparts emotionally. Furthermore, they rely heavily on firsthand, mainly oral information (cf. Lewis 2010: 29 ff.). Russia tends to be more multi-active, but it also shares some linear-active characteristics.

Reactive cultures: Individuals belonging to this culture category are mostly characterised by their ways of communicating. They are patient. While communicating, they prefer to listen to the other's position first, before reacting to it by formulating their own position. They are introverted and distrust words. They attach great importance to nonverbal communication. They observe and listen instead of talking and acting first. The preferred mode of communication is monologue. They expect a high degree of knowledge of their counterparts and, therefore, they do not provide all information. Instead, they rely on the counterpart to complete the missing information (cf. Lewis 2010: 32 ff.)[55].

Communication and interaction between these categories can be difficult, especially between individuals from linear-active and multi-active cultures, because of the different attitudes towards time, communication mode, and information gathering (cf. Lewis 2010: 38 f.).

Now that the four main cultural theories guiding the present research have been introduced, a brief overview of the "cultural divergence vs. convergence debate" will follow in the remainder of this chapter.

55 Japan and Finland are typical representatives of reactive cultures.

Diverging views on tendencies of cultural development – cultural divergence and convergence with respect to the new generation

Are cultural differences around the world decreasing, with different cultures converging towards a global culture? Are national cultures becoming obsolete? *(convergence thesis)* or are there significant cultural differences around the world that prevail even in the face of globalisation? Are national cultures even becoming more pronounced *(divergence thesis)*? These questions represent the convergence-divergence debate regarding the development of similarities and differences in cultures worldwide (cf. Yaeger *et al.* 2006: 22; Nederveen Pieterse 2009: 1). This debate originates from the comparative management literature of the 1960s proclaiming the *convergence thesis,* i.e. management practices and philosophies around the world becoming more similar (cf. Hofstede 2001: 34). Globalisation and the ongoing technological progress are assumed to be the main drivers of the *convergence thesis* (cf. Hofstede 2001: 34; Rofe 2003: 2511 f.; Leung *et al.* 2005: 358 ff.).

One of the most prominent representatives of the opposite tendency, namely *divergence thesis,* is Hofstede. He argues that cultures, in particular national cultures, are extremely stable over time (cf. Hofstede 2001: 34). Hofstede (2001: 34) admits that technological progress is indeed a powerful force, leading to similar developments across societies and eventually perhaps to cultural change. At the same time, he argues that technological progress is not powerful enough to completely erase cultural differences and may even foster differences, considering that new technologies are interpreted based on the prevalent values of a particular culture (Hofstede 2001: 34).

As mentioned above, the *divergence thesis* is challenged by globalisation and accelerated technological progress. Even though globalisation is not a new phenomenon, e.g. note the history of the Roman Empire, globalisation today is characterised by its high pace, not least because of the aforementioned technological progress (cf. Husted 2003: 430). Since the beginning of the 1980s the concept of globalisation has been discussed heavily in popular scientific media as well as in the scientific literature (cf. Clark/Knowles 2003: 361; Kutschker/Schmid 2006: 153). Globalisation has become an ideogram of the age and the 21st century (cf. Clark/Knowles 2003: 361). It can be defined as "the process by which economic, political, cultural, social, and other relevant systems of nations are integrating into World Systems [...]" (Clark/Knowles 2003: 368).

Fang (2005: 84 f.) argues that the most significant consequence of globalisation is that national cultures are no longer "black boxes". He compares the present development with the situation Hofstede and most of his colleagues faced while they emphasised the differences in cultures based on dimensions (cf. Fang 2005: 84). In his opinion, at that time the Cold War characterised and separated the world and with the absence of technological innovations such as the Internet, few cultures were informed about other cultures (cf. Fang 2005: 84 f.). Growing globalisation, causing increased world trade and business activity, accelerated technological progress, and the associated converging utilisation of and access to all relevant media as well as increased opportunities to travel in business and private life, resulted in more transparent cultures (cf. Bird/Stevens 2003: 397; Fang 2005: 85). Tastes and trends are spread across the world and lead to converging consumer behaviours and needs (cf. Bird/Stevens 2003: 398; De Mooij 2003: 183). Therefore, many researchers argue that globalisation and technological progress give rise to a commonly accepted global culture, while national cultures are moving towards growing obsolescence (cf. Bird/Stevens 2003: 396). "The Internet is used for communication, creating new virtual communities. Universities offer similar programmes, students are prescribed the same textbooks. A new global culture is thus arising especially among people in international business" (Prašnikar/Pahor/Vidmar Svetlik 2008: 9).

Recalling that culture is learned and derives from the social environment, it seems obvious that today's increasingly globally shared experiences will lead, to some extent, to a convergence of national cultures (cf. Fang 2005: 85). However, jumping to the conclusion of the emergence of a global culture because of the increased standardisation of practices around the world is highly superficial (cf. Husted 2003: 429; Leung *et al.* 2005: 359). Therefore, it seems safe to say that converging practices around the world do not automatically lead to the obsolescence of national cultures (cf. Felser 2010: 29).

Bird and Stevens (2003) present yet another idea based on the analysis of existing research papers on the topic. They describe an emerging global culture next to already existing cultures. The membership in this global culture is self-selected, because those who attach themselves to other members of the global culture become members themselves (cf. Bird/Stevens 2003: 400). The sense of belonging to this new emerging global culture does not depend on direct contact or interaction with this culture and its members because of the widespread utilisation of various technologies, which enable a certain degree of enculturation without direct contact (cf. Bird/Stevens 2003: 400 f.). The members of this new emerging global culture are characterised as follows (cf. Bird/Stevens 2003: 401 f.):

- educated;
- connected (travel and communication);
- self-confident;
- pragmatic;
- not intimidated by national boundaries and cultures;
- democratic and participatory (towards life in general);
- individualistic but inclusive;
- flexible and open; and
- starting from a position of trust (when initiating relationships).

The emergence of a new global culture does not necessarily lead to the obsolescence of national cultures because members of the global culture still retain much of their home cultures (cf. Bird/Stevens 2003: 401). The members of this global culture may internalise two cultures and develop a jointly influenced set of values, attitudes, and beliefs that serves as a lens through which the world is understood. In this respect, Axelrod (1997: 205) remarks that "the likelihood that a given cultural feature will spread from one individual (or group) to another depends on how many other features they may already have in common. Similarity leads to interaction, and interaction leads to [..] more similarity".

The idea of an emerging global culture seems to be a plausible approach, but one should keep in mind that it is in part restricted to industrialised states. Leung *et al.* (2005: 358 f.) point out that our world is only partially globalised. Furthermore, various technological developments are still not accessible in many parts of the world. Therefore, more time will be needed before a truly global culture is able to emerge (if at all). It is however undeniable that the business environment represents one of the factors that causes significant changes in the value system of an individual towards the global orientation (cf. Praśnikar/Pahor/Vidmar Svetlik 2008: 10).

Recalling the *convergence vs. divergence debate,* an interesting approach concerning the relevance of cultural influence on generations is proposed by Edmunds and Turner (2005: 566), who argue that owing to technological developments a global generation is emerging, because "defining moments" are now perceived similarly around the world. They suggest as one such instance the attack on the World Trade Center on 9/11. This major cultural trauma in the US spread to a global level, thereby creating a new global generation (cf. Edmunds/Turner 2005: 570). However, this statement has not yet been tested (cf. Parry/Urwin 2011: 90 f.).

The emergence of a global generation may be associated with the emergence of a global culture as proposed by Bird and Stevens (2003). However, as previously mentioned, not all individuals belong to this emerging global culture (cf. Bird/Stevens 2003: 399). Therefore, membership of a global generation has to be seen critically as well. It is possible, for instance, that the events of 9/11 constitute the defining moment for a new global generation, but not all individuals around the world may have perceived these events in the same way (cf. Parry/Urwin 2011: 90 f.). Furthermore, it is assumed that every individual is confronted with these events because of technological developments and globalisation. However, as previously mentioned, not all parts of the world are globalised and technologised to the same extent (cf. Leung *et al.* 2005: 358). Therefore, it may be assumed that individuals who tend to belong to a global culture belong to a global generation as well. However, belonging to a global generation based on having experienced the same events in formative years does not necessarily imply that the influence of national culture is negligible or that it has completely disappeared. Rather, generational and cultural effects may exist in parallel and interact with each other, thereby influencing the values, attitudes, and beliefs of individuals or groups of individuals. Which effect prevails thus depends on the particular context.

Therefore, it can be assumed that since Gen Y has grown up parallel with rapid technological advancements, this generation may have the most similarities across nations. This seems to be especially true regarding those Gen Yers who also belong to the global culture. Nevertheless, since national culture is perceived to be relatively stable over time even from a dynamic perspective, the assumption should be made that national influences still count for Gen Y. The question that remains is to what extent these national influences still exist. The present study seeks to gain more in-depth insights into this topic.

2.4 Research gaps and research questions

Overall, the methodological problem in intercultural research is that the authors often merely enumerate what they consider to be important for HRM in a particular country without applying any basic theoretical concepts. This characterises the general problem of comparative management research, namely a lack of theory (cf. Pieper 1990: 20). "The lack of a theoretical foundation is [...] the result of different approaches to comparative management, which [...] could not be combined into a single theoretical concept" (Pieper 1990: 20). According to Colbert (2004: 341),

> without good theory, the field of SHRM [Strategic Human Resource Management] could be characterized as plethora of statements regarding empirical relationships and/or prescriptions for practice that fail to explain why these relationships exist or should exist. [...] A stronger theoretical foundation will help to [...] improve the focus and effectiveness of HRM research and practice, and it will help organizations to thrive more effectively in their particular operating contexts (Colbert 2004: 341).

"Another consideration for future research is the need to test competing cultural models" (Matsumoto/Hee Yoo 2006: 239).

As previously indicated, most studies of generational differences and characteristics have been performed within the US (cf. Parry/Urwin 2011: 91). Little research has been conducted on the disparities of different generations around the world due to culture (cf. Covri/Bigi/Ng 2007: 2 f.; Macky *et al.* 2008: 860 among others). The results of US studies have often been transferred to other cultural contexts without question (cf. Bruch/Kunze/Boehm 2010: 94). It is assumed that these findings are globally appropriate, or at least transferable, to the western world (cf. Parry/Urwin 2011: 91). On the surface, this might be acceptable, but when considering what accounts for a generation, several concerns arise, especially when considering non-western countries. According to Eisner (2005: 14), future research should look into the initial employment expectations of Gen Y graduates with different majors, aspiring to work in different industries, and, most importantly, living in geographic areas other than the USA. The analysis of academic articles, practitioner-targeted publications, and bibliographies provides evidence that research on the management of Gen Y has begun (cf. Eisner 2005: 4). Nevertheless, no information has been found about how national culture influences Gen Y and thereby how it affects the process of shaping graduates' initial employment expectations[56].

> Practically speaking, organizations may experience and respond to generational challenges in many ways, yet popular approaches to understanding these phenomena, witnessed in a growing number of 'generational toolkits', provide only simplistic characterizations of generations [...] (Joshi *et al.* 2010: 393).

"Attitudes, values, and beliefs can serve as important context variables that may unpackage cultural differences" (Matsumoto/Hee Yoo 2006: 242).

Furthermore, there has been little theory-based comparative research on graduates' initial employment expectations in different institutional settings, e.g. different countries, and no research at all comparing university graduates in Russia and Switzerland. Moreover, some European academics (e.g. Brewster 1993: 763 ff.) argue for a specific European HRM model, which implies that, for instance, American approaches to HRM processes cannot be applied in European settings and, therefore, that each institutional setting requires its own HRM model with unique HR processes. Delery (1998: 290) further argues that although the RBV of the firm provides a rational background explaining the importance of HR to firm competitiveness and effectiveness, it does not describe the HR processes that support and ensure this sustained competitive advantage. Therefore, based

56 The existence of a research gap in this field was confirmed by Geert Hofstede himself during the worldwide webinar (online seminar) in which the author took part on the 7th of October 2010. The author addressed to Professor Hofstede a question concerning the applicability of his cultural dimensions to certain generational cohorts (to Gen Y among others). After the prioritisation of questions that were sent in, this question was chosen first to be answered. The moderators of the webinar Catherine Mercer Bing and Jerry Vastano (2010) contacted Hofstede for an answer. According to Geert Hofstede, there is a huge potential for research in this field since nobody has tested the applicability of his dimensions to Gen Y so far.

on RBV arguments, there is a clear demand to focus on several HR functions that are vital for the sustained competitive advantage of any firm.

It became clear from the secondary analysis of the scientific literature that the managerial implications of Gen Y's entry into the workplace are complex and should be investigated within a cross-national context.

> Given that most cross-cultural research is really cross-national, one needs to consider all the relevant sources that could potentially produce observed between-country differences. Some may be cultural, some may not, and it will be important for research in the future to rule out the possibility that noncultural sources contribute to observed group differences (Matsumoto/Hee Yoo 2006: 237).

In this respect, there is a need to verify: first, the relevant core characteristics of Gen Y; second, Gen Y's initial employment expectations in terms of the importance of certain EB attributes according to nationality and/or belonging to Gen Y; and third, what elements should be included in recruitment marketing strategies in order to make employer branding efforts efficient with respect to today's intercultural environment.

This book seeks to contribute to the literature, management practice, and business education in this field by closing the gap through primary and secondary research. It examines cross-nationally the characteristics of young potential entrants to the workplace, Gen Y, and aims to deliver strategic implications for employer branding and recruitment marketing strategies for Gen Y. Based on the current state of the research, the following research questions were formulated:

- What underlying EB attributes are important for Gen Y university graduates?
- How does national culture affect Gen Y and its employment expectations?
- Are there any significant differences in the initial employment expectations of Gen Y university graduates of different nationalities (Switzerland vs. Russia) in terms of the importance of certain EB attributes[57]?
- What paradigm has a stronger influence in terms of shaping the initial employment expectations of Gen Y: cultural or generational?
- What elements should modern employer branding strategies for Gen Y comprise?

57 Convergence vs. divergence thesis.

The focus of the study comprises the information side of recruitment marketing, namely "all measures of information retrieval [..] on which HR-manager relies when determining HR-objectives and deciding upon deployment of action parameters" (cf. Thom 2010: 234). This book examines one specific part of the information side that is of high importance for today's recruitment marketing, i.e. it focuses on the way students of different nationalities moving from higher education into the labour market construct their expectations towards their first potential employers. In particular, it explores the ways Swiss and Russian graduates perceive the extent to which initial employment expectations vary across these nations and it examines the orientations and attitudes the students of two different nationalities have on the issue of EB attributes.

EB attributes

On the basis of the reflections presented above, it is clear that the EB fulfils several functions that have a great impact on a candidate's decision-making during the application and recruitment process (cf. Petkovic 2008: 68, see also chapter 2.1.2.1)[58]. According to Branham (2005: 59), in order to become an EOC, employer branding engagement practices should aim at matching candidates' expectations with work realities. Therefore, an elaborate list of EB attributes was proposed by the author to assess the importance of the job and organisational attributes relevant for Gen Y. In line with Hieronimus, Schaefer and Schröder (2005: 14), identifying the

58 The employer branding strategy must reach internal as well as external target groups (cf. Andratschke/Regier/Huber 2009: 20). The main difference between internal and external employer branding is the group of people that the communication activities are directed at. External employer branding focuses on the potential labour market with the goal of attracting the right potentials and encouraging them to apply for a position in the company. The goal of internal employer branding is to create a working environment in order to retain and develop well-qualified and committed employees (cf. Classen 1995: 27). It is important to note that internal and external employer branding are highly interlinked and that they influence one another: "By earning a reputation for sustaining the same values internally as your brand promises externally, or simply by creating a highly recognizable internal brand, potential employees are predisposed to give increased weight to your company's intangibles when seeking employment or considering an offer" (Hunt/Landry n/a: 35). In return, the appearance on the external labour market influences the self-confidence and expectations of current employees (cf. Classen 1995: 27). The focus of this book lies in shaping an efficient external employer branding strategy, but the importance of the internal branding strategy and its strategic and operative interconnection with the external employer branding strategy must always be kept in mind.

job and organisational attributes (see also Chapman *et al.* 2005: 929) that best distinguish a company in the eyes of Gen Y graduates can improve the cost effectiveness of the recruiting process.

Since an EB displays a group of attributes that make it holistic, a final bundle of benefits that have been identified throughout a thorough literature analysis and explorative studies as most relevant for Gen Yers consists of the following 19 EB attributes to be measured in the empirical part of the study (see also chapter 2.2):

- Prestige (Lyons/Duxbury/Higgins 2005: 67; Cennamo/Gardner 2008: 902; Knox/Freeman 2006: 703; Headhunter 2010)
- Good reference for future career (Bruch/Kunze/Boehm 2010: 109; Kienbaum 2010; Knox/Freeman 2006: 703; Deloitte 2010: 15)
- High level of CSR (Tapscott 2009; Universum 2011; PricewaterhouseCoopers 2008; Lyons/Duxbury/Higgins 2005: 63; Twenge 2010: 204; Twenge *et al.* 2010: 17; Deloitte 2011: 10; Schiendorfer 2011: 9)
- Culture that respects one's individuality (Twenge/Campbell 2008: 864; Knox/Freeman 2006: 703; Deloitte 2010: 15; Schiendorfer 2011: 9; Herman/Gioia 2000: 9 ff.)
- Culture that values diversity among personnel (Twenge 2010: 206; Deloitte 2010: 15; Herman/Gioia 2000: 9 ff.)
- Culture that supports equality between sexes (Twenge 2010: 206; Deloitte 2010: 15; Schiendorfer 2011: 9)
- Culture that accepts (underrepresented) minorities (Twenge 2010: 206; Deloitte 2010: 15)
- Challenging work (Tapscott 2009; Kienbaum 2010; Branham 2000: 19 ff.)
- Opportunities for relocation abroad and international travel (Universum 2010-2011; Knox/Freeman 2006: 703; Schiendorfer 2011: 9)
- Secure employment (Universum 2011; Bristow *et al.* 2011: 78)
- Flexible working conditions (Tapscott 2009; Hershatter/Epstein 2010: 220 f.)
- Good work/life balance (Twenge *et al.* 2010; Ng/Schweitzer/Lyons 2010; Deal/Altman/Rogelberg 2010: 196)
- Attractive geographic location (Universum 2011)

- Friendly work environment (Ng/Schweitzer/Lyons 2010: 283; Twenge *et al.* 2010: 205; Martin 2005: 40, Lyons/Duxbury/Higgins 2005: 68; Tapscott 2009; Knox/Freeman 2006: 703;)
- Performance-related bonus (Ng/Schweitzer/Lyons 2010: 282; StepStone 2011: 7)
- Professional training and education (Broadbridge/Maxwell/Ogden 2009: 412 f.; Terjesen/Vinnicombe/Freeman 2007: 517; Bristow *et al.* 2011: 78; Ramachandran/Artiuch 2007: 24; Knox/Freeman 2006: 703: Headhunter 2010; Schiendorfer 2011: 9; Adachi *et al.* 2012: 11)
- Personal mentoring/coaching (Broadbridge/Maxwell/Ogden 2009: 412 f.; Terjesen/Vinnicombe/Freeman 2007: 517; Branham 2005: 59; Adachi *et al.* 2012: 11)
- Leadership opportunities (Wong *et al.* 2008: 7; Adachi *et al.* 2012: 11; Herman/Gioia 2000: 9 ff.)
- Good possibilities for rapid promotion (Ng/Schweitzer/Lyons 2010: 289; Bristow *et al.* 2011: 78; Headhunter 2010; StepStone 2011; Branham 2000: 19 ff.; Tulgan 2009: 153 ff.)

The necessity to test the importance of the abovementioned EB attributes is substantiated because of the lack of target-oriented research in this area. As Sutherland, Torricelli and Karg (2002: 15) put it:

> Many of the criteria listed are anecdotal. Surveys that have been conducted draw their results from potential employees who are not necessarily knowledge workers. Other writings discuss criteria but not in the context of attracting employees to organisations but rather as general criteria around attraction and retention of knowledge workers. It is apparent that more work needs to be done to gather empirical data on this topic to validate the criteria that have been outlined in the writings (Sutherland/Torricelli/Karg 2002: 15).

Generation Y construct and nationality

Since there exist different generational classifications across countries, the generation Y phenomenon is measured by a specifically developed Gen Y construct that is operationalised later in the research (see chapter 4.1.1). The national dimension of culture is analysed by including the nationality factor into the research model, thus assessing the strength of cultural influence on each of group of Gen Yers (see chapter 4.2).

To sum up, although employees' expectations play a crucial role in the dynamics of the economy, there have been few direct scientific tests of the employment expectations of Gen Y university graduates because they are rarely observed as the starting point for recruitment marketing and employer branding activities. Therefore, there is a lack of scientific basis with respect to both graduates' initial employment expectations and the cultural backgrounds influencing these expectations. Hence, a study of the initial employment expectations of final year students of different nationalities before entering the labour market would assist in gauging the difference (if any) in the assigned weight to the EB attributes across nationalities. In terms of using cultural theories, this doctoral study represents an application of several cultural theories as well as Gen Y theory to the domain of recruitment marketing.

The book seeks to contribute to the business and management literature, practice, and education through primary and secondary research addressing these core questions and proposing research-based and theory-driven solutions. Javidan *et al.* (2006a: 911) present arguments in favour of such an approach:

> [..] We need to know more about when two cultures come in contact, which culture dimensions are key in this relationship. Undoubtedly, some are more important than others, but which and under what conditions? [...] we need to discover how different cultural dimensions interact as well as understanding the relative importance of each as they contribute to many societal outcomes (Javidan *et al.* 2006a: 911).

3

CONCEPTUAL FRAMEWORK

After having formulated the research questions, the decision-oriented conceptual framework integrating the majority of possible factors that might be relevant for the employer branding strategies to target Gen Y is elaborated. The conceptual framework presented in this chapter serves for describing and explaining real phenomena through terms and hypothetical assumptions (cf. Grochla 1978: 62 f.).

The development of the conceptual framework regarding the influence of culture on generation Y's expectations towards their employers and the recommendations derived thereof are based on a factual-analytical research strategy. This research strategy is designed to pervade complex situations, thereby developing an appropriate basis for action (cf. Grochla 1978: 72). Recruiting Gen Y in a global context represents a highly complex situation because of the manifold influencing variables. This research strategy helps conceptually simulate reality, thus elucidating relations and deriving corresponding recommendations (cf. Grochla 1978: 72). After the empirical part of the research has been completed and the results obtained, the conceptual framework developed in this chapter will be enlarged through the research findings to be applied to solving real problems (cf. Zaugg 2002: 5). Based on this conceptual framework, which may also be applied to the analysis of other generational cohorts, recommendations for the successful recruitment of the generation being studied can be developed.

Based on Grochla (1978: 23), the conceptual framework applied in this study consists of three main building blocks: (1) external, organisational, and employee factors; (2) indirect and direct action parameters, which are influenced by external, organisational, and employee factors but at the same time influence organisational and employee factors; and (3) effectiveness and efficiency criteria that assist in evaluating possible courses of action.

In the following, these elements of the conceptual framework are explained and the relations between them clarified.

3.1 External factors

All organisations operate in a particular environment to which they are inextricably connected. When thinking in terms of an integrative conceptual framework, certain exogenous and endogenous factors should be given consideration. Exogenous factors include industry characteristics and technology, the nature of competitors and the extent and speed of change, country and other regional characteristics such as political, economic, and sociocultural conditions, and legal requirements. Endogenous factors include the degree of internationalisation and structure of international operations and the competitive strategy being used (cf. Brewster/Sparrow/Harris 2005: 2).

According to Duncan (1972: 314), the external environment is "the totality of physical and social factors that are taken directly into consideration in the decision-making behaviour of individuals in the organization". These external dimensions influence the inputs of an organisation, affect the way organisational outputs are perceived, and are of large importance for organisational processes. Therefore, the external setting provides multiple contexts that influence the way the organisation operates (general environment and task environment).

External factors impose restrictions on the organisation that predetermine the range of available courses of action and place certain limits on the freedom of organisational decision-makers and employees to act and react to a certain event. According to Thom (1987: 343), these so-called contingency factors should not be viewed as absolute and unchangeable. Rather, they take the form of stipulations for current decisions. External factors may include, for example, government policies and legislation[59], economic forecasts, industry-related policies, social unrest, educational reforms, demographic forecasts and changes, and competitor recruitment[60].

The organisational environment that contains elements outside the organisational boundaries that are relevant to its operations is made up by a general environment (macro environment) and a task environment (micro environment). The macro environment is less proximal to the focal organisation and includes general factors that influence a broader geographic region with many organisations operating in a particular country.

59 "Heterogeneous legal requirements usually lead to differentiated products. Trade barriers have a more indirect effect. These usually lead to local production in the host country which often makes the local adaptation of products less expensive" (Grünig/Morschett 2012: 293).

60 "The presence of many national or global competitors influences a company's own market offer and its competitive situation" (Grünig/Morschett 2012: 293).

Kubicek and Thom (1976: 3988) divide these general factors into five subsystems: economic, political, sociocultural, technological, and physical-environmental. "Local geographies have many differences – different labor markets, different workforce demographics, different employee motivations and cultures, and different leadership styles" (Bersin 2011: 10).

Economic environmental factors refer to the economic environment of a particular country or region, namely its level of economic development (e.g. Switzerland as an industrialised developed economy vs. Russia as a member of the BRICS countries). Further, the level of intensive current and potential future-oriented cooperation between countries is an important indicator of an economically benevolent situation, which is the case for Switzerland and Russia. The job market situation and future trends in the employment market (demand vs. supply of the qualified workforce) are described by shortages in the qualified workforce in both (Swiss and Russian) markets, whereas in Russia the situation is more precarious because of persistent "brain drain" problems.

Political factors provide other important framework parameters within which an organisation operates, and these comprise all existing constitutional and legal regulations. In some countries such as Russia, this environment is restrictive and significantly influences all aspects of the organisation; in other countries such as Switzerland, the political-legal context is more permissive and fosters entrepreneurship (cf. Baumueller 2007: 216). Moreover, recruitment processes can be affected by restrictive immigration policies as in Switzerland (where there are strictly set restrictive quotas on the level of cantons for companies concerning the recruitment of third-country nationals, i.e. citizens who hold other than EU citizenship).

The sociocultural situation is shaped by the phenomena discussed earlier in the book, i.e. demographic changes, the convergence vs. divergence debate at the level of national culture, and generational paradigms (see chapters 1.1.2, 1.1.3, 2.2 and 2.3). Depending on these factors, a multinational corporation operating in a particular country may have to adapt its structures and management processes (e.g. HR practices of attracting, recruiting, and selecting).

The technological situation refers to the level of technological development of the environment, which provides opportunities as well as places constraints on the organisational activity not only in a specific location but also at a global scale. Therefore, it is important for the organisation to know the technological shrewdness of its workforce and its customers in order to be able to set up realistic requirements for potential employees in terms of technological literacy (cf. Baumueller 2007: 217). Today's technological advancement redefines not only the way the recruitment process is accomplished. It also endows potential employees with a unique opportunity to verify the authenticity of organisational communication and, correspondingly, a firm's EB.

The physical-environmental situation refers to all the natural and artificial resources that are relevant for organisational operations, e.g. mineral resources, infrastructure, degree of environmental pollution, etc. (cf. Baumueller 2007: 217). In this respect, it seems relevant to mention the still strong dependence of the Russian economy on its natural resources, predominantly oil and gas. This fact explains the desire of many Russian graduates to work for such companies as Gasprom (cf. Universum 2011). Switzerland, on the contrary, has almost no natural resources; its economy is knowledge-based and the majority of enterprises operate in the service sector. Furthermore, in terms of infrastructure, Switzerland has one of the densest transport networks in the world, whereas in Russia predominantly only big cities have good infrastructure. The specialists responsible for the employer branding campaign should consider this fact since, for instance, geographic location can significantly influence the degree of employer attractiveness in the eyes of potential employees.

The task environment is characterised by its proximity to and direct influence on the particular organisation. The entities that make up the task environment of the organisation include direct and potential competitors, customers, employees, shareholders, and other stakeholders (cf. Kubicek/Thom 1976: 3992). In turn, the organisation influences its surrounding task environment (competitors and other stakeholders such as customers, employees, and shareholders). Thus, the relationship between an organisation as such and its environment represents a complex network of interdependencies, which is particularly important to consider for the functioning of multinational corporations (cf. Duncan 1972: 314).

3.2 Organisational and employee factors

While the external environment of an organisation includes factors that are beyond the direct and immediate control of the company, organisational and employee factors as well as action parameters lie within the reach of organisational control. Factors such as a company's history and tradition, its growth path and size, its resources, capabilities and competencies, and the characteristics and capabilities of its members are subject to a more direct influence (see Thom 1987: 343).

Various organisational and employee factors characterise a company. They are specific to each particular company and should be considered to be key factors influencing the elaboration of employer branding strategies and structuring of recruitment processes. In the following, the factors that are particularly relevant for recruitment marketing will be enumerated.

Every organisation differs in terms of the size and complexity of its structures, management systems, and processes, degree of financial power, and innovative capacity, which often depend on belonging to a particular industry sector. These organisational factors are reflected in the EB, create a particular employer image among the public, and determine the degree of employer attractiveness among potential and current employees. The EVP should be regarded as one of the most important factors that an organisation possesses, since through its EVP it can send a clear message to its potential workforce in the recruitment marketing process. However, many companies, as mentioned earlier in the thesis, rely on chance rather than on a thorough analysis and relevant data when defining their EVPs (see chapter 2.1.2).

Employee factors represent the cognitive map of an organisation that is located in the minds of individuals who work, want to work, or have worked for the company (cf. Baumueller 2007: 224). There are also plenty of relevant employee factors but only those most important for recruitment marketing will be mentioned further. First, when embarking on a new strategy to implement the employer branding philosophy in the recruitment process, an organisation has to be aware of the labour intensity ratio. Labour-intensive companies require either a large number of employees or a large number of hours worked by employees, or both, in order to be successful. Labour intensity may be quantified by taking a ratio of the cost of labour (i.e. wages and salaries) as a proportion of the total capital cost of producing the good or service. The higher the ratio, the higher labour intensity is. Labour-intensive companies can control costs in bad economies by laying off workers (cf. Farlex Financial Dictionary 2011: online). These reflections show that before deciding on other employee factors that are relevant for the company, HR specialists must first be clear about the number of employees, their qualifications, and their workload forecasts before they start addressing their potential workforce.

After labour intensity has been calculated, the characteristics of the potential workforce (in this case, university graduates) have to be defined. Educational background is one important factor with respect to the level of education. It further helps decide on the cooperation strategy with educational institutions (cf. Baumueller 2007: 231). Other characteristics of graduates, such as years of practical experience or number of internships, personal career goals, and an open mindset, also represent important employee factors. The degree of cultural and generational diversity among the workforce that is aspired to in the organisation should also be clarified beforehand.

Today, many organisations have embraced the benefits that diversity brings. Diversity among employees delivers the necessary proportion of group heterogeneity and fosters diversity in the group's cognitive base (cf. Baumueller 2007: 237). Cultural diversity has become one of the distinguishing marks of Gen Y employees. Therefore, modern employer branding strategies that aim to recruit Gen Y employees should be conceptualised around the idea of harvesting the benefits of diversity (cf. Thom/Hubschmid 2011a: 18 ff.).

Alumni networks manifest in the degree of interconnection between the former, current, and future workforce. They thus represent a strong instrument for employer branding communication and therefore should be a focus of employer branding activities. Through alumni networks, many potential employees learn about their future EOCs. Therefore, such networks offer an important platform where potential employees can compare their employment expectations with the employment reality.

3.3 Action parameters

Action parameters are divided into two groups: indirect and direct. Indirect action parameters are of long-term nature and do not directly influence the achievement of organisational goals, whereas direct action parameters instantaneously contribute to the achievement of organisational goals (cf. Zaugg 1996: 94; Zaugg 2002: 8).

3.3.1 Indirect action parameters

The famous triangle "corporate strategy – corporate structure – corporate culture" constitutes the core of every organisation. This triangle is highly specific for each company.

> The difference between an international and a national company is not in the documents and their names but in the content. In particular, the corporate strategy of an international company will be considerably more complex than one of a domestic company (Grünig/Morschett 2012: 93).

Without going into the detail of these three notions, it is important to stress at this point the following facts that are relevant for the recruitment marketing strategy for Gen Y. First, the employer branding strategy should be intertwined with and stem from the overall corporate strategy. Only when the commitment of the top management is guaranteed would it be possible to elaborate and put in practice a viable employer branding strategy. Therefore, an employer branding strategy should be an indispensable part of the recruitment corporate strategy. Second, corporate structure influences the way in which recruitment marketing initiatives are implemented. In order to react quickly to the changing environment and adapt the recruitment and employer branding strategy accordingly, corporate structure should be flexible enough and display a certain degree of interconnectedness. Finally, corporate culture[61]

61 Deal and Kennedy (2000) allege that the social and business environment has a significant influence on the corporate culture. It is sufficient to analyse the culture of Russian and Swiss companies to see the difference due to political systems and accepted social norms. For example, in large Russian enterprises, communication culture is highly hierarchical and such enterprises are viewed as more attractive stable employers that are able to survive in a volatile economic situation or even in a financial crisis. In Switzerland, on the contrary, owing to the traditions of direct democracy, employees are used to communicating in a more informal way and they thus view small and medium-sized enterprises as attractive employers that provide creative and flexible work environments. Therefore, it is not surprising that corporate cultures of companies operating in different countries differ because they are subject to different political systems and different national cultures from which they recruit their workforces.

should serve as one of the attraction factors for Gen Yers. When looking for a job, Gen Yers want first of all to have a culture fit with the organisation they want to work for. Therefore, it is in the interest of the organisation to create a corporate culture that attracts the right Gen Yers. Corporate culture[61] is one of the important indirect action parameters that should find its manifestation in the definition of the EVP (see chapter 2.1.2).

3.3.2 Direct action parameters

As mentioned above, direct action parameters directly influence the attainment of the goals of a launched recruitment marketing campaign. Therefore, a thoroughly elaborated approach to employer branding, methods of implementing defined strategies, and a carefully developed recruitment concept for Gen Y are necessary for the overall success of the employer branding campaign. Target-group segmentation helps choose the suitable recruitment channels and define RJPs. RJPs – providing the potential employee with true information about a particular job – are emphasised to influence recruitment outcomes (cf. Werner/DeSimone 2009: 259).

The review of the recruitment literature showed several important factors. *Job and organisational characteristics* – referred to as *instrumental attributes* – have been detected as influencing perceived organisational attraction (cf. Carless/Imber 2007: 328). In connection with the person–environment fit theory, job and organisational characteristics are of even more importance. *Perceived PJ and PO fit* predict the extent to which a particular job and the associated organisation are regarded as beneficial and attractive, thereby influencing actual job choice (cf. Carless 2005: 422). Besides instrumental attributes, *symbolic attributes* influence organisational attraction as well (cf. Lievens/Highhouse 2003: 76). It is argued that individuals ascribe certain personality traits to an organisation and evaluate the perceived fit between their own personalities and the perceived organisational personality. Again, this perceived fit influences organisational attraction and thus actual job choice (cf. Slaughter/Greguras 2009: 13). Furthermore, recruitment is influenced by *recruitment sources*, recruiter characteristics, RJPs, and the perceptions of the recruitment process itself. Different recruitment sources lead to the attraction of different individuals and, therefore, cause different recruitment outcomes (cf. Breaugh/Macan/Grambow 2008: 58). Further, recruiters and their particular behaviours, attitudes, and so on are also assumed to influence recruitment outcomes (cf. Chapman *et al.* 2005: 929). A final important factor to recruitment and its outcomes is the general *treatment during the recruitment process*.

The importance of these single factors (direct action parameters) strongly depends on the individual's expectations towards the employer. The expectations of Gen Yers are further influenced by *generational effects*. These effects indicate, as previously mentioned, that members of a generation develop common generational characteristics based upon their shared experiences. These generational characteristics constitute "[…] relatively enduring values, attitudes, preferences, and behavior […]" (Kupperschmidt 2000: 66), thereby serving as a lens through which the world is seen and interpreted.

However, generational effects are not the only influence on Gen Y's expectations towards the employer: *contextual effects* also play another important role. For instance, *culture* and its manifestations also shape an individual's expectations towards an employer. The values, attitudes, and behaviour determined by belonging to a particular culture serve as another lens through which the target group sees and interprets the importance of different job and organisational attributes.

3.4 Effectiveness and efficiency indicators

"Metrics are the language of business. Anything that can be measures can be improved. Without metrics, it's difficult to understand exactly where to focus your efforts for obtaining job orders, making placements, and increasing revenue."

Donald E. Breckenridge Jr., President and CEO of Sendouts[62]

The final element of the conceptual framework aims at assessing the effectiveness and efficiency of employer branding strategies. The shortest and best-known distinction between the meanings of the terms *effectiveness* and *efficiency* was coined by Drucker (1974: 45) who described *effectiveness* as "doing the right things" and *efficiency* as "doing the things right". According to

62 Sendouts is the leading provider of recruiting software for third-party recruiting and staffing firms.

Huselid, Jackson and Schuler (1997: 171 ff.), a detailed determination of effectiveness and efficiency criteria is important. Thom and Wenger (2010: 25 ff.) also point out that while the criteria of effectiveness represent absolute measures that help estimate whether a particular strategy is a suitable way to achieve a predefined objective, efficiency criteria are relative measures that assess whether a particular course of action is better suited for problem-solving and realising a specific objective compared with an alternative.

Without clarity about how to assess HR effectiveness, it would be impossible to recognise how HR in general and particularly HR processes contribute to competitive advantage. As such, those responsible for HR processes in an organisation would never become full business partners. First, it is important to define the domain of HR assessment, which may include the HR department as a whole or specific HR or employer branding practices. Second, after the domain has been clarified, it is important to be explicit about the concept and assumptions underlying the assessment process. Third, all HR assessments should be broken down into parts because of the ambiguity and numerous intervening variables surrounding the process (cf. Ulrich 2002: 301 f.) For instance, HR activities generate HR outcomes (e.g. employer attractiveness, employee satisfaction, motivation, commitment, involvement, trust, loyalty, engagement, etc.), which in turn affect firm performance (productivity of qualified personnel, market share and market value, profits, etc.).

The difference between *effectiveness and efficiency* is always highlighted in the German-speaking literature on HRM. Having analysed the control process of recruitment presented by Scholz (2000), the author proposes that the effectiveness of recruitment and recruitment marketing should be defined as the number of recruited employees that the organisation wants to recruit (meaning that the requirement profile of a certain position corresponds to the competence profile of a candidate) and the number of recruited employees that stay after the probation period with the firm, respectively. The efficiency rates of the recruitment and employer branding process ensure the so-called efficiency ratio (input–output relation) of the recruitment process (time and effort, costs for media use, etc.). Effective and efficient employer branding should enable a perfect match between the offer of a position in a particular company and the expectations of a certain group of candidates that match the corporate culture and are able to identify themselves with the organisation.

HR practices and the people involved in them generate costs that can and should be managed. Hence, managing costs ultimately leads to better organisational performance and determines HR effectiveness. First, it is necessary to specify the particular HR practice, e.g. employer branding process. Second, the activities associated with this process should be identified. Third, a cost/benefit analysis for each activity should be carried out. Finally, overall indices relevant for the process should be created. These steps help translate HR practices into financial results so that they are likely to be understood by business executives and other important decision-makers in the company (cf. Ulrich 2002: 309). Furthermore, it is worth monitoring the results over time: a longitudinal analysis helps trace how HR practices change over time in terms of effectiveness (cf. Ulrich 2002: 310). Employer branding specialists should prove that their strategies and, above all, activities affect the bottom line. If they are able to show this, there will be no need to outsource employer branding activities to external constituencies.

Although the recruiting process may have subtleties specific to a certain industry and type of organisation (see chapters 3.2 and 3.3), underlying metrics represent key steps for effectiveness and efficiency process evaluation. For instance, these steps can include position–received applications coverage ratio, response time, quality of candidates submitted, quality of candidates interviewed, quality of hire, job order fill ratio, and time to fill the position. Key performance indicators (KPIs) to evaluate the success of employer branding activities may further include application versus acceptance ratios, attrition rates, average tenure/retention rates, cost per hire, employee engagement, employee referral rate of new recruits, external talent attraction indices/rankings, and the number of applicants considered to be the right potentials.

In terms of the evaluation of recruitment channels, HR metrics are also essential. Tracking applicants, qualified candidates, and recruits (per recruitment source and channel) helps understand how effective a certain recruitment channel is in terms of recruitment marketing metrics (views, clicks, number of applicants).

Branham (2005: 65 f.) proposes creating a so-called EOC scorecard rather than trying solely to benchmark oneself against other employers. Creating such a scorecard demands tracking year-on-year improvements by creating specific dashboards of EB indicators. This can be realised by tracking the measures of the four dimensions of talent management: attraction, selection, engaging, and sustaining engagement. The measures of attraction proposed by Branham (2005) include:

- number of applicants
- ratio of employment applicants to open positions
- application versus acceptance ratios
- percentage of applicants considered "A" candidates
- average number of days to fill vacancies
- ratio of acceptances to offers
- applicant dropout rate
- number of recruiting sources used
- percentage of new hire referrals who stay at least six months
- average monthly percentage of open positions[63]
- attrition rates
- average tenure/retention rates
- cost per hire
- employee engagement
- employee referral rate of new recruits
- external talent attraction indices/rankings
- promotion of internal candidates into key roles
- quality of recruits
- sourcing effectiveness.

Each company should elaborate on a specific list of KPIs as a part of its EOC scorecard, reassess and readapt it on a regular basis because of continuous changes in the macro and micro environment that influence employer branding strategies, and raise the need for permanent feedback and the adjustment of the employer branding campaign based on clearly defined indicators as a part of solid HR metrics. For instance, certain indicators are comparably easy to collect, e.g. number of applications especially for key functions, relative number of notices of cancelations during the pro-

63 EOCs normally "have ratios of employment applicants to open positions of at least 20 to 1, some as high as 100 to 1" (Branham 2005: 65).

bation period, reasons why new employees chose their new employers[64], feedback on behalf of recruiters and potential employees concerning recruitment decisions, and the popularity of the employer in general. In particular, the number of notices of cancelations during the probation period is an indicator that expectations were not met. Such "corporate dropouts" could originate, for instance, from communicating qualities in line with the employer branding that fall short of the real employer's characteristics. Therefore, it is useful to survey closer the reasons why someone leaves the company and to ensure the authenticity of promises delivered through an employer branding campaign. If an employee leaves the company because of disappointment over the conditions of employment, then the decision can most likely be traced back to an inefficient and ill-conceived employer branding strategy. If an employee simply received a better offer, then it is a matter of perceived positioning within the marketplace. In this case, employer branding plays a role at a different level. If, however, an employee leaves the company for situational and/or personal reasons, it has hardly anything to do with the EB.

If HR and employer branding specialists engage actively with elaborating on company-specific effectiveness and efficiency criteria for evaluating employer branding initiatives, they will be able to prove that HR can be a profit and not only a cost centre and deliver performance at the level of a strategic partner. "Human Resources can demonstrate ROI [return on investment] by highlighting how recruiting costs can be reduced, turnover can be addressed and better communication between the senior leaders and the workforce can create a culture of transparency and recognition" (Ruettimann 2011: 15).

Fig. 14 presents the conceptual framework for recruitment marketing that integrates the majority of the reflections discussed above. This will be enlarged later with the results of the empirical study.

64 In particular, new employees are a good source of feedback. At the beginning, they perceive the company neutrally. Correspondingly, it is important to collect employees' data on decision-making during the recruitment process as well as within their first days at work (cf. Trost 2009: 70 ff.).

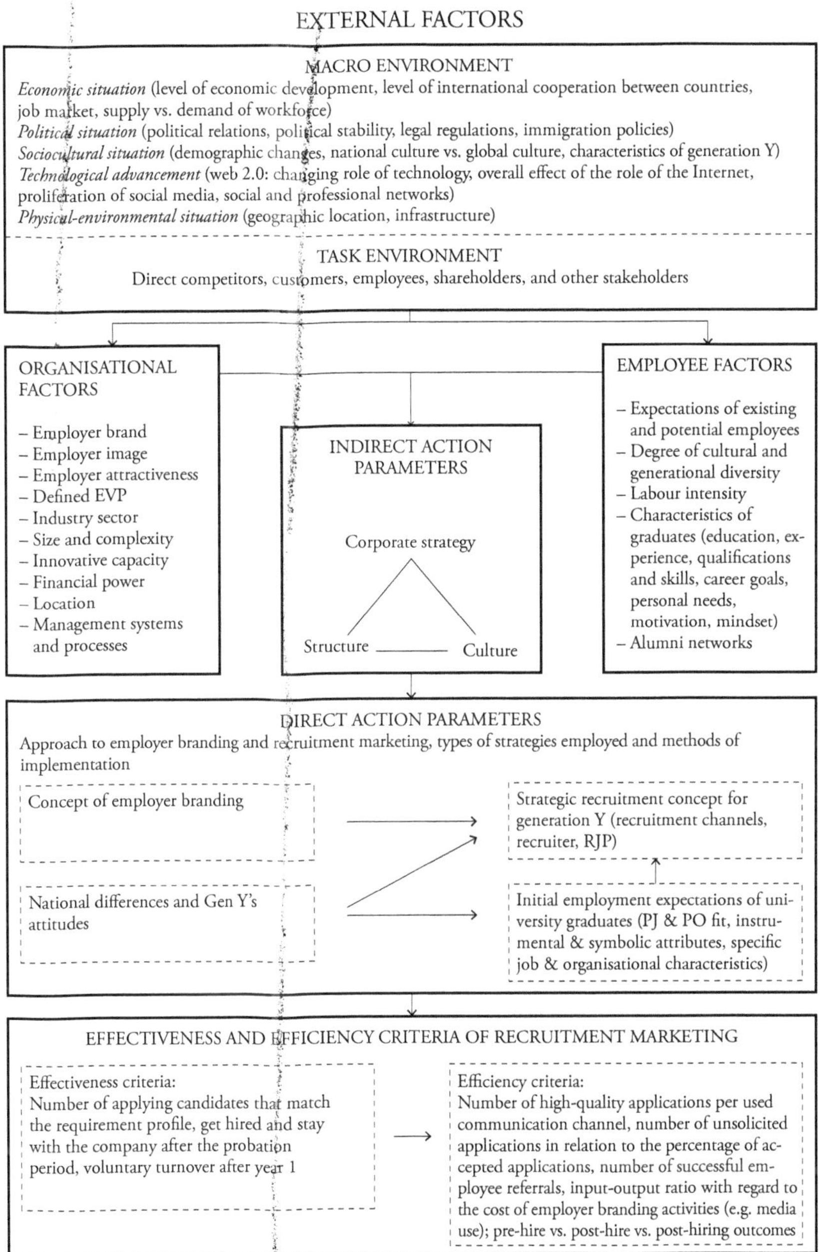

Fig. 14: Conceptual framework for recruitment marketing (cf. Hubschmid 2011: 39, Hubschmid/Thom 2010: 115 ff. based on dimensions developed by Kubicek/Thom 1976: 3977 ff., further expanded by Zaugg 2002: 5)

4

DEVELOPMENT OF THE RESEARCH MODEL

> Cross-cultural research [...] brings with it a host of complex methodological issues that researchers must address. [...] By far the most important concept that researchers need to be aware of when conducting cross-cultural research is *equivalence*, which we define as a state or condition of similarity in conceptual meaning and empirical method between cultures that allows comparisons to be meaningful. Equivalence needs to be established as much as possible for all aspects of research, including sampling methods and characteristics, language, data-collection procedures, theoretical framework, and meaningfulness and relevance of hypotheses (Matsumoto/Hee Yoo 2006: 243).

After having carefully assessed the theoretical bases in the previous chapters, the author has chosen to evaluate the importance of the 19 EB attributes[65] (see chapter 2.4) that are important for Gen Yers by performing a cross-sectional study[66]. The number of attributes defines the number of hypotheses to be tested in the empirical part of the research, whereas the author's reflections (i.e. 19 hypotheses[67]) will be tested at three levels of reasoning. First, the author assumes that *Generation Y attitudes* influence the importance of certain EB attributes that an ideal employer and an ideal future job should possess. Second, the author alleges that *nationality* influences the importance of certain EB attributes that an ideal employer

65 Undoubtedly, many more attributes make up a holistic employer brand. However, it was decided to include only 19 in the research for reasons of practicable survey length, among others.

66 The next best step in order to examine generational differences and characteristics is cross-sectional surveys, which investigate different groups of people at a particular point in time (cf. Lerner 2002: 498; Levenson 2010: 258). This kind of design is widely used, primarily because it requires less time and money as well as commitment by respondents compared with longitudinal and time-lag designs (cf. Lerner 2002: 498). Examples of cross-sectional studies are those conducted by Lyons, Duxbury and Higgins (2005), Cennamo and Gardner (2008), Wong *et al.* (2008) and Real, Mitnick and Maloney (2010). Cross-sectional designs have also been applied in qualitative studies using e.g. in-depth interviews to disclose generational differences and characteristics (cf. Parry/Urwin 2010: 9). Examples of this kind of research are the studies conducted by Broadbridge, Maxwell and Ogden (2009) and Gursoy, Maier and Chi (2008). When using a cross-sectional design, regardless of whether surveys or interviews are being conducted, one has to keep in mind that any differences observed across different groups of people may be merely driven by life-stage, age, or mixture effects rather than exclusively by generational effects (cf. Levenson 2010: 259).

67 The number of hypotheses is justified since the dissertation represents a monograph, which allows for a holistic study and evaluation of a large number of assumptions. Further, an explorative study (two expert interviews) prior to the quantitative study was conducted in April 2011 in Bern (with Dr Stefan Girschik, Group COO of Rehau) and in Moscow (with Irina Kombacheva, Director of the Employer Branding department of the Headhunter Group of Companies), which also helped set the priorities among various EB attributes. Finally, many of the chosen attributes have already been subjected to tests in different cultures, although not necessarily among Gen Yers.

should possess, whereas the assumptions concerning the importance of certain EB attributes to Russian or Swiss graduates have their theoretical foundations in the comparative culture research discussed in previous chapters. Finally, the author argues that *nationality moderates* the relationship between certain EB attributes and Gen Y attitudes, such that this relationship is stronger or weaker depending on nationality (see the theoretical reasoning in chapter 4.2). Joshi *et al.* (2010: 397) support this attitudinal approach: "Age-based generations would represent a unique and collective set of attitudes and values that emerge as a result of the successive 'coming of age' of birth year cohorts".

First, the process of defining the central constructs should take place because of the often incorrect use of variables included in these constructs (cf. Josiam 2009: 9). Researchers can generate scale items using either a deductive or an inductive approach (cf. Hinkin 1995: 968 ff.). The former entails the development of a classification schema or typology prior to data collection and following a thorough review of the literature. This enables researchers to develop a theoretical definition of a construct, which is then used to guide the development of scale items (cf. Schwab 1980: 3 ff.). Yoo and Donthu (2001) and Narver and Slater (1990) indicate that based on information generated from previous studies, a pool of items related to each construct can readily be formulated. By contrast, an inductive approach involves identifying constructs and possible scale items based on qualitative insights gleaned from respondents (cf. Hinkin 1995: 969 ff.). This approach is often used when there is limited theory or knowledge in relation to the topic. In this research, the deductive approach will be dominantly applied since it allows for a more precise description of the constructs being measured.

There are two schools of thought in cross-cultural comparative research regarding measurement procedures: quantitative and qualitative. Quantitative approaches assume that culture can be measured by traditional methods of empirical social science[68], whereas qualitative approaches use interpretive methods of ethnomethodology (cf. Pieper 1990: 21). The quantitative research method will be used in this empirical study.

68 Hofstede (1980) is an excellent example of this school of thought.

This is a form of conclusive research that involves a broad sample and uses structured data collection procedures. The main phases of the research are defined as follows: sampling procedure (the target group, reason for the selection of this target group); pilot study (i.e. 20 students who are about to graduate, so-called convenience sample); data collection in Russia and in Switzerland (types, sources, nature, and forms of data); data processing and analysis; and discussion of the results.

A review of the secondary literature provided the author with a theoretical foundation of the main relevant concepts and theories of culture, Gen Y, EB, and the nature of graduates' employment expectations, among others. According to Berthon, Ewing and Hah (2005: 168), it makes sense to investigate employer attractiveness deriving the sample of students in their final years of studies. Therefore, the research target group comprises final year students in both countries working towards their Master's degree. According to Sutherland, Torricelli and Karg (2002: 16), this choice is justified because they represent an important group of knowledge workers since they are viewed as achievement-oriented individuals aspiring to Master's degrees.

4.1 Overview of the research model and operationalisation of the main constructs

"In empirical research, we look for measures of the constructs that describe mental programs; that is, we have to *operationalize* them. We need to find observable phenomena from which constructs can be inferred" (Hofstede 2001: 4).

4.1.1 Operationalisation of the independent variable (IV) Gen Y

Firstly, participants rated their agreement with the following statements (items) that were chosen to measure Gen Y attitudes:

It is important to have access to online social and professional networks, private email, and voice over Internet protocol apps throughout the working day
It is important to have a job that offers the possibility to work from home (home office) or other places through virtual private networks

It is important to have a challenging job that allows me to be innovative and have fun
It is important to work for an organisation that has a culture that allows me to have a different opinion
It is important to have leaders who will support my personal development
It is important to work for an organisation that has an open feedback culture (feedback on a regular basis)
It is important to have work/life balance
It is important to spend private time with colleagues
It is important to gain feedback via a salary corresponding to my performance
It is important to have the possibility of time-out (regeneration phase) after a period of intensive work
It is important to work for a company with high ethical standards

Fig. 15: Operationalisation of the IV Gen Y (own representation)

This scale was developed based on the thorough literature analysis presented earlier in the thesis (see chapter 2.2). Different researchers attribute Gen Yers with different characteristics. Therefore, to avoid contradictions throughout the research, the most common characteristics of Gen Y were chosen to measure the construct of Gen Y attitudes. The scale used to measure the degree of agreement with the statement was a seven-point Likert scale with variations from "strongly disagree" to "strongly agree".

To account for variance in the responses and considering the diverging opinions in the literature regarding the biological age of Gen Yers (see discussion in chapter 2.2), the decision was made to measure the construct *Generation Y attitudes* independent of the biological age of the representatives of this generational cohort. The construct was thus operationalised and measured by means of a thoroughly developed scale. This scale was based on the literature review of generation Y and was represented by 11 questions in the questionnaire (see *Fig. 15*). The final measurement was based on 10 statements following the exclusion of one of the statements to improve the scale reliability (Cronbach's Alpha value; for details refer to chapter 5.2).

4.1.2 Measurement of dependent variables (DVs)

EB was measured by 19 items using another seven-point Likert scale ranging from "very unimportant" to "very important". The attributes that Gen Yers look for in potential employers, the importance of which was tested in the empirical part of this study, were chosen following the thorough literature review and based on the secondary data available from numerous studies[69]. Certain attributes such as *culture that supports equality between sexes* and *secure employment* were included in the research partly because of the substantial media interest in the results of these two attributes. The current economic situation and discussion on the relevance of *gender quotas,* especially in the Swiss environment, provided further reason for including these two attributes in the current research. As a result, the importance of the following 19 attributes (items) was tested:

- prestige
- a good reference for future career
- a high level of CSR
- a culture that respects one's individuality
- a culture that values diversity among personnel
- a culture that supports equality between sexes
- a culture that accepts (underrepresented) minorities
- challenging work
- opportunities for relocation abroad and international travel
- secure employment
- flexible working conditions
- good work/life balance
- an attractive geographic location
- a friendly work environment
- a performance-related bonus

69 Data from certain research (e.g. the detailed results of the studies conducted by the consulting firm in the field of employer branding Universum) were provided to the author on request. Further, the elaboration of the scale for the operationalisation of the EB construct was also possible thanks to the intense collaboration with Universum Communications throughout 2011.

- professional training and education
- personal mentoring/coaching
- leadership opportunities
- good possibilities for rapid promotion

As stated above, the assumptions regarding the importance of certain EB attributes to Russian and Swiss graduates were made based on existing cultural research, mainly on the four cultural theories discussed earlier in the thesis (see chapter 2.3).

To test for the potential of the moderating effect of a certain nationality on the importance of EB attributes for Gen Yers, the author chose to search for interaction effects in all 19 cases[70]. This level of hypothetical reasoning represents the most valuable and demanding part of the research at both theoretical and empirical levels.

4.2 Generation of hypotheses

Hypotheses at three levels of reasoning were then generated. At the first level of reasoning, it was decided to assess if Gen Y attitudes influence the importance of the 19 EB attributes that were carefully identified and discussed earlier in the thesis. Based on the literature on Gen Y, the hypotheses at the first level of reasoning were formulated consistently assuming that all the EB attributes mentioned below are important to those graduates that score high on Gen Y attitudes independent of national differences.

Gen Y attitudes influence the importance of an employer attribute:
H1a: prestige
H1b: a good reference for future career
H1c: a high level of CSR
H1d: a culture that respects individuality
H1e: a culture that values diversity among personnel
H1f: a culture that supports equality between sexes
H1g: a culture that accepts (underrepresented) minorities
H1h: challenging work

70 There are two IVs in this study, namely Gen Y attitudes and nationality, whereas nationality assumes the role of the moderator. The 19 EB attributes represent 19 DVs, while gender and age are the two control variables.

H1i: opportunities for relocation abroad and international travel
H1j: secure employment
H1k: flexible working conditions
H1l: good work/life balance
H1m: an attractive geographic location
H1n: a friendly work environment
H1o: a performance-related bonus
H1p: sponsorship of professional training and development
H1q: personal mentoring/coaching
H1r: leadership opportunities
H1s: good possibilities for rapid promotion

The goal of the formulation of the hypotheses at the second level of reasoning was to assess for which nation each of the 19 EB attributes studied was more important. Following the hypotheses, H2a–H2s were thus formulated. The author's assumptions were substantiated by the findings that stem from the four cultural studies discussed earlier (the works of Hofstede, GLOBE, Trompenaars and Hampden-Turner, and Lewis; see chapter 2.3)[71]. According to De Mooij and Hofstede (2010: 88), the variety of the manifestations of Hofstede's dimensions should be considered before setting hypotheses according to a particular research question. According to Javidan *et al.* (2006a: 910), "No single researcher or research team [..] should own the cross-cultural research field!". It is for this reason that the author decided to depart from the assumptions of these four theories (Hofstede, GLOBE, Trompenaars and Hampden-Turner, and Lewis) during the phase of hypotheses generation and base her arguments in terms of the direction of the hypotheses on the findings of these four well-known research projects. Javidan *et al.* (2006a: 911) offer their support of such a research decision: "Our advice regarding which particular cultural dimensions to focus on is that it depends entirely on the research question of interest".

71 The following hypotheses as well as the arguments in favour of certain tendencies that are described further are based on the statements of the aforementioned researchers regarding a particular culture. They gave the author of this thesis a starting point for her reflections on cultural influences on the importance of the chosen EB attributes that will be subject to statistical verification.

H2a: For Russian graduates, the attribute prestige is more important than it is for their Swiss counterparts.

This assumption was made based on the findings of the study of Trompenaars and Hampden-Turner (2010: 105 f.), who postulate that Russians have a stronger tendency to *ascription* and status. In addition, the findings from the GLOBE study characterise Russians through higher *power distance* scores. Therefore, it seems to be logical to assume that Russian graduates ascribe more importance to the attribute *prestige* and based on their national preferences strive to work for prestigious corporations.

H2b: For Swiss graduates, the attribute a good reference for future career is more important than it is for their Russian counterparts.

The assumption is made based on the findings of the GLOBE study, which delivers higher scores on *the uncertainty avoidance* dimension for the Germanic cluster[72]. This means that Swiss graduates might strive to increase the probability of future career success by assuming that their present jobs will contribute to their career successes in the future. In addition, the representatives of the Germanic cluster score higher on the dimension of *future orientation,* which postulates that their behaviour is future-oriented and therefore that they tend to plan their career paths. Furthermore, owing to higher scores on the dimension of *performance orientation,* the representatives of the Germanic cluster are looking for gratification in the future for the results achieved in their previous jobs. Based on the findings of Trompenaars and Hampden-Turner, Swiss society is characterised by more *specificity* in their professional aspirations, i.e. Swiss representatives tend to strongly believe that their successes in the future depend on the results they achieve in their previous jobs. *Achievement orientation* is also higher for the Swiss. Finally, in their *attitudes to time* the Swiss are described as future-oriented and guided by the synchronic perception of time, which unites past, present, and future. This observation of Trompenaars and Hampden-Turner is obviously relevant for their job expectations.

72 The results of the GLOBE study on the dimension of uncertainty avoidance have been used to substantiate the author's assumptions since they are new compared with the findings of Hofstede and thus they tend to reflect modern tendencies in the societies studied.

H2c: For Swiss graduates, a high level of CSR is more important than it is for their Russian counterparts.

The assumption of the higher importance of CSR issues for Swiss graduates stems from the results of the GLOBE and Trompenaars and Hampden-Turner studies. Scores on the *future orientation* dimension for the Germanic cluster in the GLOBE study are higher. Trompenaars and Hampden-Turner offer evidence that in *attitudes to environment* the Swiss believe that they are responsible for the environment and can influence it. These assertions give the right to affirm that the Swiss ascribe more importance to the CSR agendas of their future employers than their Russian counterparts, who believe that they cannot change the environment.

H2d: For Swiss graduates, a culture that respects individuality is more important than it is for their Russian counterparts.

Sufficient arguments from the presented cultural studies substantiate this assumption. First, according to Hofstede's research, Swiss respondents deliver much higher scores on the dimension of *individualism* than Russians. In addition, they score lower on the *power distance* dimension, meaning that they prefer a culture that respects the individuality of every employee, independent of the position one holds in the company. Second, in the GLOBE study the representatives of the Germanic cluster score lower on the dimensions of *institutional* and *in-group and family collectivism* than the representatives of the Eastern Europe cluster. Third, in the study of Trompenaars and Hampden-Turner the Swiss score higher on the dimension of *individualism*, although the difference between the scores for the two countries is much smaller than it is in the studies of Hofstede and GLOBE.

H2e: For Swiss graduates, a culture that values diversity among personnel is more important than it is for their Russian counterparts.

The assumption that a diverse workforce is more valued by Swiss graduates stems from the scores for the two countries based on the theories of Hofstede and Trompenaars and Hampden-Turner. The low scores for the Swiss on the *uncertainty avoidance* dimension allow us to assume that Swiss society embraces diversity and cultivates tolerance for it. Further, the high scores for the Swiss on the dimension of *individualism* provide solid grounds to conclude that in Swiss society, an individual stands in the centre and, therefore, diversity is taken as an attribute of individualistic culture. The results of Trompenaars and Hampden-Turner also present evidence that the representatives of the Germanic cluster score higher on the dimension of *individualism* while being guided by the *universalistic approach* to the job, which implies the importance of rules and competences rather than relationships in the working world. This logic allows us to conclude that tolerance to diversity is more important for Swiss graduates, since no matter how diverse the employment pool might be, the results and contribution to the bottom line of the organisation is what counts most.

H2f: For Russian graduates, a culture that supports equality between sexes is more important than it is for their Swiss counterparts.

One of the arguments in favour of this assumption comes from the GLOBE study. The scores for the representatives of the Eastern Europe cluster on the dimension of *gender egalitarianism* are significantly higher than those for the Germanic cluster. In addition, it is a well-established fact that gender egalitarianism and the emancipation of women was a typical characteristic of Eastern European societies under Soviet rule that has been and is still taken as a matter of course among graduates in Russia[73]. Moreover, the lower scores on the *masculinity* dimension for Russians signify that in the working world there is a clear aspiration for equality between sexes in terms of an appreciation of feminine values such as constructive teamwork between the representatives of both sexes.

H2g: For Swiss graduates, a culture that accepts (underrepresented) minorities is more important than it is for their Russian counterparts.

The evidence from different cultural theories allows us to make this assumption. First, in Hofstede's model Switzerland scores lower on the dimension of *power distance*, which allows us to conclude that the acceptance of human inequality in society is low. Therefore, the Swiss tend to

73 Women face less discrimination in Russia than they do elsewhere (cf. Ramachandran/Artiuch 2007: 24).

have a culture that accepts underrepresented minorities and which shows that it lives up to societal values of human equality. The GLOBE's results further prove that social relationships in an organisation are characterised by assertiveness and not by belonging to a certain minority, which in certain cultural frameworks means being an outcast. Finally, Trompenaars and Hampden-Turner show that the representatives of the Germanic cluster consider themselves to be masters of their own fate through *their attitudes to environment,* meaning that members of different minority groups are welcome to develop their talents in the organisation.

H2h: For Swiss graduates, challenging work is more important than it is for their Russian counterparts[74].

Relying on the results from the studies of Hofstede, GLOBE, and Trompenaars and Hampden-Turner, the Swiss score higher on the *masculinity dimension* (Hofstede), which signifies achievement orientation in terms of work values. According to the results of the GLOBE study, the representatives of the Germanic cluster are characterised by higher *performance orientation* and *assertiveness* than their counterparts from the Eastern Europe cluster. Trompenaars and Hampden-Turner deliver proof of the distinctive orientation towards *achievement* among the Swiss as opposed to *ascription,* which is more typical for Russians.

H2i: For Swiss graduates, opportunities for relocation abroad and international travel are more important than they are for their Russian counterparts.

This assumption is based, first, on the *masculine* orientation of Swiss society that emphasises ego-related goals that encourage experimenting in order to be successful in the job. The lower *uncertainty avoidance* scores (compared with those for Russians) in Hofstede's model also support this assumption. The higher *performance orientation* and higher *assertiveness* scores for the Germanic cluster in the GLOBE study as well as the higher scores on *achievement orientation* in the study of Trompenaars and Hampden-Turner deliver additional support for this assumption.

74 As the survey conducted by Accenture in 2008 among university graduates from developed and emerging economies shows, interesting and challenging work is more important for graduates from developed economies, whereas flexible working hours are viewed as more important for graduates from emerging markets (cf. Farley/Malkani/Smith 2008: 5).

H2j: For Swiss graduates, secure employment is more important than it is for their Russian counterparts.
According to the results of the GLOBE study, the Germanic cluster scores higher on the *uncertainty avoidance* and *future orientation* dimensions, which implies a societal need for security in the future. Trompenaars and Hampden-Turner provide evidence that Swiss society is more long-term-oriented regarding their *synchronic* attitudes towards time as opposed to the *sequential* view of time among Russians. Moreover, because Swiss culture belongs to the cluster of *linear-active* cultures, as can be derived from Lewis's theory, schedules and security are important while working.

H2k: For Russian graduates, flexible working conditions are more important than they are for their Swiss counterparts.
The following arguments provide grounds for the assumption about the higher importance of flexible working hours for Russians: according to Hofstede, low scores on the *masculinity* dimension signify a preference for fewer worked hours. The GLOBE study concludes that lower *performance orientation,* which is typical for the Eastern Europe cluster, encourages flexibility in working conditions. On Trompenaars and Hampden-Turner's dimension of *attitude to time,* the sequential view of time encourages the acceptance of flexible working conditions since the focus is put on a certain moment in time. Finally, Lewis's categorisation of Russia as a *multi-active* society delivers evidence of the unimportance of strict schedules, which allows doing several things at a time in a job.

H2l: For Swiss graduates, good work/life balance is more important than it is for their Russian counterparts.
According to the results of the study by Trompenaars and Hampden-Turner, Switzerland scores high on the dimension of *specificity* (as opposed to *diffusion*), meaning that in Swiss society work and private life are strongly separated. Lewis adds further proof in favour of the importance of good work/life balance for the Swiss: Switzerland's belonging to the *linear-active* cluster of cultures means that social and professional lives are not interwoven, thereby allowing for a clear separation of working and spare time, i.e. the importance of good work/life balance is intertwined with cultural values.

H2m: For Russian graduates, an attractive geographic location is more important than it is for their Swiss counterparts.
Russian society scores higher on the dimension of *power distance* in both Hofstede's study and the GLOBE study. This signifies the importance of prestige in society, also in terms of such an EB attribute as an attractive geographic location. Trompenaars and Hampden-Turner specify a higher tendency to *ascription* in Russian society; therefore, an attractive geographic location might be the sign of the higher status of an employee. Furthermore, taking into consideration the enormous territory of Russia, not every location is viewed as attractive. The most attractive locations can be found in the European part of Russia, with Moscow and St. Petersburg heading the list of most attractive geographic locations to work in.

H2n: For Russian graduates, a friendly work environment is more important than it is for their Swiss counterparts.
Low scores on Hofstede's dimensions of *individualism* and *masculinity,* higher scores on the GLOBE's dimensions of *humane orientation, institutional,* and *in-group collectivism,* higher scores on the *emotional dimension* of Trompenaars and Hampden-Turner, and Russia's membership of the cluster of *multi-active* cultures according to Lewis's model allows us to conclude that for Russians a friendly work environment is more important than it is for Swiss. Russians confront their counterparts on the job emotionally and rely on oral information.

H2o: For Swiss graduates, a performance-related bonus is more important than it is for their Russian counterparts.
There is evidence from several dimensions for the assumption stated above. The high scores of Switzerland on Hofstede's dimensions of *masculinity* and *individualism* signify the achievement orientation of employees. The high scores on *performance* and *future orientation* as well as *assertiveness* in the GLOBE study reinforce this assumption. Trompenaars and Hampden-Turner deliver further proof by showing that Switzerland scores higher on *achievement orientation* and *individualism;* further, the Swiss consider themselves to be more the *masters of their own fate* compared with Russians. Finally, Lewis's placement of Switzerland into the category of *linear-active*

societies implies that the Swiss are job-oriented while working, i.e. they strive to achieve results and expect the appropriate grati-fication for that.

H2p: For Swiss graduates, sponsorship of professional training and development is more important than it is for their Russian counterparts.
The same high scores on the same dimensions that were used to explain *H2o* apply for *H2p*. The overall achievement orientation of the Swiss allows us to say that they believe what happens to them is their own doing, and, therefore, all EB attributes that provide them with the opportunity for personal and professional development are rated as highly important in such a masculine, individualistic, performance-oriented, and future-oriented society.

H2q: For Russian graduates, personal mentoring/coaching is more important than it is for their Swiss counterparts.
Coaching and mentoring is a two-way communication between a mentor and a mentee. The efficiency of this relationship can only be guaranteed if there is mutual understanding at the interpersonal level between the mentor and the mentee. On the GLOBE's dimension of *humane orientation,* the representatives of the Eastern Europe cluster score higher than their counterparts from the Germanic cluster, thus signifying the higher importance of a humane relationship in Eastern European countries. Trompenaars and Hampden-Turner highlight the importance of the dimension of *emotionality* for Russians. Lewis, through his placement of Russia into the category of *multi-active* cultures, delivers further evidence for the importance of the emotional dimension in Russian society. Finally, the personal mentoring/coaching concept was a well-established instrument of personnel management in the planned economies of the former Soviet system. Therefore, Russians are used to it and ascribe high importance to this employer attribute.

H2r: For Swiss graduates, leadership opportunities are more important than they are for their Russian counterparts.
Based on the high scores of Hofstede's dimensions of *individualism* and *masculinity,* it seems logical to assume that the Swiss ascribe more impor-

tance to leadership opportunities than Russians do. The Germanic cluster in the GLOBE study is characterised by high scores on the *assertiveness* dimension, while in Trompenaars and Hampden-Turner's model Switzerland scores high on the *achievement* dimension. All these arguments give us the right to assume that leadership opportunities are more important in Swiss than in Russian culture.

H2s: For Russian graduates, good possibilities for rapid promotion are more important than they are for their Swiss counterparts.

Based on the high scores on the dimensions of *power distance* in both models (Hofstede and GLOBE), it is assumed that rapid promotion for Russians is more important than for Swiss since through promotion they acquire status privileges and prestige in the job. Trompenaars and Hampden-Turner support this assumption by providing high scores for Russian society on the *ascription* dimension.

At the first level of reasoning *(H1a–H1s),* the author hypothesises that Gen Y attitudes influence the importance of all EB attributes. At the second level of reasoning *(H2a–H2s),* the author hypothesises for what nationality a certain EB attribute is more important based on the cultural influences derived from comparative cultural studies. At the third level of reasoning *(H3a–H3s),* the research objective is to assume that nationality reinforces the importance of the 19 EB attributes for each of the respective nationalities. Based on these assumptions, the following hypotheses are formulated:

H3a: Nationality moderates the relationship between Gen Y attitudes and the attribute prestige, such that this relationship is stronger for Russian graduates.

H3b: Nationality moderates the relationship between Gen Y attitudes and the attribute a good reference for future career, such that this relationship is stronger for Swiss graduates.

H3c: Nationality moderates the relationship between Gen Y attitudes and the attribute a high level of CSR, such that this relationship is stronger for Swiss graduates.

H3d: Nationality moderates the relationship between Gen Y attitudes and the attribute a culture that respects individuality, such that this relationship is stronger for Swiss graduates.

H3e: Nationality moderates the relationship between Gen Y attitudes and the attribute a culture that values diversity among personnel, such that this relationship is stronger for Swiss graduates.

H3f: Nationality moderates the relationship between Gen Y attitudes and the attribute a culture that supports equality between sexes, such that this relationship is stronger for Russian graduates.

H3g: Nationality moderates the relationship between Gen Y attitudes and the attribute a culture that accepts (underrepresented) minorities, such that this relationship is stronger for Swiss graduates.

H3h: Nationality moderates the relationship between Gen Y attitudes and the attribute challenging work, such that this relationship is stronger for Swiss graduates.

H3i: Nationality moderates the relationship between Gen Y attitudes and the attribute opportunities for relocation abroad and international travel, such that this relationship is stronger for Swiss graduates.

H3j: Nationality moderates the relationship between Gen Y attitudes and the attribute secure employment, such that this relationship is stronger for Swiss graduates.

H3k: Nationality moderates the relationship between Gen Y attitudes and the attribute flexible working conditions, such that this relationship is stronger for Russian graduates.

H3l: Nationality moderates the relationship between Gen Y attitudes and the attribute good work/life balance, such that this relationship is stronger for Swiss graduates.

H3m: Nationality moderates the relationship between Gen Y attitudes and the attribute an attractive geographic location, such that this relationship is stronger for Russian graduates.

H3n: Nationality moderates the relationship between Gen Y attitudes and the attribute a friendly work environment, such that this relationship is stronger for Russian graduates.

H3o: Nationality moderates the relationship between Gen Y attitudes and the attribute a performance-related bonus, such that this relationship is stronger for Swiss graduates.

H3p: Nationality moderates the relationship between Gen Y attitudes and the attribute sponsorship of professional training and development, such that this relationship is stronger for Swiss graduates.

H3q: Nationality moderates the relationship between Gen Y attitudes and the attribute personal mentoring/coaching, such that this relationship is stronger for Russian graduates.

H3r: Nationality moderates the relationship between Gen Y attitudes and the attribute leadership opportunities, such that this relationship is stronger for Swiss graduates.

H3s: Nationality moderates the relationship between Gen Y attitudes and the attribute good possibilities for rapid promotion, such that this relationship is stronger for Russian graduates.

In the next chapter, the empirical setting as well as the methods of the empirical research used to analyse the collected data and to test the hypotheses formulated above are described.

5

METHODS OF EMPIRICAL RESEARCH

5.1 Empirical setting, sample description, and data collection

The empirical setting of this study is represented by the faculties of Economics and Business Administration of five universities in the German-speaking part of Switzerland – Bern, Fribourg, Zurich, Basel, St. Gallen – and two universities in Moscow – Moscow State University, named after Lomonosov, and the national research university/Higher School of Economics. The sample description according to age and gender is presented in *Fig. 16.* The student sample most likely represents the value orientations of the next generation of employees and managers.

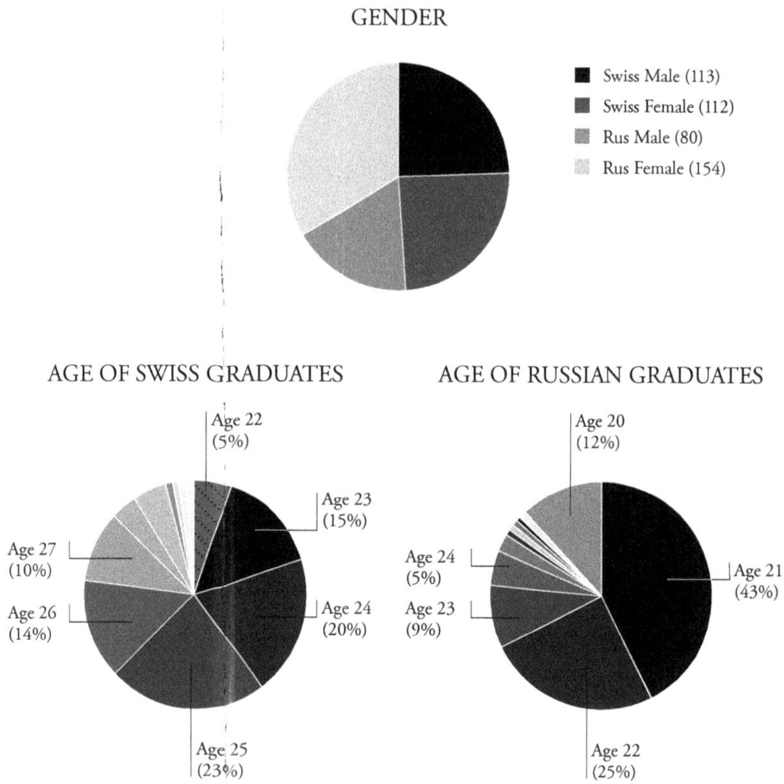

Fig. 16: Sample description according to age and gender

The data for this study were gathered during April and May 2011 from two groups of students, namely final year Master's students in business administration and economics in two universities in Moscow and five universities in the German-speaking part of Switzerland. In total, 600 questionnaires in English[75] were distributed to students during class time, with 555 returned either during class or by return mail in both countries.

Because the author was interested in the attitudes of young potential jobseekers from Russia and Switzerland, she limited her sample to respondents who were either of Russian or of Swiss nationality. The final dataset consisted of 459 questionnaires (N=459: 225 in Switzerland, 234 in Russia), excluding respondents holding nationalities other than Russian or Swiss and eliminating three outliers[76]). In the Russian sample the majority of respondents were women (154) versus 80 men[77]; therefore, the sample was skewed towards women. The Swiss sample was more balanced in terms of gender representation (112 women versus 113 men). The age of respondents ranged between 20 and 30 years old. The scales used in the self-administered questionnaire[78] were developed based on literature analysis as well as expert discussions in Bern and Moscow prior to data collection, and then pre-tested on a specifically chosen sample. In order to provide a substantiated basis for further research, a first pre-test of the questionnaire was conducted to determine its effectiveness and to implement any changes concerning wording, format, or order that may prove necessary (cf. Ruane 2004: 141).

The statistical analysis after the performed data cleansing and eval-uation of the model was carried out using SPSS (version 19) in the following three steps:

75 Establishing linguistic equivalence is necessary, since one of the most important areas in which equivalence needs to be ascertained is in measurement. "Measurement equivalence refers to the degree to which measures used to collect data in different cultures are equally valid and reliable" (Matsumoto/Hee Yoo 2006: 243).

76 To assure that the model satisfies the regression assumptions (for more details, refer to chapter 6.3).

77 This sample reflects, however, the general pattern of gender representation among students in business and economics in Moscow universities.

78 Self-administered questionnaires are questionnaires that are completed by respondents themselves and are, as such, cheaper and faster to administer, not subject to interviewer bias, and more convenient for respondents (cf. Bryman/Bell 2003: 142 f.).

1. Descriptive statistics showing the percentage of the importance of a certain EB attribute to all respondents regardless of their nationality. No sample split was made at this stage (except for cross-tables for recruitment channels and events to illuminate the difference).
2. Bivariate correlations performed in two blocks: between Gen Y attitudes and the 19 EB attributes as well as between nationality and the same EB attributes (requiring no sample split either).
3. Hierarchical moderated multiple regressions (MMRs) to look for possible significant interactions between the variables and to check for the possible moderating effect of nationality.

5.2 Construct validity and scale reliability

> The general problem of all operationalizations is how to achieve *validity* – that is, correspondence between the observed behavior and the underlying constructs. [...] To achieve good construct validity [..] we need *both* good measurements *and* good theory (Hofstede 2001: 4).

Validity shows that a study measures what it intended to measure (content validity[79]), and the way the study structure fits to the theories behind it (construct validity) (cf. Johns/Lee-Ross 1998; Sekaran 2003). Johns and Lee-Ross (1998) point out further that it is necessary to test face validity, i.e. to conduct a pilot study. Following this suggestion, 25 Master's students were asked prior to the main data collection phase to fill in the questionnaires. The test showed that 95% of respondents understood what they were being asked.

Before running any data tests, a researcher is obliged to make sure that the collected data are reliable. As a consequence, the first test concerns the reliability of the data. The reliability of each construct was determined by calculating the Cronbach's Alpha of each scale (EB construct and Gen Y construct). Cronbach's Alpha was applied because it delivers an applicable estimation of reliability. In the literature, a value of at least 0.8 can be interpreted as reliable. In some cases, a value of 0.7 is also considered to be good. Overall, the values of Crobach's Alpha provide a rough orientation for the interpretation of the results (cf. Cronbach 1951: 299).

79 "Content validity is the extent to which an instrument covers the universe of relevant aspects of the phenomenon studied [...]" (Hofstede 1996: 197).

Table 3 presents the statistics of item-scale for Gen Y and gives a brief overview how the construct of Gen Y was operationalised for the study.

	Mean of the scale if item left out	Variance of the scale if item left out	Corrected item-scale correlation	Cronbach's Alpha if item left out
It is important to have access to online social and professional networks, private email, and voice over internet protocol apps throughout the working day	58.46	31.776	.240	.699
It is important to have a job that offers the possibility to work from home (home office) or other places through virtual private networks	58.62	30.525	.325	.681
It is important to have a challenging job that allows me to be innovative and have fun	57.58	33.348	.390	.671
It is important to work for an organisation that has a culture that allows me to have a different opinion	57.70	32.648	.401	.668
It is important to have leaders who will support my personal development	57.63	33.040	.369	.672
It is important to work for an organisation that has an open feedback culture (feedback on a regular basis)	57.62	32.859	.413	.667
It is important to have work/life balance	57.41	33.398	.368	.674
It is important to spend private time with colleagues	58.74	30.581	.336	.679
It is important to gain feedback via a salary corresponding to my performance	57.97	32.883	.287	.684
It is important to have the possibility of time-out (regeneration phase) after a period of intensive work	57.92	31.341	.460	.657
It is important to work for a company with high ethical standards	57.99	31.989	.341	.675

Table 3: Statistics of item-scale Gen Y

The Gen Y construct was measured with the help of 10 statements. The first statement was left out, which improved the reliability of the scale (Cronbach's Alpha = 0.7).

The EB construct was built up by the 19 items (EB attributes). The value of Cronbach's Alpha (0.8) supports the assumption of the author that the chosen 19 items present a reliable scale to measure EB as a holistic concept made up of different attributes (see *Table 4*).

Cronbach's Alpha	Number of items
.788	19

Table 4: Reliability statistics for the EB construct

5.3 MMR, interaction effects, and simple slopes analysis

The type of regression analysis used in this study is hierarchical MMR. MMR models are used to identify factors that change the relationship between IVs and DVs. This analysis is widely used in marketing, where the moderating effect is estimated by including an additional exogenous variable (cf. AikenWest 1991).

> The moderation model tests whether the prediction of a dependent variable, Y, from an independent variable, X, differs across levels of a third variable, Z. Moderator variables affect the strength and/or direction of the relation between a predictor and an outcome: enhancing, reducing, or changing the influence of the predictor (Fairchild/MacKinnon 2009: 4).

Moderation effects are tested with multiple regression analysis and are most often discussed as an interaction between variables, where the effects of one variable depend on the other variable in the analysis (cf. Fairchild/MacKinnon 2009: 4).

Hierarchical regression (also referred to as sequential regression) differs from simple multiple regression in the way that the IVs are entered into the regression in steps or blocks in a predetermined order, thus not letting the computer decide, as would be the case for stepwise regression (cf. Pallant 2007: 160). Following this pattern, age and gender were entered into the analysis in the first block. This has the effect of statistically controlling for these variables. In the second step, the other two IVs – the standardised Z-value[80] for *Gen Y*

80 Standardisation is a useful transformation in statistics. Standardising data on one scale is necessary so a comparison can take place. Sometimes called "converting to Z-scores" or "taking Z-scores", it has the effect of transforming the original distribution to one in which the mean becomes zero and the standard deviation becomes 1. Therefore, the Z-score is known as a common yardstick for all types of data. A Z-score quantifies the original score in terms of the number of standard deviations that that score is from the mean of the distribution. The formula for converting from an original or "raw" score to a Z-score is (cf. Wannacott/Wannacott 1990: 129 ff., 295):

$$Z = \frac{X-\mu}{\sigma} \text{ or } Z = \frac{\text{score - mean}}{\text{standard deviation}}$$

attitudes and *nationality* – were added into the equation. The difference is that the possible effect of age and gender was removed and thus it was possible to see whether the second block of IVs explained some of the remaining variance in the DV, which is a certain EB attribute.

The interaction term (made up of one continuous variable Gen Y that was standardised and one binary moderator [nationality] that was left unstandardised[81]) was not standardised (Dawson 2011). After having calculated the interaction term, the author used the "two-way with all options" Excel worksheet from the website of Jeremy Dawson. After having entered all the necessary data, the researcher received the plot she needed in order to carry out a simple slopes test.

Interactions are often used in studies of organisational psychology and they have recently been adopted for analysis in research papers on organisational attractiveness (for more details, see Schreurs *et al.* 2009: 36 ff.; Kausel/Slaughter 2010: 3 ff.). The simplest interaction is that between a dummy variable (nationality) and a continuous variable (Gen Y attitudes). In the regression analysis, the independent continuous variable *Gen Y* was used as the first focal predictor and dichotomous variable *Nation* as a moderator. It was decided to check for two-way interactions between nationality and Gen Y attitudes. Two-way interactions in this case imply that a relationship between an IV *(Gen Y attitudes)* and a DV (a particular *EB attribute*) is moderated by a third variable (a particular *nationality*).

To follow up on the moderating effect, simple slopes tests were conducted. Following the procedure outlined by Aiken and West (1991), regression lines were plotted at lower (i.e. 1) and higher levels (i.e. 2), showing the weak and strong levels of Gen Y attitudes. *Fig. 17* shows the relationship between the variables in the basic moderation model.

81 It is best not to standardise a binary moderator (Dawson 2011). Although in terms of the significance, it does not matter if it has been standardised, the plot will not be quite right in the case of the standardisation of a binary moderator. Therefore, the author worked with a standardised continuous variable and a non-standardised binary moderator and then calculated the interaction between these two. This decision was taken after Jeremy Dawson provided the author with expert opinion on the issue (from the email correspondence between Dr Jeremy Dawson and Elena Hubschmid on the 18th of October 2011).

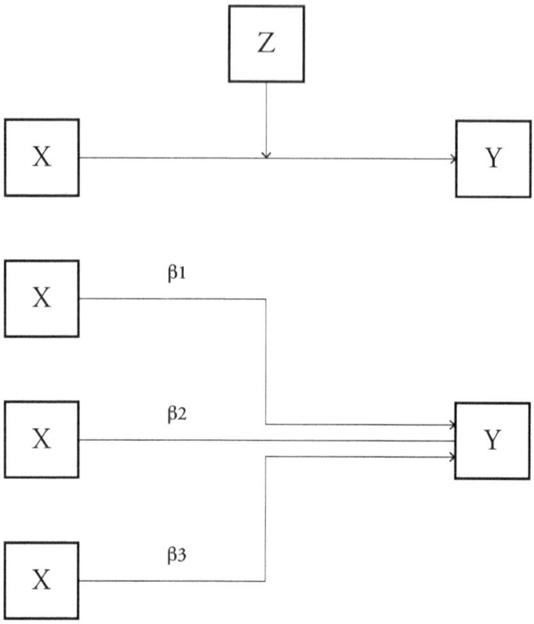

Fig. 17: The basic moderation model (cf. Fairchild/MacKinnon 2009: 4)[82]

When significant interactions have been shown, it is necessary to conduct a simple slopes test to check for the significance of the moderating effect of each nationality. For this purpose, specially designed Excel macros developed by Jeremy Dawson were used (cf. Dawson 2011: online). The graph obtained (after the significance of the slopes had been calculated) helps plot the interactions and present the significance of the strength of the relationship between the IV and DV in a comprehensible manner.

82 A regression equation forms the basic moderation model:
"Y= i5+ β1X+β2Z+β3XZ+e5
where β1 is the coefficient relating to the IV, X, to the outcome, Y, when Z = 0, β2 is the coefficient relating to the moderator variable, Z, to the outcome when X = 0, i5 is the intercept in the equation, and e5 is the residual in the equation. The regression coefficient for the interaction term, β3, provides an estimate of the moderation effect. If β3 is statistically different from zero, there is significant moderation of the X-Y relation in the data. Plotting interaction effects aids in the interpretation of moderation to show how the slope of Y on X is dependent on the value of the moderator variable. Regression slopes that correspond to the prediction of Y from X at a single value of Z are termed simple slopes" (Fairchild/MacKinnon 2009: 4).

6

RESULTS OF THE STUDY

In the following section, the main results of the study are presented, starting with the results obtained by means of descriptive statistics, followed by the representation of tables of bivariate correlations. Finally, the results of the hypothesis tests obtained by means of MMR and the interaction plots are presented.

6.1 Descriptive statistics

The frequency tables for EB attributes showed the percentage of respondents that ascribe different levels of importance to these 19 items. The categories *"very important"* and *"important"* have been summarised into one category and the results are presented in *Table 5*. The overall attitude is highly positive, falling between the "important" and "very important" responses to the item measurements.

EB ATTRIBUTE	Percentage of respondents who marked the attribute as *"very important"* or *"important"*
Prestige	55%
A good reference for future career	80%
High level of CSR	66%
Culture that respects my individuality	82%
Culture that values diversity among its personnel	61%
Culture that supports equality between sexes	63%
Culture that accepts (underrepresented) minorities	46%
Challenging work	77%
Opportunities for relocation abroad and international travel	53%
Secure employment	67%
Flexible working conditions	72%
Good work/life balance	84%
An attractive geographic location	59%
A friendly work environment	91%
A performance-related bonus	61%
Sponsorship of professional training and development	78%
Personal mentoring/coaching	66%
Leadership opportunities	76%
Good possibilities for rapid promotion	67%

Table 5: Percentage of respondents who assigned a high level of importance to EB attributes

Table 5 shows that the majority of respondents (more than 70%) view such attributes as *good reference for future career* (80%), *culture that respects my individuality* (82%), *challenging work* (77%), *flexible working conditions* (72%), *good work/life balance* (84%), *a friendly work environment* (91%), *sponsorship of professional training and development* (78%), and *leadership opportunities* (76%) as very important or important in their future jobs. The top three attributes confirm the opinion from the literature on generation Y, namely that it ascribes great importance to a culture that respects the individuality of all employees, especially their own individuality (82% of respondents), good work/life balance (84%), and a friendly work environment (91%).

The cross-tables for the recruitment channels below show the differences between the levels of importance that Russian and Swiss graduates assign to different recruitment channels. Respondents were asked to rate all the channels mentioned below:

- *Online:* employer websites, job boards, social networks, professional networks, targeted messages/notifications, direct mailings, live webinars with employers;
- *In-person:* career fairs, employer presentations at universities, events sponsored by the employer, support of graduation theses, personal contacts; and
- *Print:* advertisements in magazines and newspapers, career guides and books, career magazines for students, recruitment brochures.

In *Figs. 18* and *19,* selected results from this section of the survey for online and in-person recruitment channels are graphically depicted. The overall trend shows that print channels are significantly losing their importance as recruitment channels for Gen Y.

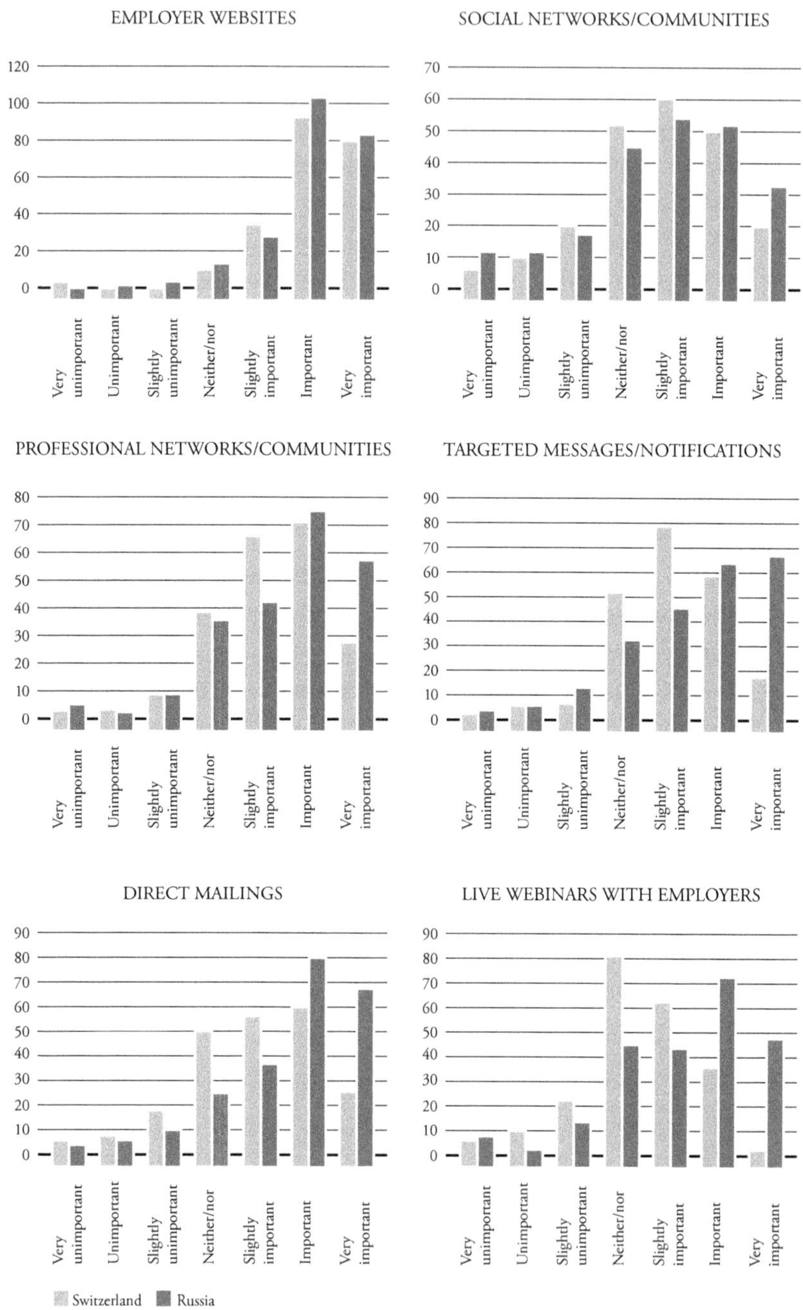

Fig. 18: Comparison of the importance of selected online recruitment channels to Swiss and Russian graduates

Fig. 18 shows that generally graduates of both nationalities ascribe a high level of importance to such online recruitment channels as employer websites and social networks. Russian graduates even view professional networks/communities as a "very important" channel of communication. More Russians than Swiss prefer targeted messages/notifications as a channel of communication with potential employers. Further, more Russian graduates prefer direct mailings and more Russians would like to communicate with potential employers via participation in live webinars. Interestingly, this pattern shows that technological changes influence the behaviour and preferences of graduates in a country with an emerging economy stronger than in the industrialised country, thus supporting the assumption of the strong potential for change in the behaviour patterns that technology provokes.

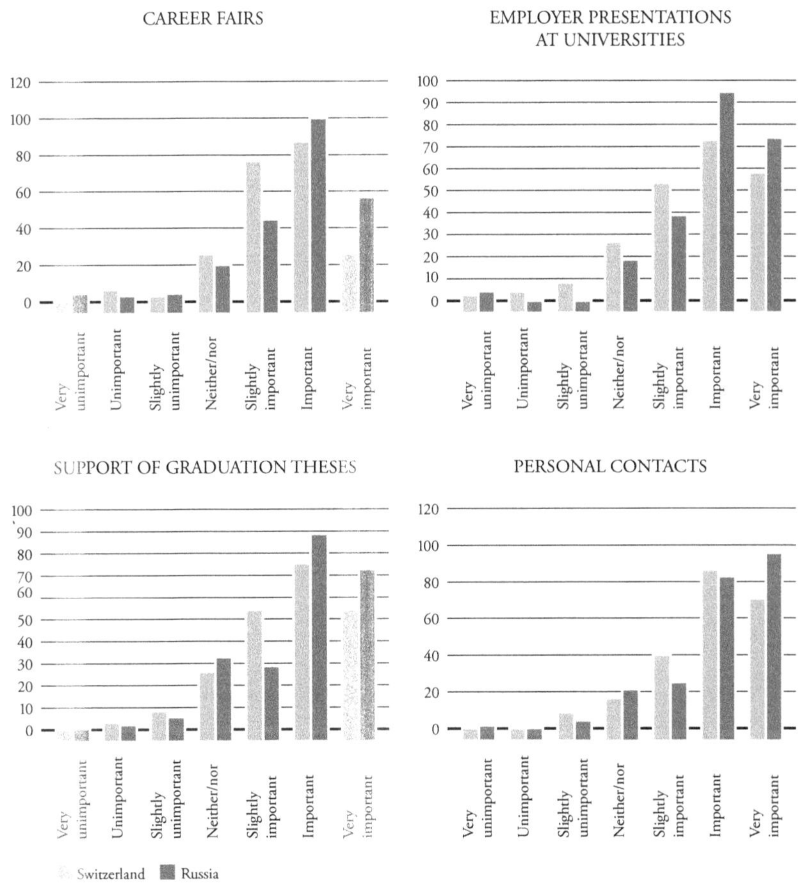

Fig. 19: Comparison of the importance of selected in-person recruitment channels to Swiss and Russian graduates

When observing the importance of in-person recruitment channels, career fairs, employer presentations at universities, support of graduation theses, and personal contacts are viewed as either "important" or "very important " by both groups of graduates overall with Russian graduates again assigning a higher level of importance to all channels in this category. This answer pattern is in favour of the postulation derived from comparative cultural studies, namely that Russians tend to rate personal factors higher than the Swiss.

Referring to the assumption derived from the scientific literature that a certain generation experiences particular "defining moments" that shape their attitudes, values, and preferences (cf. Hoepflinger 1999: 10; Oertel 2007: 18; Lindquist 2008: 56; Franz 2009: 25), the results of the survey tend to prove this assumption but only partially. *Fig. 20* shows that as Schewe and Meredith (2004: 51 ff.) put it, differences exist according to a cultural setting and events that shape a particular nation in a certain moment in time might be given different weights.

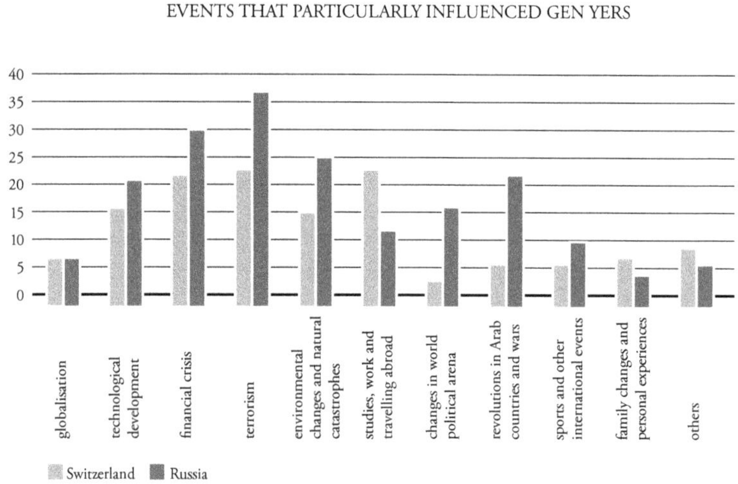

Fig. 20: "Defining generational moments" for Swiss and Russian graduates

Respondents' cohort memberships and their reported significant events were analysed through cross-tabulations to determine if the cited events differed by nationality. Individuals reported events that occurred during their early to young adulthood years. According to cohort theory, these events influence the formation of values in a way that each generation can be distinguished by unique values and beliefs. Another factor that according to Adachi *et al.* (2012: 14) influences the perceived importance of economic and political events worldwide across this generation is hyperconnectivity. "The euro crisis is a textbook example of how increased connectedness, interdependence, and scale can turn a local problem into a global threat" (Adachi *et al.* 2012: 14).

The answer pattern *(Fig. 20)* shows that Russian graduates are influenced by economic and political changes as well as by technological development more strongly than their Swiss counterparts are. The uprising of young well-educated Gen Yers in Russia as a reaction to election fraud at the end of 2011 and beginning of 2012 supports this perspective. Interestingly, the Swiss are more influenced by their studies or work experiences abroad[83] than Russians, supporting the assumption that there exist different groups of Gen Yers who embrace their belonging to the global culture and those who are rather nationally oriented.

6.2 Bivariate correlations

The next step of the analysis was represented by checking for significant correlations in two blocks, namely between Gen Y attitudes and the 19 EB attributes and between nationality and the 19 EB attributes. The relationship between EB attributes and Gen Y attitudes was investigated using Pearson's product-moment correlation coefficient. This correlation coefficient (r) represents the linear relationship between two variables. The significance level calculated for each correlation is a primary source of information about the reliability of the correlation. The test of significance is based on the assumption that the distribution of residual values (i.e. the deviations from the regression line) for the DV Y follows the normal distribution and that the variability in residual values is the same for all values of the IV X (cf. Field 2009: 179). The results of the performed analysis on the existence of bivariate correlations are given in *Tables 6* and *7*.

83 Obviously, they and/or their parents have a sounder material basis for that.

EB ATTRIBUTES		Gen Y
My ideal employer is associated with prestige	Pearson Significance (two-tailed) N	.207** .000 456
My ideal employer is associated with a good reference for future career	Pearson Significance (two-tailed) N	.139** .003 454
My ideal employer is associated with a high level of CSR	Pearson Significance (two-tailed) N	.440** .000 456
My ideal employer has a culture that respects my individuality	Pearson Significance (two-tailed) N	.293** .000 457
My ideal employer has a culture that values diversity among its personnel	Pearson Significance (two-tailed) N	.373** .000 456
My ideal employer has a culture that supports equality between sexes	Pearson Significance (two-tailed) N	.334** .000 458
My ideal employer has a culture that accepts (underrepresented) minorities	Pearson Significance (two-tailed) N	.298** .000 457
My ideal job profile is characterised by challenging work	Pearson Significance (two-tailed) N	.277** .000 458
My ideal job profile is characterised by opportunities for relocation abroad and international travel	Pearson Significance (two-tailed) N	.142** .002 459
My ideal job profile is characterised by secure employment	Pearson Significance (two-tailed) N	.236** .000 457

My ideal job profile is characterised by flexible working conditions	Pearson Significance (two-tailed) N	.436** .000 459
My ideal job profile is characterised by good work/life balance	Pearson Significance (two-tailed) N	.388** .000 458
My ideal job profile is characterised by an attractive geographic location	Pearson Significance (two-tailed) N	.263** .000 458
My ideal job profile is characterised by a friendly work environment	Pearson Significance (two-tailed) N	.419** .000 458
My ideal working condition is associated with a performance-related bonus	Pearson Significance (two-tailed) N	.207** .000 458
My ideal working condition is associated with sponsorship of professional training and development	Pearson Significance (two-tailed) N	.365** .000 458
My ideal working condition is associated with mentoring/coaching	Pearson Significance (two-tailed) N	.448** .000 458
My ideal working condition is associated with leadership opportunities	Pearson Significance (two-tailed) N	.312** .000 457
My ideal working condition is associated with good possibilities for rapid promotion	Pearson Significance (two-tailed) N	.202** .000 458

** Correlation is significant at the 0.01 level (two-tailed).

Table 6: Bivariate correlations between Gen Y attitudes and EB attributes

As can be seen from the results presented in *Table 6*, the correlations between Gen Y and all 19 EB attributes are highly significant for two-tailed probabilities. Moreover, the correlation coefficient value is positive in all 19 cases, meaning that high scores on Gen Y attitudes are associated with high scores on each of the EB attributes (cf. Pallant 2007: 131 f.). The strength of the relationship is either small (r= .10 to .29) or medium (r=.30 to .49) with the strongest relationship between *CSR* (r=.44), *flexible working conditions* (r=.436), *a friendly work environment* (r=.419), *and mentoring/coaching* (r=.448).

EB ATTRIBUTES		Nation
My ideal employer is associated with prestige	Pearson	.345**
	Significance (two-tailed)	.000
	N	456
My ideal employer is associated with a good reference for future career	Pearson	.082
	Significance (two-tailed)	.082
	N	454
My ideal employer is associated with a high level of CSR	Pearson	-.039
	Significance (two-tailed)	.409
	N	456
My ideal employer has a culture that respects my individuality	Pearson	-.075
	Significance (two-tailed)	.110
	N	457
My ideal employer has a culture that values diversity among its personnel	Pearson	-.230**
	Significance (two-tailed)	.000
	N	456
My ideal employer has a culture that supports equality between sexes	Pearson	-.238**
	Significance (two-tailed)	.000
	N	458

My ideal employer has a culture that accepts (underrepresented) minorities	Pearson Significance (two-tailed) N	-.387** .000 457
My ideal job profile is characterised by challenging work	Pearson Significance (two-tailed) N	-.322** .000 458
My ideal job profile is characterised by opportunities for relocation abroad and international travel	Pearson Significance (two-tailed) N	.174** .000 459
My ideal job profile is characterised by secure employment	Pearson Significance (two-tailed) N	.097* .038 457
My ideal job profile is characterised by flexible working conditions	Pearson Significance (two-tailed) N	-.209** .000 459
My ideal job profile is characterised by good work/life balance	Pearson Significance (two-tailed) N	-.159** .001 458
My ideal job profile is characterised by an attractive geographic location	Pearson Significance (two-tailed) N	.110* .019 458
My ideal job profile is characterised by a friendly work environment	Pearson Significance (two-tailed) N	-.085 .070 458
My ideal working condition is associated with a performance-related bonus	Pearson Significance (two-tailed) N	.412** .000 458
My ideal working condition is associated with sponsorship of professional training and development	Pearson Significance (two-tailed) N	.067 .154 458

My ideal working condition is associated with mentoring/coaching	Pearson Significance (two-tailed) N	-.143** .002 458
My ideal working condition is associated with leadership opportunities	Pearson Significance (two-tailed) N	.090 .054 457
My ideal working condition is associated with good possibilities for rapid promotion	Pearson Significance (two-tailed) N	.487** .000 458

** Correlation is significant at the 0.01 level (two-tailed).
* Correlation is significant at the 0.05 level (two-tailed).

Table 7: Bivariate correlations between Gen Y attitudes and nationality

All correlations except three are significant for two-tailed probabilities at the 0.01, 0.05, and 0.1[84] levels (see *Table 7*). No significant correlations are shown for nationality and CSR, nationality and culture that respects individuality, and nationality and sponsorship of professional training and development. A positive significant correlation can be seen between nationality and prestige (r=.345), performance-related bonus (r=.412), and good possibilities for rapid promotion (r=.487), which signifies that the Russian nationality correlates with high scores on these three attributes. A significant negative correlation coefficient was shown in eight cases. This indicated that the Swiss nationality correlated with the following EB attributes (although the strength of the relationship was predominantly small): a culture that values diversity among personnel (r=-.23), a culture that supports equality between the sexes (r=-.238), a culture that accepts (underrepresented) minorities (r=-.387), challenging work (r=-.322), flexible working conditions (r=-.209), good work/life balance (r=-.159), a friendly work environment (r=-.085), and mentoring/coaching (r=-0.143).

6.3 Evaluation of the model

Hierarchical multiple regression was used to assess the ability of two measures (Gen Y attitudes and nationality) to predict the importance

84 Allowing for two-tailed probabilities with a big N (cf. Pallant 2007: 133).

of the 19 EB attributes, after controlling for the influence of age and gender. Preliminary analyses were conducted to ensure no violation of the assumptions of normality, linearity, multicollinearity, and homoscedasticity[85]. In *Table 8*, the main results from the multiple regression are presented in a way that summarises the contribution of the model as well as of each of the IVs to the explanation of the variance in the importance of each of the 19 EB attributes being explored. *Age* and *gender* were entered in Step 1, explaining a certain amount of variance in the importance of an EB attribute (see column 2). After the entry of the *Gen Y attitudes* and *nationality* variables in Step 2, the percentage of the total variance explained by the model appears in column 3. Column 4 shows the additional percentage of variance in the importance of a certain EB attribute that was explained by adding the two additional variables in block 2 of the hierarchical regression, i.e. *Gen Y attitudes* and *nationality.* In the last column on the right, the unique contribution of each of the IVs (if any) is presented, after the overlapping effects of all other variables have been statistically removed.

85 The regression model requires the independence of the error terms and random, patternless residuals imply independent errors. When checking for the independence of residuals, deviations from a centralised rectangle on a scatterplot were shown. However, this does not represent a violation of the regression assumptions in this particular case. The pattern in the residuals in this particular case could be explained as follows: the scale 1 to 7 in the responses was treated as an interval scale, while 1 to 7 was in fact an ordinal scale with the intervals between the values of the variable not being spaced equally. It is undeniable that there is definitely a difference in the spaces between "important" and "slightly important" and "unimportant" and "slightly unimportant". There is in fact no well-defined numerical difference between the levels of importance. Further, three outliers were excluded (ages: 47, 42, 37), although the author did not remove those who were born earlier than 1979 to provide for the variance in the responses on the Gen Y attitudes scale. Note that the author was testing for Gen Y attitudes, which sometimes do not correlate with biological age. The Mahalanobis distances (critical chi-square value for four independent variables = 8.47) (cf. Pallant 2007: 157; extracted and adapted from Tabachnik and Fidell 1996) compared with the distances in the values of the other cases. However, Cook's distance for all cases was < 1; therefore, there was no real need to delete these points since they do not have a large effect on the regression analysis. However, three outliers were deleted and thus removed from the analysis to improve the overall fit of the model. According to Field (2009: 219), "one should still be interested in studying such points to understand why they did not fit the model".

DV	Percentage of explained variance (R square Model 1) in the importance of an attribute after Step 1 (age and gender)	Total variance explained by the model (R square Model 2) as a whole after Step 2 (Gen Y attitudes and nationality) Significance levels at p<0.001 if not indicated otherwise	Additional percentage of variance explained by the two control measures Gen Y attitudes and nationality factor (R square change) Significance levels at p<0.001 if not indicated otherwise	Unique contribution (if any) of each IV
Prestige	11%	19.3% F(4.446) =26.65	8.8% Fchange(2.446) =24.4	Nationality beta=0.28 Gen Y beta=0.25
Good reference for future career	2%	4.1% F(4.444) =4.69, p<0.01	1.9% Fchange(2.444)=4.7, p<0.01	Gen Y beta=0.139, p<0.01
High level of CSR	1.5%	19.8% F(4.446)=27.47	18.4% Fchange(2.446)=51.1	Gen Y beta=0.429
Culture that respects my individuality	0%	9.6% F(4.447)=11.85	9.5% Fchange(2.447) =23.38	Gen Y beta=0.286 Nationality beta=-0.131, p<0.05
Culture that values diversity among personnel	0%	19.8% F(4.446)=27.45	19.4% Fchange(2.446) =54.038	Gen Y beta=0.361 Nationality beta=-0.308 Age beta=-0.168, p<0.01
Culture that supports equality between sexes	14%	28.3% F(4.448)=44.19	14.1% Fchange(2.448) =44.069	Nationality beta=-0.352 Gender beta=0.349 Gen Y beta=0.251 Age beta=-0.111, p<0.05
Culture that accepts (under-represented) minorities	9%	26.4% F(4.447)=40.118	17.5% Fchange(2.447) =53.121	Nationality beta=-0.448 Gen Y beta=0.231 Gender beta=0.202
Challenging work	3%	17.2% F(4.448)=23.346	14% Fchange(2.448) =37.797	Nationality beta=-0.333 Gen Y beta=0.262
Opportunities for relocation abroad and international travel	2.5%	5.8% F(4.449)=6.914	3.4% Fchange(2.449) =8.020	Gen Y beta=0.162, p<0.01 Nationality beta=0.151, p<0.05

Secure employment	4.5%	9.1% F(4.447)=11.237	4.6% Fchange(2.447) =11.329	Gen Y beta=0.217 Gender beta=0.151, p<0.01
Flexible working conditions	1.6%	22.5% F(4.449)=32.552	20.9% Fchange(2.449) =60.568	Gen Y beta=0.433 Nationality beta=-0.170, p<0.01
Good work/ life balance	1.3%	17.1% F(4.448)=23.176	15.8% Fchange(2.448) =42.800	Gen Y beta=0.368 Nationality beta=-0.177, p<0.01
Attractive geographic location	2.4%	9% F(4.448)=11.135	6.6% Fchange(2.448) =16.316	Gen Y beta=0.261
Friendly work environment	2.1%	18.8% F(4.448)=25.987	16.7% Fchange(2.448) =46.049	Gen Y beta=0.396 Nationality beta=-0.116, p<0.05
Performance-related bonus	13%	26.6% F(4.448)=40.560	13.9% Fchange(2.448) =42.490	Nationality beta=0.400 Gen Y beta=0.270 Gender beta=0.195
Professional training and development	0.5%	14.3% F(4.448)=18.671	13.8% F(2.448)=36.047	Gen Y beta=0.377
Personal mentoring/ coaching	1.6%	21.4% F(4.448)=30.416	19.8% Fchange(2.448) =56.265	Gen Y beta=0.437
Leadership opportunities	1%	11.8% F(4.447)=14.927	10.9% Fchange(2.447) =27.505	Gen Y beta=0.334
Good possibilities for rapid promotion	15%	29.9% F(4.448)=47.664	15.2% Fchange(2.448) =48.523	Nationality beta=0.458 Gen Y beta=0.243

Table 8: Evaluation of the model and contribution of each IV

Interestingly, Gen Y makes a significant contribution to the equation concerning the prediction of the DV in all 19 cases. Furthermore, there are several interesting results to report concerning the contribution of other IVs to the model. From *Table 8* (see beta coefficients), it appears that the variable *Gen Y attitudes* makes the strongest unique contribution (beta > 0.350) to explaining the importance of *a high level of CSR, culture that values diversity among personnel, flexible working conditions, good work/life balance, friendly work environment, professional training and development, personal mentoring/coaching,* and *leadership opportunities.* By contrast, the *nationality factor* makes no significant contribution to the importance of CSR, professional training and development, personal mentoring/coaching, and leadership opportunities. At the same time, the variable *nationality* makes a stronger contribution to explaining DVs such as *prestige, culture that supports equality between sexes, culture that accepts (underrepresented) minorities, challenging work, performance-related bonus,* and *good possibilities for rapid promotion.*

Additionally, the estimation of the model showed that apart from the IVs Gen Y and nationality other IVs also contributed to the explanation of the importance of a certain EB attribute to graduates. For example, both *age* and *gender* make a significant contribution to explaining the importance of the variable *culture that supports equality between sexes.* Gender also makes a significant contribution in the case of the variables *culture that accepts (underrepresented) minorities, secure employment,* and *performance-related bonus.*

6.4 Results of the hypothesis tests

The results of the hypothesis tests at the three mentioned levels of reasoning discussed in chapter 4.2 are presented in *Tables 9, 10,* and *11*[86].

86 The V-mark stands for the acceptance of a hypothesis, whereas the X-sign means that a hypothesis was rejected.

No.	Hypothesis (starting from Gen Y attitudes as the IV)	Result of the hypothesis test	Levels of sig. α defined as p-value =0.05 and =0.1
H1a	*Gen Y attitudes influence the importance of an employer attribute:* "prestige"	✓	0.012
H1b	... a good reference for future career	✓	0.001
H1c	... a high level of CSR	✓	0.000
H1d	... culture that respects my individuality	✓	0.000
H1e	... culture that values diversity among its personnel	✓	0.000
H1f	... culture that supports equality between sexes	✓	0.000
H1g	... culture that accepts (under-represented) minorities	✓	0.001
H1h	... challenging work	✓	0.000
H1i	... opportunities for relocation abroad and international travel	✓	0.001
H1j	... secure employment	✓	0.001
H1k	... flexible working conditions	✓	0.000
H1l	... good work/life balance	✓	0.000
H1m	... an attractive geographic location	✗	0.105
H1n	... a friendly work environment	✓	0.001
H1o	... a performance-related bonus	✓	0.105
H1p	... sponsorship of professional training and development	✓	0.001
H1q	... personal mentoring/coaching	✓	0.000
H1r	... leadership opportunities	✓	0.000
H1s	... good possibilities for rapid promotion	✓	0.000

Table 9: Results of the hypothesis tests at the first level of reasoning

Apart from H1m, which contains the EB attribute *geographic location,* all other hypotheses were accepted at the first level of reasoning, signifying that Gen Y attitudes do indeed influence the importance of the other 18 remaining EB attributes. The fact that the hypothesis that includes the importance of the EB attribute geographic location was rejected with regard to Gen Y attitudes can be explained by the growing importance of remote working. Gen Yers prefer to work from home and conduct virtual meetings with other team members, which means that the physical geographic location of the office matters less for students as long as they score high on the Gen Y attitudes.

No.	Hypothesis (starting from Nationality as the IV)	Result of the hypothesis test	Levels of sig. α defined as p-value =0.05 and =0.1	Regression coefficient B unstandardised + or - [87]
H2a	*For Russian graduates, the attribute* "prestige" is more important	✓	0.000	+
H2b	*For Swiss graduates, the attribute* "a good reference for future career" is more important	✗	0.826	
H2c	*For Swiss graduates, the attribute* "a high level of CSR" is more important	✗	0.398	
H2d	*For Swiss graduates, the attribute* "culture that respects my individuality" is more important	✓	0.065	-
H2e	*For Swiss graduates, the attribute* "culture that values diversity among its personnel" is more important	✓	0.000	-
H2f	*For Russian graduates, the attribute* "culture that supports equality between sexes" is more important	✗	0.000	-

87 A (+) sign of the regression coefficient means the EB attribute is more important to Russian graduates; a (-) sign signifies the greater importance of an EB attribute to Swiss graduates (because of the coding process).

H2g	*For Swiss graduates, the attribute* "culture that accepts (underrepresented) minorities" is more important	✓	0.000	-
H2h	*For Swiss graduates, the attribute* "challenging work" is more important	✓	0.000	-
H2i	*For Swiss graduates, the attribute* "opportunities for relocation abroad and international travel" is more important	✗	0.009	+
H2j	*For Swiss graduates, the attribute* "secure employment" is more important	✗	0.181	
H2k	*For Russian graduates, the attribute* "flexible working conditions" is more important	✗	0.006	-
H2l	*For Swiss graduates, the attribute* "good work/life balance" is more important	✓	0.002	-
H2m	*For Russian graduates, the attribute* "an attractive geographic location" is more important	✗	0.215	
H2n	*For Russian graduates, the attribute* "a friendly work environment" is more important	✗	0.028	-
H2o	*For Swiss graduates, the attribute* "a performance-related bonus" is more important	✗	0.000	+
H2p	*For Swiss graduates, the attribute* "sponsorship of professional training and development" is more important	✗	0.073	+
H2q	*For Russian graduates, the attribute* "personal mentoring/coaching" is more important	✗	0.119	
H2r	*For Swiss graduates, the attribute* "leadership opportunities" is more important	✗	0.071	+
H2s	*For Russian graduates, the attribute* "good possibilities for rapid promotion" is more important	✓	0.000	+

Table 10: Results of the hypothesis tests at the second level of reasoning

Seven hypotheses out of 19 concerning the importance of a certain EB attribute according to nationality were accepted at the second level of reasoning. The remaining 12 were rejected either because *nationality* does not exercise significant influence on the importance of an attribute or because the attribute is more important to the graduates of the other nationality than that assumed in the hypothesis.

The rejection of H2b, containing the EB attribute of *a good reference for future career,* means that this attribute is no longer more important to Swiss graduates, but that the importance of this attribute is growing among Russian students the more they become Gen Yers. This can be traced back to the growing individualism in Russian society, especially among Gen Yers, and the growing interest in career prospects. Surprisingly, graduates view *CSR* as an important attribute that their future employers should possess independent of nationality. The rejection of H2c, stating that this attribute is more important to Swiss graduates, signifies a paradigm shift in the way that Gen Yers view their future employers independent of nationality. With regard to the recent discussions in Switzerland concerning the role and place of women in management positions, it is not surprising that Swiss graduates consider the attribute *equality between sexes*[88] no less important that their Russian counterparts, where equality between sexes exists because of the Soviet legacy of an egalitarian society. This justifies the rejection of H2f. H2i, stating that the attribute *opportunities for relocation abroad and international travel* was more important to Swiss graduates, was rejected. This signifies that as Russian Gen Yers have the opportunity to study and work abroad, they look for possibilities to gain experience that is more international with their future employers. *Secure employment* (H2j) seems to be important to graduates of both nationalities. It must be stated though that the importance of this EB attribute depends largely on the macro-economic situation in the country of residence as well as on the overall situation in the job market and cannot be easily explained as a result of national differences[89]. *Flexible working conditions* (H2k) seem to be no less important to Swiss graduates than to their Russian counterparts, signifying again that Gen Y in general expects flexible working conditions

88 There is a certain gender effect involved (see Table 8).

89 Moreover, a certain gender effect has to be considered (see Table 8).

from employers. Further, possessing a Russian nationality alone does not imply that an *attractive geographic location* (H2m) is more important to Russians than to the Swiss, pointing out again that technological advancement makes the role of this EB attribute far less important to the young generation of graduates than for their parents. Swiss graduates view the EB attribute *a friendly work environment* (H2n) as no less important than their Russian counterparts do; this EB attribute is highly influenced by Gen Y attitudes and to a lesser extent by nationality (see also *Table 8*). Interestingly, *a performance-related bonus*[90], *sponsorship of professional training and development,* and *leadership opportunities* (H2o, H2p, H2r) are becoming more important to Russian graduates. This can also be explained by the transformation processes in Russian society: a new generation of graduates is evolving as more individualistic and performance-oriented as well as more career-oriented[91]. At the same time, the attribute *personal mentoring/coaching* (H2q), which was discussed in the theoretical part of the book as typical of Soviet society, is no longer more important to Russian graduates. Swiss graduates expect personal mentoring and coaching programmes from their employers – a fact that confirms the very strong influence of Gen Y attitudes.

6.5 Interaction effects and the analysis of simple slopes

After having looked at the level of importance that certain EB attributes possess in the eyes of graduates depending on the overall belonging to generation Y and later, to a certain nationality, the results of the tests for possible interaction effects between Gen Y attitudes, nationality, and EB attributes are discussed further. The 19 EB attributes were chosen to be tested for the possible presence of significant two-way interactions (cf. Aiken/West 1991) between Gen Y, nation, and EB attributes and to control for the moderating effect of nationality.

90 There is a certain gender effect involved (see Table 8).

91 In terms of status orientation, which is said to be typical of Russian society according to the arguments derived from the cultural theories, the acceptance of H2s confirms this statement, signifying that to Russian graduates good possibilities for rapid promotion represent an important EB attribute when choosing an employer.

As mentioned before, the main purpose of the research was to control for the moderating effect of nationality in the relationship between Gen Y attitudes and the 19 EB attributes. The results of the hypothesis tests at the third level of reasoning are summarised in *Table 11* and are followed by *Figs. 21–28,* which plot the results of the simple slopes analysis (cf. Dawson/Richter 2006; Dawson 2011: online).

No.	Hypothesis	Result of the hypothesis test	Levels of sig. α, p-value =0.05 and =0.1	Result of the simple slopes test
H3a	*Nationality moderates the relationship between* Gen Y attitudes and *"prestige"*, such that this relationship is stronger for *Russian* graduates	✗	0.233	
H3b	… *"a good reference for future career"*, such that this relationship is stronger for *Swiss* graduates	✓	0.067	CH: 0.002 RU: 0.335
H3c	… *"a high level of CSR"*, such that this relationship is stronger for *Swiss* graduates	✗	0.992	
H3d	…*"a culture that respects my individuality"*, such that this relationship is stronger for *Swiss* graduates	✓	0.015	CH: 0.000 RU: 0.000 Swiss slope is steeper (see *Fig. 22*)
H3e	…*"a culture that values diversity among its personnel"*, such that this relationship is stronger for *Swiss* graduates	✗	0.382	
H3f	…*"a culture that supports equality between sexes"*, such that this relationship is stronger for *Russian* graduates	✗	0.198	
H3g	…*"a culture that accepts (underrepresented) minorities"*, such that this relationship is stronger for *Swiss* graduates	✓	0.074	CH: 0.000 RU: 0.001

H3h	...*"challenging work"*, such that this relationship is stronger for *Swiss* graduates	✗	0.322	
H3i	...*"opportunities for relocation abroad and international travel"*, such that this relationship is stronger for *Swiss* graduates	✓	0.057	CH: 0.000 RU: 0.139
H3j	...*"secure employment"*, such that this relationship is stronger for *Swiss* graduates	✗	0.524	
H3k	...*"flexible working conditions"*, such that this relationship is stronger for *Russian* graduates	✗	0.597	
H3l	...*"good work/life balance"*, such that this relationship is stronger for *Swiss* graduates	✗	0.273	
H3m	...*"an attractive geographic location"*, such that this relationship is stronger for *Russian* graduates	✓	0.013	CH: 0.102 RU: 0.000
H3n	...*"a friendly work environment"*, such that this relationship is stronger for *Russian* graduates	✓	0.003	CH: 0.001 RU: 0.000
H3o	...*"a performance-related bonus"*, such that this relationship is stronger for *Swiss* graduates	✓	0.009	CH: 0.000 RU: 0.001
H3p	...*"sponsorship of professional training and development"*, such that this relationship is stronger for *Swiss* graduates	✗	0.135	
H3q	...*"personal mentoring/coaching"*, such that this relationship is stronger for *Russian* graduates	✗	0.687	
H3r	...*"leadership opportunities"*, such that this relationship is stronger for *Swiss* graduates	✗	0.671	
H3s	... *"good possibilities for rapid promotion"*, such that this relationship is stronger for *Russian* graduates	✗	0.069	CH: 0.000 RU: 0.000 Swiss slope is steeper (see *Fig. 28*)

Table 11: Results of the hypothesis tests at the third level of reasoning

Eight significant two-way interactions out of 19 were shown, of which *the hypothesised strength of the relationship was approved in seven of eight hypotheses* where the interaction was significant:

- *11 hypotheses* where there was no significant interaction were automatically rejected; and
- in *one hypothesis,* the interaction was significant, but the relationship seemed to be stronger for the other nationality than that assumed in the hypothesis (H3s).

Of the 19 cases, direct significant two-way interactions were shown in eight cases with regard to the following EB attributes: *a good reference for future career, a culture that respects my individuality, a culture that accepts (underrepresented) minorities, opportunities for relocation abroad and international travel, an attractive geographic location, a friendly work environment, a performance-related bonus,* and *good possibilities for rapid promotion.*

In the following, these eight significant two-way interactions are plotted using the Excel macros of Dawson (2011) and the meaning of the difference in the steepness of simple slopes (where appropriate) is explained. *Figs. 21–28* show how Gen Y attitudes[92] and nationality interact to affect the importance of these eight EB attributes.

92 Gen Y=1 means that graduates score low on Gen Y attitudes, thus signifying that they feel less like belonging to generation Y. Gen Y=2 indicates a high score on Gen Y attitudes, thus signifying that respondents scored highly on this scale, namely they view themselves as typical representatives of generation Y.

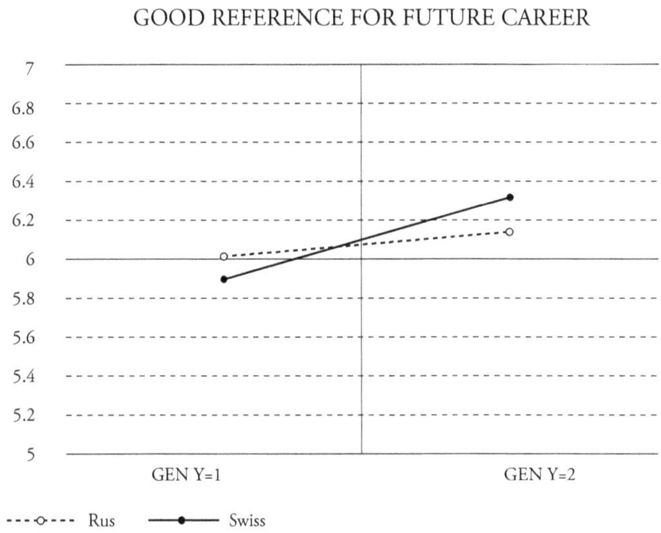

Fig. 21: Two-way interaction between Gen Y attitudes and nationality with respect to a good reference for future career

Gen Y attitudes exercise significant influence on the importance of the attribute *a good reference for future career,* as presented in the analysis performed at the first level of reasoning. At the second level of reasoning, the hypothesis that nationality influences the importance of the EB attribute *good reference for future career* was rejected. However, when checking for an interaction effect between these two and the importance of this EB attribute, it seems that more Swiss graduates feel like Gen Y, (i.e. they ascribe a high level of importance to Gen Y attitudes in the questionnaire), the more important *a good reference for future career* becomes to them *(p=0.002).* For Russian graduates, no significant interaction effect was shown *(p=0.335),* i.e. nationality with regard to Russian graduates does not moderate the relationship between belonging to Gen Y and the importance Russian graduates ascribe to the EB attribute *good reference for future career.* More specifically, the slope for Russian graduates was not significant neither when Gen Y attitudes are weak nor strong; in other words, Russian graduates with both weak and strong levels of Gen Y attitudes found this attribute to be equally important. *Hence, H3b is supported.*

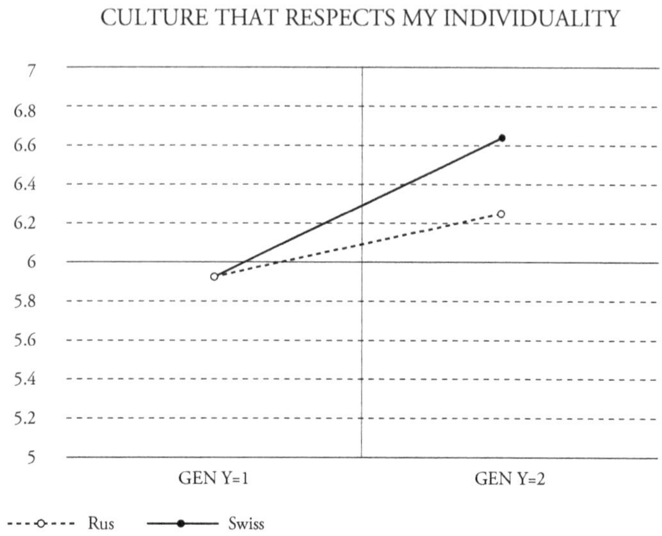

Fig. 22: Two-way interaction between Gen Y attitudes and nationality with respect to a culture that respects individuality

Gen Y attitudes postulate the importance of the attribute *culture that respects my individuality.* Swiss nationality signifies that the importance of this attribute is higher for Swiss graduates than for their Russian counterparts. However, when testing for the interaction effect, the research showed that both Swiss and Russian graduates ascribe more importance to this attribute the more they feel like Gen Y. In *Fig. 22*, the Swiss slope seems to be steeper (meaning that the moderating effect of nationality is stronger for the Swiss); however, the simple slopes tests were significant in both cases ($p=0.000$ for both slopes), i.e. for both nationalities. In this particular case, the research confirms that Gen Y attitudes are indeed changing Russian culture in the way that Gen Yers in Russia value the attribute "individuality" more than previous generations. The Swiss slope, however, is a little steeper. On these grounds, *H3d is supported.*

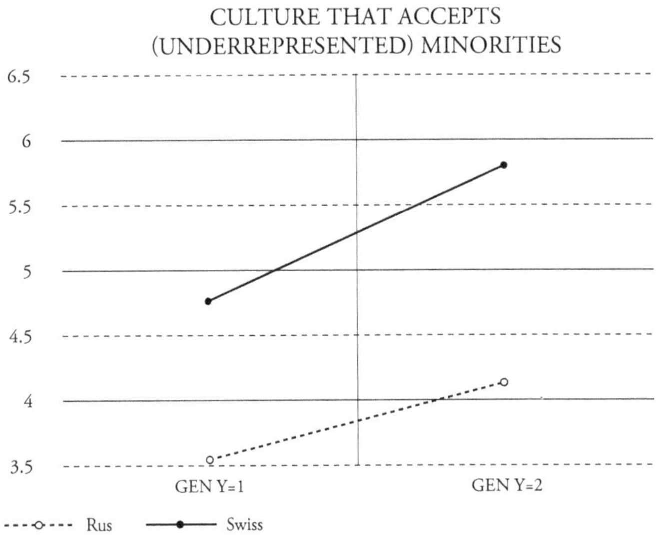

Fig. 23: Two-way interaction between Gen Y attitudes and nationality with respect to a culture that accepts (underrepresented) minorities

Gen Y attitudes exercise significant influence on the importance of the EB attribute *culture that respects (underrepresented) minorities.* Swiss nationality also influences significantly the importance of this EB attribute, so that it is more important to Swiss graduates than to Russians. It can be viewed in *Fig. 23* that the Swiss in general ascribe more importance to this EB attribute (even though they feel less like Gen Y) than do Russians. However, the simple slopes analysis shows the significance of both slopes, although the Swiss slope seems to be steeper (thus signifying that the moderating effect of nationality is stronger for Swiss graduates, $p= 0.000$ *vs.* $p=0.001$ for Russians). Therefore, there has been a significant shift in the development of a national culture in Russia among Gen Yers, confirming that Gen Y attitudes are changing the national characteristics, so that the graduates of both nationalities ascribe more importance to this EB attribute the more they feel like they are part of generation Y. *This statistical analysis provides support for H3g.*

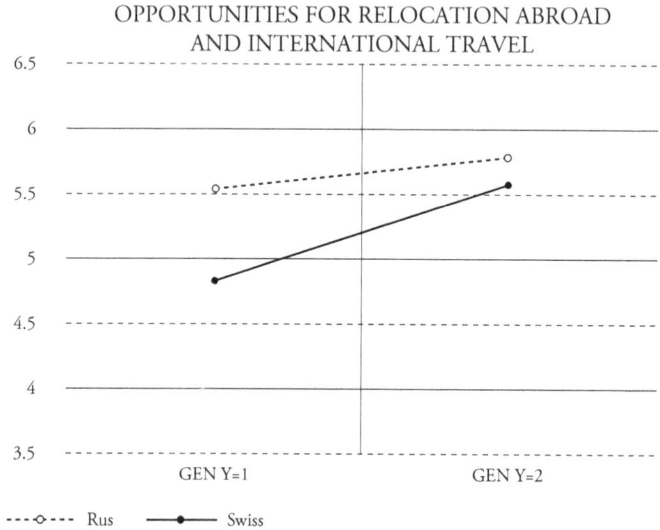

Fig. 24: Two-way interaction between Gen Y attitudes and nationality with respect to opportunities for relocation abroad and international travel

As can be viewed from the hypothesis tests at the first level of reasoning, Gen Y attitudes influence the importance of the EB attribute *opportunities for relocation abroad and international travel,* meaning that Gen Yers strive to gain more international experience and pursue international career paths. At the second level of reasoning, it was shown that this EB attribute is more important to Russian graduates. *Fig. 24* clearly shows that the national influence for Russians on the importance of this EB attribute is stronger than for Swiss nationals the less they feel they belong to Gen Y. The moderating effect is significant only for the Swiss slope *(p=0.000)* vs. the Russian slope *(p=0.139)*. Thus, the importance of opportunities abroad becomes more relevant to Swiss graduates the more they refer to themselves as Gen Y, reaching almost the same level of importance as their Russian counterparts ascribe to this EB attribute when they refer to themselves as Gen Y. The results from the test at the third level of reasoning (as opposed to the second level of reasoning where the assumptions were made on the basis of nationality) show that Swiss Gen Yers are eager to travel and acquire international experience since they might consider their own country (despite its international image) to be too small to seek employment. These results advocate a significant shift among Swiss graduates with respect to the importance of the EB attribute *opportunities for relocation abroad and international travel* and confirm the assumption of the strong influences of Gen Y attitudes that are changing the national Swiss paradigm within a new generation of graduates. *H3i is, therefore, supported.*

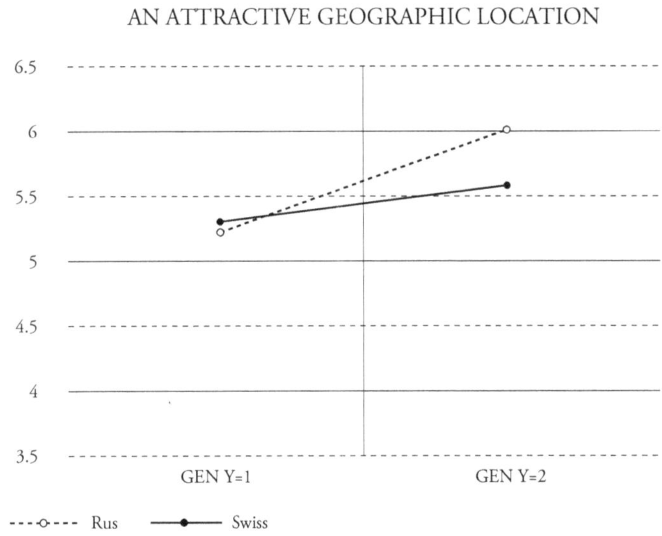

Fig. 25: Two-way interaction between Gen Y attitudes and nationality with respect to an attractive geographic location

As indicated in *Table 9,* the only attribute for which the importance is not influenced by Gen Y attitudes is geographic location (H1m). This was explained by growing technological advancement and the new opportunities for Gen Y to practice remote working efficiently while not being physically present in the office. At the second level of reasoning, the level of importance that the national factor might exercise on the importance of the EB attribute *attractive geographic location* was not significant, either. However, the test for the presence of interaction effects at the third level of reasoning showed a significant two-way interaction for the Russian slope *(p=0.000)*. This result confirms the trend towards the growing importance of an attractive geographic location for Russian graduates, signifying that for Russian Gen Yers working for a company that offers employment in an attractive geographic location is more important than for their Swiss counterparts (the Swiss slope is not significant, *p=0.102*). This can be explained by the fact that apart from Moscow and St. Petersburg few places in Russia are viewed as attractive geographic locations and Russian Gen Yers value this attribute highly enough to apply for a particular position within a certain company or to accept a job offer. Switzerland in general is viewed as an attractive geographic location; therefore, neither Gen Y attitudes nor being Swiss influences the importance of this EB attribute to Swiss graduates. Hence, *H3m is supported.*

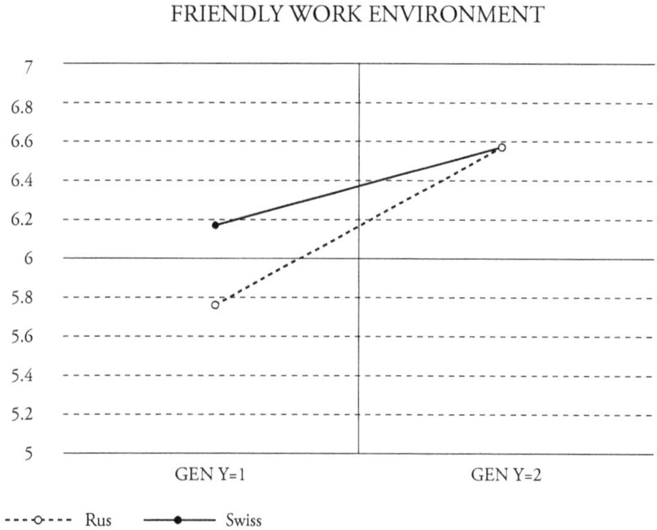

Fig. 26: Two-way interaction between Gen Y attitudes and nationality with respect to a friendly work environment

Gen Y attitudes significantly influence the importance of the EB attribute *friendly work environment.* As far as the nationality factor is concerned, for the Swiss this EB attribute was marked as more important than for Russians (this can be also seen in *Fig. 26* when Gen Y=1). However, when testing for the interaction effects between Gen Y attitudes and nationality, the picture changes. Both slopes are significant, meaning that the more both Russian *(p=0.000)* and Swiss *(p=0.001)* graduates show their belonging to Gen Y, the more important the EB attribute *friendly work environment* becomes. In *Fig. 26*, the Russian slope, however, is steeper, signifying that the moderating effect of nationality is stronger for Russian graduates. On the graph, the two slopes intersect each other when Gen Y attitudes within both groups of graduates are strongly manifested (Gen Y=2). This again provides evidence that Gen Y graduates, in this very case almost independent of national differences, strive to work in a congenial and friendly atmosphere and have fun at work, and thus delivers further empirical evidence for the support of the assumption derived from the literature on Gen Y. *The statistics deliver support for H3n.*

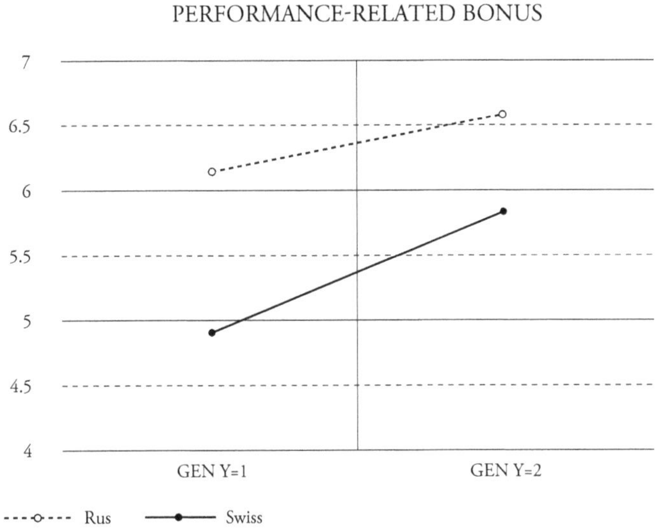

Fig. 27: Two-way interaction between Gen Y attitudes and nationality with respect to a performance-related bonus

Gen Y attitudes significantly influence the importance of the EB attribute *performance-related bonus.* The role of the national factor shows that this EB attribute seems to be more important to Russians than to the Swiss, indicating that the national assumption about low performance orientation in Russian society no longer holds true (even when graduates themselves feel less like Gen Y). The interaction seemed to be significant for both nations, i.e. in this particular case, nation does moderate the relationship between Gen Y attitudes and the importance of the EB attribute *performance-related bonus.* This attribute becomes more important to the graduates of both nationalities the more they feel as though they belong to Gen Y. The Swiss slope is slightly more significant (*p-value 0.000 vs. 0.001* for the Russian slope), meaning that for the Swiss belonging to Gen Y and holding onto Gen Y attitudes have a stronger influence on the importance of this EB attribute. The less Swiss graduates feel like Gen Y, the less important is the performance-related bonus (value 4.8 on the graph), whereas for Russians a performance-related bonus is more important even when they do not express high agreement with Gen Y attitudes (value 6.2 on the graph). This concludes that Gen Y attitudes have a stronger influence in Swiss culture, whereas in Russia the national factor itself stresses the importance of new performance-oriented dimensions (in opposition to the theoretical statements from the previous cultural research). *Thus, H3o is supported.*

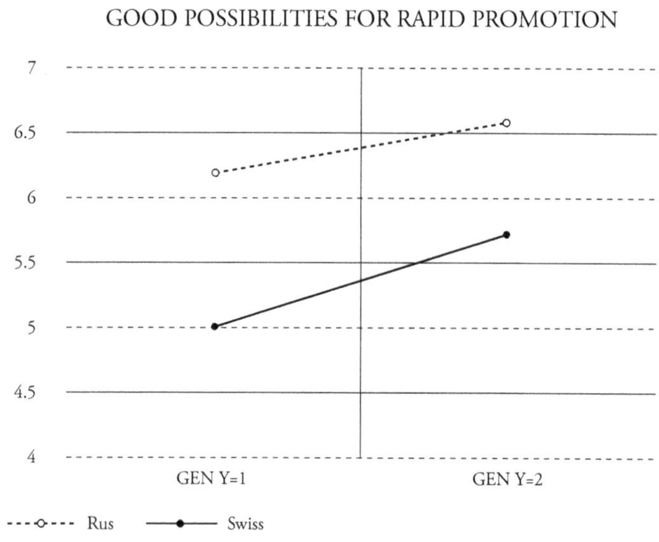

Fig. 28: Two-way interaction between Gen Y attitudes and nationality with respect to good possibilities for rapid promotion

As can be seen from the hypothesis test conducted at the first level of reasoning, Gen Y attitudes exercise significant influence on the importance of the EB attribute *good possibilities for rapid promotion.* Further, the analysis at the second level of reasoning confirmed the hypothesis that this EB attribute is more important to Russian graduates than to Swiss graduates (supported by the results of the analysis at the third level of reasoning even when they feel less like Gen Y; see *Fig. 28*). At the third level of reasoning, when checking for interaction effects, the interaction for both nationalities seemed to be significant, because the p-value of the simple slopes was highly significant *($p=0.000$)*. The Swiss slope is a little steeper on the graph, which again signifies that the influence of Gen Y attitudes on the importance of this particular EB attribute is stronger for Swiss nationals. This statement can be also traced by looking at the values of the importance of this EB attribute when Gen Y=1. The difference in values for the Swiss slope (5 to 5.7) represents a more significant shift than the difference between 6.2 and 6.6 (Russian slope). Further, the importance of the possibilities for rapid promotion is higher for the group of Russian graduates who feel less like Gen Y. In other words, this observation signifies that this EB attribute is more strongly influenced by the national factor in the case of Russian graduates than is the case for their Swiss counterparts, for whom Gen Y has a stronger influence on the importance of the *possibilities for rapid promotion*[93]. The moderating effect in the relationship between Gen Y attitudes, nationality, and this EB attribute (steepness of the slope), however, is stronger for the Swiss sample, meaning that nationality intensifies the change in the proclaimed importance of the EB attribute *good possibilities for rapid promotion* among Swiss Gen Yers. *Thus, H3s is rejected because of the result of the simple slopes test.*

In chapter 7, the discussion of the results and presentation of the practical and theoretical implications follow. The limitations of the conducted research are also considered.

93 Although the difference in the significance (p-value) of the slopes is very small.

7

DISCUSSION AND RECOMMENDATIONS

"Domestic identity of people is going to decrease. Look at what our children are doing online, how they communicate worldwide. Virtual mobility will be huge in the future."

James H. Wall[94]

94 Global Managing Director, Talent Solutions and Chief Diversity Officer at Deloitte.

To date, as previously mentioned, very little research has been conducted on the cultural differences of Gen Yers around the world. Owing to this relative lack of research, US findings on generational differences and characteristics have mostly been adapted to other parts of the world without second guessing. The results obtained from the present research show clearly that understanding the differences between the expectations of graduates in developed and emerging economies is a key element in the success of any organisation's employer branding strategy. This knowledge can provide employers with the ability to compete and achieve high performance in a multi-polar globalised world, in which an environment is marked by multiple centres of economic power (cf. Farley/Malkani/Smith 2008: 3).

The purpose of the present study was twofold. First, the author sought to advance our understanding of the concepts of Gen Y by means of the operationalisation of this construct and of the EB through the definition of the EB attributes that are important to Gen Y individuals. Second, the author sought to gain insight into the importance of nationality as a factor that moderates the strength of the relationship between Gen Y attitudes and EB attributes by means of the development of an appropriate research instrument. The results from the empirical part of the study highlight the importance of using a differentiated approach while integrating certain EB attributes into the holistic EB.

The study focused on the ways students from two different nationalities in the process of transitioning from higher education into the labour market prioritise their employment expectations. Through a thorough literature review and secondary analysis of the quantitative data from most recent studies of the topic, the author attempted to identify the EB attributes that make employers attractive to Gen Y graduates of different nationalities. This knowledge on what today's graduates are looking for when selecting an employer is a first step to ensuring that a company strives to satisfy these needs and meets the expectations in order to attain the status of an EOC.

The next step involved the development of a statistical research model that reflected and was able to analyse the possible interaction between *Gen Y attitudes, nationality,* and *EB attributes.* In particular, the central aim of the present study was to examine the existence and strength of the moderating influence of nationality on the relationship between Gen Y attitudes and the importance of certain EB attributes. EB was measured by means of 19 identified items given priority based on the literature analysis on Gen Y, cultural theories (Hofstede, GLOBE, Trompenaars/Hampden-Turner, Lewis), and recent scientific papers that discuss the contemporary situation on the job market. Hypotheses were formulated at three levels of reasoning, represented by 19 hypotheses at each level. At the third level of reasoning, the assumption was made that the strength of the relationship between Gen Y attitudes and the chosen EB attributes is moderated by nationality such that this relationship is stronger or weaker because of a particular nationality (cf. chapter 4.2 and *Table 11*).

The author's final intent was to answer the question of whether the target market of Gen Yers can and should be segmented according to nationality and to present recommendations with regard to cross-national employer branding activities in the recruitment process targeting Gen Y. This study presented the results of a cross-national analysis of employment expectations of Swiss German and Russian university graduates and attempted to answer the question of what differences should be taken into account when creating employer branding strategies in the context of international recruitment marketing. A brief comparison of generation Y's expectations and characteristics in the German-speaking world and Russia showed that while on the surface there are many parallels between Gen Yers in both cultural areas, at deeper levels culturally induced differences regarding the importance of certain EB attributes remain. Therefore, it gives the author the right to assume that individuals and their expectations remain, to a certain degree, influenced by national specifics. Moreover, the results of the study showed a partial shift in certain cultural dimensions, providing evidence that culture is also a dynamic construct and that certain national characteristics tend to change over time. This allowed the author to question several of the statements derived from existing cultural theories.

This research showed that Gen Yers in different locations associate their potential employers with a common set of core values but that the importance they ascribe to each EB attribute under the drivers of employer attractiveness, as rooted in their cultural backgrounds, differs. MMR analysis at the third level of reasoning showed eight significant two-way interactions out of 19, of which the hypothesised strength of the relationship was approved in seven where the interaction was significant. These compelling results support the intention of the author to show the significance of the varying relationship between Gen Y attitudes and the importance of different EB attributes according to nationality. As a result, it is indispensable to analyse the relation of the representatives of the target group separately towards every particular EB attribute[95].

In summary, the results extend previous research by demonstrating that Gen Y graduates of different nationalities should be viewed as coming from certain cultural contexts despite the fact that they possess common Gen Y characteristics. Likewise, the performed research proves that Gen Y attitudes exercise very strong influence over the importance of certain EB attributes and sometimes even neutralise the effects that arise due to nationality. This provides sound grounds for supporting the view of Bird and Stevens (2003: 400 ff.), who assume that a global culture to which Gen Yers belong exists parallel to national cultures, of which Gen Yers to a certain extent remain a part. It seems to be reasonable for organisations to direct their attention to developments such as the emergence of a global culture and a global generation. This development of a global culture and generation can be traced to ongoing globalisation and technological progress. Members of this global culture and global generation have similar characteristics and, therefore, share expectations towards employers. However, it has to be taken into consideration that this may be because these individuals are by nature more globally oriented than their national counterparts.

7.1 Practical implications

The issues addressed in this research have several practical implications. As such, this research may help practitioners in deciding what EB attributes should be included when creating a holistic EB for their companies and

95 The percentage of explained variance that each IV contributes to the whole model should be taken into account (for more details, consult chapter 7.3 on the limitations of the performed research).

how this EB should be conceived in respect to the characteristics of the target group of graduates they want to reach as their future employees. It can be said that the research defined the essential elements for practical implementation of employer branding strategies to target Gen Y and that HR and employer branding practitioners should follow when creating employer branding strategies to attract Gen Y graduates in the context of international recruitment marketing. In order to successfully recruit Gen Yers in a cross-national context, organisations have to take into account the influences of both generational and national effects when developing their employer branding strategies.

As indicated earlier in the book, contextual effects consist of several factors. The nationality effect represents one example. The complexity of these contextual effects all but eliminates the possibility to provide specific recommendations. Instead, in this chapter very high-level recommendations – generally relevant for the recruitment of Gen Y – will be summarised. These will subsequently have to be adjusted to the specific context a particular organisation faces in the real world[96].

7.1.1 Target group segmentation

Recruitment activities and campaigns should be designed according to the characteristics of the prospective applicant population. Hence, target group segmentation is an absolute must from the very beginning and this represents a starting point in every employer branding campaign. In this case, a particular segment of university graduates in economics was subjected to analysis. It is obvious that not all Gen Yers belong to this target group.

Organisations seeking to recruit from a diverse talent pool of young university graduates need to have a bundle of options to meet the different expectations of the talent pool. Companies should start gathering and using talent market data to define their KPIs (see chapter 3.4) in order to implement smart talent segmentation and plan their communication and employer branding activities in an efficient way. An organisation should

96 Trost (2009: 68 ff.) identifies the following four critical success factors of employer branding campaigns: inclusion of the target group, brand champion, sustainability, and control. The author of this research develops further practical implications based on the obtained results from the performed study. See also Hubschmid (2012: 81 f.).

explicitly highlight the EB attributes that are important to the target group during the recruitment process via the appropriate recruitment channels.

Further, the target group should approve of the campaign, otherwise it will miss its effect. By including the target group at an early stage of the employer branding processes, its specific insights can be taken into account and the campaign can be adjusted accordingly (see also Trost 2009: 68 f.).

7.1.2 The importance of Gen Y attitudes

Many companies have realised that it is not just getting more difficult to recruit well-qualified graduates, but that they are also at constant risk of losing their talented Gen Yers to competitors (cf. Sutherland/Torricelli/Karg 2002: 14). Therefore, when conceptualising and putting into practice an employer branding strategy, the specificities of Gen Y employees must be taken into account because of the strong influence that Gen Y attitudes exert on the importance of EB attributes (cf. chapters 6.1, 6.2, and 6.5). "Companies that adapt their compensation packages and job structures to respond to the needs and expectations of Generation Y will be better positioned to attract the employees they need and want" (Schnorbach 2009: 34). The first step, however, is to actually know what Gen Yers are looking for when selecting an employer and what kinds of company attributes they value (cf. Sutherland/Torricelli/Karg 2002: 15).

This research approved of the statement made by Macleod (2008: 2) that Gen Y is characterised by its own unique place in history and brings its own set of experiences and expectations to the workplace. The results of the statistical analysis showed that Gen Y attitudes represent a very influential factor in shaping the employment expectations of the younger generation. Gen Yers are focused on developing their skills, progressing in their careers, and giving something back to society through their work and existing CSR initiatives (see chapter 6.2). Independent of nationality, they value an organisational culture that respects individuality and provides a friendly work environment. They also bring their own set of aspirations to the world of work, both in terms of development and support through mentoring/coaching programmes as well as in terms of career progression (see also Wilton 2008: 81).

It can be said that despite the complexity of the contextual effects, generational effects influence the importance of certain EB attributes independent of cultural background. There are some prevalent expectations of Gen Y towards the employer, which may be only slightly different across cultures, especially among students. Therefore, these characteristics should serve as an important building block for the development of a recruitment marketing strategy aimed at Gen Y employees.

7.1.3 Assessment of the nationality factor

In terms of the nationality factor, the particular context primarily affects the way an organisation communicates and represents itself as an EOC (cf. *Figs. 18* and *19*). Performing a differentiated employer branding strategy according to national differences among Gen Yers while accentuating the common characteristics of the emerging global culture that unite them should be ensured.

Despite the general characteristics of Gen Y both in Russia and in Switzerland, one major difference could influence the initial employment expectations of Russian and Swiss university graduates. Gen Y in Switzerland was raised in times of economic growth and prosperity, whereas Gen Y in Russia grew up in times of political, economic, and social change and instability (cf. Guriev/Tsivinsky 2010: 12). As the results of this study showed, Russian and Swiss Gen Yers assign different importance to defining generational moments (see *Fig. 20*). Nevertheless, Naumov and Puffer (2000: 717) allege that the young generation in Russia

> [...] had limited experience in the welfare system and collectivist ideology promoted by the former communist regime, and had been exposed from the early age to Western market-oriented and social values. Thus it is not surprising that the profiles of this younger generation tended to converge toward those in Western developed countries more than the other groups of Russians [..] (Naumov/Puffer 2000: 717).

The tests at the third level of reasoning proved this statement in terms of the importance of EB attributes such as *a culture that respects individuality and accepts minorities, a friendly work environment, and a performance-related bonus* among others for both groups of graduates.

In this respect, it should be kept in mind that nationality does not stand for some static bundle of stable characteristics (cf. *Table 10*). The national dimension of culture is a dynamic construct that evolves with time as well as technological and economic progress. Therefore, the change in cultural specifics should always be monitored and considered within the employer branding framework in order to ensure the realistic assessment of the cultural attributes of the younger generation.

7.1.4 A clear strategy and the team behind employer branding efforts

There should be a clear strategy behind the employer branding philosophy. The employer branding strategy should be linked and stem from the corporate strategy[97] and have precise corporate objectives in terms of personnel demand.

> Clear strategies mean that companies do not fragment their limited resources by pursuing too many new ideas. Dynamic market development and tough competitive conditions do not change the fact that a company always needs clear ideas in order to achieve and to defend competitive advantages in attractive markets (Grünig/Kühn 2005: 47 f.).

Hence, the strategic focus of the target group of Gen Yers should be assured and substantiated using unequivocal arguments and numbers. Knowing and understanding Gen Y's preferences in respect to job profile and organisational characteristics before elaborating on and launching an employer branding strategy should be ensured. The employer branding process should be strategically viewed as an EB funnel where the position of the EB should be monitored from the familiarity via consideration to the acceptance phase within the target group.

Apart from that, the members of the board must rally behind the employer branding strategy, otherwise all efforts will get abandoned. A strong corporate position on the issue of the employer branding strategy is crucial when developing and putting into practice a strategically successful EB. The CEO of the company should take the role of EB champion in order to assure the EB's long-term success (cf. Trost 2009: 69).

To ensure the effectiveness of employer branding initiatives, the EB team should ideally include the CEO, a public relations and/or communications manager/director, a HR manager/director, a university/student

97 Ensuring the fit between corporate, product, and employer brands.

relations manager/director, and specialists who are professional statisticians and mathematicians in order to be able to calculate the strategic and operational risks based on existing data. As already mentioned, the overall support of the employer branding team must be ensured by top management, otherwise all EB initiatives run the risk of staying brilliant ideas without sound support.

7.1.5 The weight of EB attributes within the holistic EB

Because EB activities must be viewed as matching employers with employees, a differentiated approach to the EB concept must help achieve a perfect match. The era of personality targeting is underway since employer branding now means finding and attracting people who fit in with the corporate culture. Since young people focus on corporate values and images when looking for their potential employers, cultural fit (meaning PJ fit and PO fit, not solely monetary benefits) has become one of the main drivers of employee engagement among the younger generation. Therefore, distinguishing between different EB attributes that make up a holistic EB is of paramount importance and, if analysed and assessed correctly, is one of the key success factors of every EB and any employer branding campaign.

Today, the growing importance of mathematical analysis has made "soft" decision-making and intuitive strategy choice obsolete. This statement also holds true for employer branding strategies. This research has shown that the EB construct can and needs to be measured (see chapters 2.4 and 4.1.2) by breaking down a holistic EB into a bundle of EB attributes that are important to the target group. The measurement of the EB should not only be data supported and driven by mathematical algorithms created from data on past successes and failures. The performed research has shown that each measurement model should also be assessed in relation to a particular EB attribute (see *Table 8* and chapter 7.3).

7.1.6 Authentic communication

The alignment between the perceptions of an EB among the target group and internal personnel should be monitored since the authenticity and transparency of communication has a high importance for Gen Yers and is a sign of an attractive corporate culture. Any incongruity between these perceptions should be corrected by adjusting the EVP during the employer branding campaign. Therefore, using RJPs and authentic EB messages is one way of creating loyalty[98] in Gen Yers while recruiting them, thus boosting the effectiveness of recruitment marketing measures.

As mentioned earlier in the thesis, it is often argued that Gen Yers have problems staying loyal to their employers. They do, however, seem to have the capacity to be loyal towards an employer they feel is loyal towards them. Honesty is an important factor in this equation. Therefore, the employer should come across as honest during the recruitment process and be open about the potential downsides of the job and the organisation. The technological achievements and networks of Gen Yers allow them to quickly verify the level of communication transparency and the authenticity of organisational messages. Subsequently, the organisation will have to "keep its promises" or communicate openly when earlier promises change. Such open and honest communication should prove a big step towards creating sympathy and, in the long run, loyalty from Gen Y employees. Furthermore, since Gen Yers attach high importance to the social aspects of the working environment, an organisation should provide them with the opportunity to visit the company during the recruitment process and to get in touch with their potential colleagues. Sheer online recruiting, job fair contacts, or bilateral discussions between the candidate and recruiter or his/her future supervisor are not sufficient.

7.1.7 The importance of appropriate recruitment channels

Of equal importance is the selection of adequate channels to clearly communicate these values (cf. Sutherland/Torricelli/Karg 2002: 13): "The stronger the brand message appeals to top performers, the more these individuals will want to work for the company. Employer branding is, therefore, a key strategy to attracting and retaining the best" (Sutherland/Torricelli/Karg 2002: 14). In this way, the company will be able to gain a strategic competitive advantage in the competition for the right potentials.

98 Loyalty should not be seen as a lifelong state of being; it can be fostered and prolonged for a certain period.

Using Gen Y's natural affinity for technology when choosing the right recruitment channels is a certain way to secure an efficient input/output ratio of EB metrics (i.e. pre-hire, post-hire, and post-hiring recruitment outcomes; for details, see chapter 2.1.1 and Breaugh/Starke 2000: 409).

The Internet makes personality targeting affordable but there is a need for an integrated communication approach. Here, the same principle applies to reaching talent as it does to reaching customers. Therefore, organisations should use the tools that new media offers to attract the younger generation. The employer website is in this context one of the most important instruments: Gen Yers use the Internet to obtain information about the company, especially at the beginning of the recruitment process, and an appealing website may be the best advertisement. Furthermore, it is important to reduce the usage of underperforming recruiting channels to free up financial resources for new employer branding and "communication with talent" initiatives. Gen Yers are "techno-savvy" and usually connected to the virtual world via new media. They heavily rely on social media to cultivate their friendships and business contacts. Social media should thus be viewed as a communication platform with the target group rather than as a one-way channel for delivering specific messages[99]. Overall, companies should think of expanding their social media engagement by integrating social media activities in every step of the recruitment marketing process. In so doing, they should be aligned with the overall HR and business strategies, since any dissonance will be quickly spotted and criticised online (see also Strack *et al.* 2011).

The present research also showed that Gen Yers valuing individuality prefer a correspondingly individualistic approach to communication with employers (see chapter 6.1 and *Figs. 18* and *19*). The importance that Gen Yers ascribe to targeted messages and direct mailings as valuable recruitment channels should be evaluated. The results of the study provide evidence that there are, however, differences in the level of the importance of certain recruitment channels for Gen Yers between an

99 Networks such as Facebook are becoming more important for sourcing Gen Y candidates. Twitter is also becoming a powerful recruitment tool, providing a high ROI for recruiters, although professional networks such as Xing and LinkedIn still generate the highest volume of job interest and job-related activity. Companies should thus differentiate between their communication strategies according to the particular channel and type of network.

emerging economy such as Russia and an industrialised country such as Switzerland[100]. The appropriate recruitment channels should, therefore, also be assessed from a country-specific perspective.

Online channels offer unique characteristics for starting efficient employer branding strategies. If companies already have a strong EB, they should strive to highlight through social media channels the particular equity elements of their EB. For companies with a weak EB, it is recommended to raise awareness first by establishing a presence on career websites and/or social and professional networks. In this respect, it is recommended to increase the usage of recruitment channels that according to the data obtained from HR metrics perform well and match them with the appropriate technology. Identifying new channels that can provide a cost-effective ROI should also be in place and regularly monitored.

7.1.8 Personal networks of Gen Yers

Since Gen Yers are highly connected, often across national boundaries, possess a large networking potential, and are open, globally minded, and techno-savvy, a company should use these characteristics of Gen Yers to gain access to their extended networks, both online and in real life. Organisations should encourage their current Gen Y employees to use their networks to attract potential new employees. New recruits based on employee referrals might be very successful since a Gen Yer who is already working for a company can anticipate if there will be a cultural fit between a potential employee and the organisation. Hence, organisations should not miss out on this opportunity to successfully recruit Gen Yers. Using Gen Y's far-reaching networks to recruit other Gen Yers leads to successful employee referrals and, as a result, good PO matches. However, those Gen Yers who already work for the company should know the exact job profile so that cliques can be eliminated. Line and HR managers should critically analyse all suggestions, ensure that the candidate fulfils all predetermined criteria, and carry the responsibility for the final hiring decision.

The results of the survey on the importance of recruitment channels show that Gen Yers independent of nationality rate personal contacts very

100 For example, live webinars with employers, targeted messages/notifications, direct mailings, and career fairs among others are more important for Russian graduates (see *Figs. 18* and *19*).

highly in the hierarchy of possible in-person recruitment channels (cf. *Fig. 19*). These findings deliver support for the existence of a huge networking potential that Gen Y is characterised in the literature. Therefore, their far-reaching personal networks and the desire to maintain personal contacts with each other and employers should be considered in employer branding efforts.

7.1.9 The importance of employer branding metrics

According to Trost (2009: 70), one of the biggest challenges is to ensure the sustainability of the EB. Through the careful and consistent elaboration of the EVP, which reflects the expectations of the target group and how they change over time, the flexibility and continuity of the EB can be ensured.

As mentioned in chapter 3.4, efficiency and effectiveness criteria must be defined in order to monitor the success of employer branding activities regarding Gen Y. Measures such as the number of applicants (right potentials), quality of hire (feedback to the recruitment process), external talent attraction rankings (external image as an EOC), the employee engagement level of new entrants[101], cost-per-hire balance, application versus acceptance ratios, attrition rates and causes for leaving the company, promotion of internal candidates that have been recruited into key roles, sourcing effectiveness in terms of recruitment channels, and the employee referral rate of new recruits (see *Fig. 14*) should become integral for assessing employer branding strategies.

The abovementioned parameters should be measured[102] on a regular basis and compared with the rates from previous years or those of competitors (based on the availability of data[103]). Communication between existing and potential employees can also be measured by tracking communication flows between employees in certain positions through employee surveys. The periodic measurement of positive EB strengths through Internet searches and consulting firms such as Universum should be per-

101 For example, measuring the on-the-job performance of recently hired graduates after six months can give an indication of the productivity of Gen Yers and thus provide information on the effectiveness of the recruitment marketing campaign.

102 If these measurements are performed according to nationality, this can deliver the necessary data to make statements about the relevance of the nationality factor within the target group.

103 For instance, this would be possible in the case of published EOC rankings.

formed and compared with competitors. Periodically visiting sites such as glassdoor.com and kununu.com to assess possible negative EB images could also be useful in terms of the necessary modification of employer branding strategies.

Additionally, the speed with which the organisation acquires critical knowledge on relevant employer branding issues must be measured. Organisations should further measure whether this learning speed in the employer branding team and at the top of the organisation is fast enough and whether they are progressing at the same pace. The speed with which problems occur and best practices are shared throughout the employer branding process needs to be measured as well. For example, if a new approach in the employer branding strategy is highly successful and delivers good results, the time it takes for the employees working for the organisation and involved in the EB initiatives to hear about it and/or adopt it must be measured (see also Sullivan 2012: online).

Having a creative and innovative employer branding team can cause certain errors in employer branding processes. In this case, a minimum recruitment value target should be set in order to document losses. Following that, how much rapid learning occurs after each failure should be assessed. Measuring the percentage of all employees that work in the employer branding function (including top management) and the percentage of the total budget assigned to the employer branding team can give a good indication of the financial efficiency of this team (cf. Sullivan 2012: online).

Further, measuring the consistency of the internal EB and comparing it with the external EB is of high importance. It is possible to assess the level of consistency by tracking the number of open employee forums held, the number of questions discussed, and the percentage of critical questions among them. It is also possible to count the number of anonymous responses to the issues discussed on forums, where current and potential employees might be active participants. To find out if current employees understand what the organisation stands for, a sample of current workers should be periodically surveyed to see if they can list the desired values that make up the organisational culture. After data from current employees have been collected and analysed, a sample of new recruits should be surveyed in order to assess whether they act in line with corporate values and culture after, for example, six months on the job, thus ensuring cultural fit. Such measurements can indicate the extent to which new Gen Y employees have been successfully acculturated. Moreover, the improvement of internal and external employer branding processes should be measured in order to assess whether they are matching the speed of improvement in product and service development and in the marketplace[104]. Calculating the time that it takes (in months) to make major recruitment decisions and the time it takes to release weak performers as well as employees who do not fit with the organisational values may also indicate the state of the art of the employer branding strategy (see also Sullivan 2012: online).

To summarise, the major decisions in every employer branding campaign should be data supported and should have a clear algorithm behind them. In order to successfully recruit Gen Yers in a global context, organisations have to take into account the influences of both generational and contextual effects when developing their recruitment marketing strategy and perform measurements integrating these effects into the assessment formula.

Recruitment marketing is not a one-size-fits-all practice; organisations must carefully coin their recruitment marketing and EB practices on the basis of specific organisational factors and gathered data[105]. It can be said that creating a "glocal"[106] model (cf. Hilb 2001: 9 ff.) for recruitment marketing is a key priority for large organisations in forthcoming years. This applies to nationally as well as internationally operating companies.

104 Congruity between the EB, product brand, and corporate brand.

105 Another approach that may explain the biased findings about Gen Y is the interaction of generational and contextual influences. Since an individual's behaviour, attitudes, and beliefs are formed by contextual influences as well as by cultural or economic influences, one has to pay attention to these contextual factors, as they may influence the results of a particular study in advance or affect its practicability and generalisability. For example, expectations of graduates towards their employers before the economic crisis might differ from those of graduates during or after the crisis (cf. Deal/Altman/Rogelberg 2010: 194). Ng, Schweitzer and Lyons (2010: 288) assign the current economic climate as one possible reason for the more realistic expectations of Gen Yers towards their initial salaries. According to ILO statistics, 12.7% of young people worldwide are unemployed, with the highest rate of unemployment in Spain and with very low rates in Switzerland (Bauer 2012: 23). In this case, contextual influences surpass characteristics predefined through belonging to a particular generation.

106 "Glocal" means having high local flexibility and high global integration (cf. Hilb 2001: 10).

"All companies, whether already international, or going international, need a normative basis, that is a statement of the objectives and values on which to base their activities" (Grünig/Morschett 2012: 91).

An explicit conceptual framework for recruitment marketing that integrates the findings of the current research is presented in *Fig. 29.* New elements are highlighted in italics. It should be noted, however, that since generational phenomena are complex and managerial research on this topic is scarce (cf. Joshi *et al.* 2010: 409), the conceptual framework developed herein represents a first step to developing a viable agenda for future generational research in organisations, with a focus on employer branding and recruitment marketing to target Gen Y.

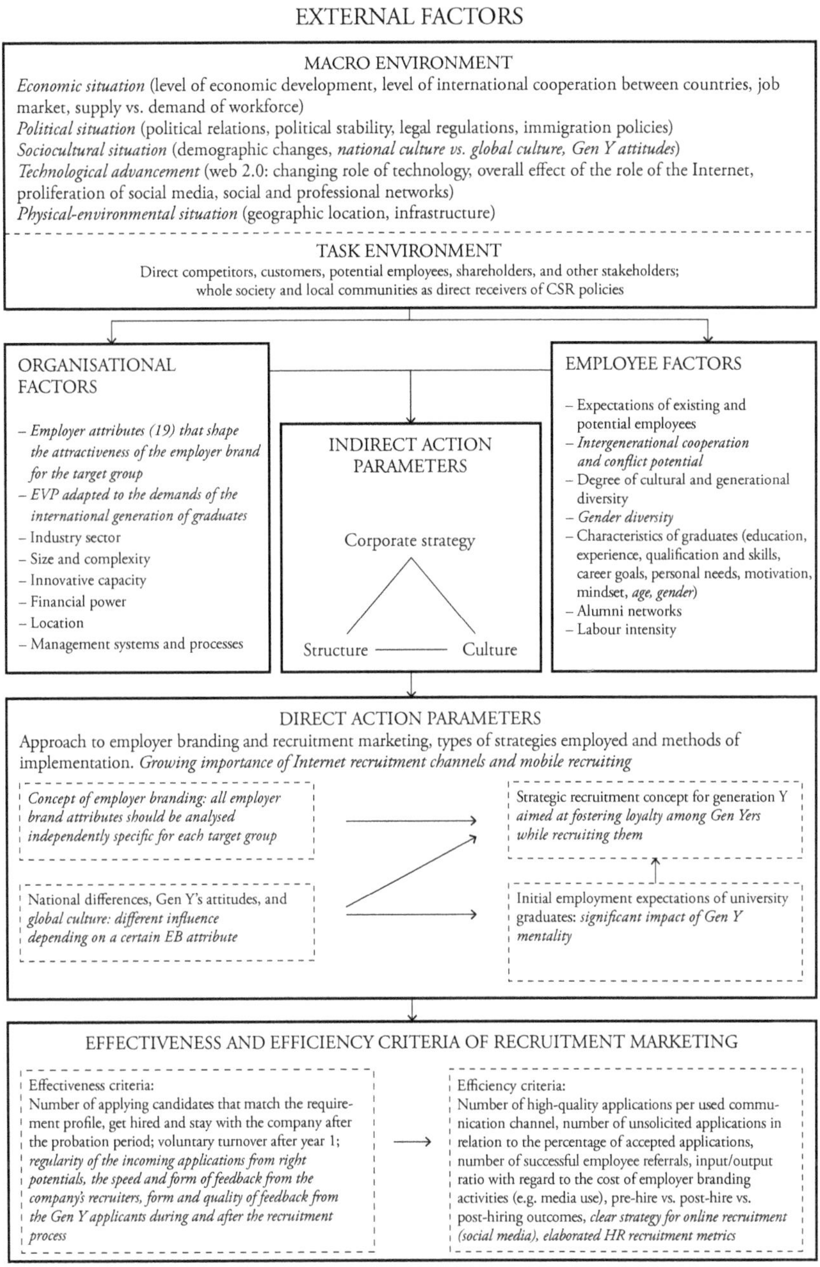

Fig. 29: Explicit conceptual framework for recruitment marketing (own representation)

7.2 Scientific appraisal of the research

In terms of the critical appraisal of the performed research, the theoretical contribution of the author should undoubtedly be highlighted. Through the extensive literature analysis, exhaustive examination of secondary studies, and profound empirical research, the author has managed to develop a theoretical research model that can be used to study the employment expectations of Gen Y, particularly those of different nationalities. With her research, she has further shown that Gen Y and culture theories have been modified through the combination of the two by opening a new dimension in management research. Thus, the present study represents the basic groundwork of an explorative nature by introducing the so-called "management theory of relativity" of the role of cultural influences within this new generation. It shows a clear demand for the development of a specific cultural theory for generation Y.

The research conducted and results obtained present a new approach to conceptualising nationality and its meaning to generation Y. The results are a significant departure from the traditional theories of culture that have been dominating comparative cultural research over decades. The study was able to demonstrate the differences as well as similarities that exist in the expectations of the university graduates of two nationalities coming from a developed and an emerging economy. It has further shown that solely traditional theories and dimensions of culture cannot capture these differences. The empirical results provided insights into the fact that cultural values and Gen Y attitudes may have significant implications for employer branding practices where Gen Y is concerned. More similarities than differences have been shown between these two groups of graduates in their employment expectations. The managerial implications that are relevant for the development of a more consistent EB for a particular target group of potential recruits have also been discussed.

Overall, the study contributes to research on the employment expectations of graduates. Using an empirical paradigm and a comparatively large sample[107] from two countries, the research demonstrates that nationality as well as belonging to generation Y can play a crucial role in influ-

107 To date, the biggest sample of these two populations in comparison (Switzerland and Russia).

encing the importance of certain EB attributes. More importantly, the research shows that the impact of certain nationalities as a moderating variable varies depending on the EB attribute subjected to analysis. In this respect, scholars have frequently noted that an EB should be conceived with caution and include elements that are important for the target group. However, they have usually failed to specify what EB attributes deserve particular attention and why. By addressing this issue, this study demonstrates that different nationalities and belonging to Gen Y (when the interaction is being modelled) can exert significant influence over the importance of separate EB attributes. In summary, this study extends the literature on Gen Y findings from a cross-national perspective by showing that the relationship between Gen Y attitudes, nationality, and the importance of EB attributes may be more complex than previously envisioned.

7.3 Limitations of the study and implications for future research

Although this research presents a set of findings that contribute to the literature on Gen Y in a cross-national context, it also has some limitations. Consequently, the conducted research has been limited by areas where further research is still needed.

The sample of respondents was derived from the subgroup of the population of graduates in economics and business administration living and studying in Moscow and in German-speaking Switzerland. Another consideration of the present study is that while Russian is the predominant culture, the Russian Federation consists of more than 100 national groups[108]. In addition, attention should be paid to the highly dynamic quality of contemporary Russian society. Hence, the main limitation to this exploratory study is its reliance on a sample gathered predominantly on campus during class time. Therefore, the generalisability of results may be a concern and thus there is potential for common method variance in future research efforts on the subject. However, this study does open up possibilities for studying the employment expectations of graduates in the same as well as in other fields of study in other universities in different countries.

108 "[...] differences within a country may be larger than between countries [...]" (Grünig/Morschett 2012: 291).

Further, nationality only constitutes one contextual influence affecting an individual's characteristics and expectations. For example, in seven out of 19 cases, the variable nationality does not make a unique significant contribution to the equation used in the model (see *Table 8*). Moreover, the total variance explained by the model varies from 4% to 30% depending on the DV, i.e. the EB attribute that was being observed. This limitation suggests that specific findings should be considered with some caution. There is vast potential to look into the possible contributions of such variables as work experience, field of study (major), and so on. It would also be worth exploring similar attitudinal variables of university graduates in other focused majors such as philosophy, art, or medicine.

The gender aspect presents many potential future research topics as well. There must be some significant and important gender differences, particularly in the use of new technology and in the acceptability of blurring the line between home and work. It is likely that Gen Y attitudes apply primarily to young men. Women are known to place greater emphasis on developing relationships and protecting their lifestyle choices. As the evaluation of the model shows (see *Table 8*), gender makes a significant contribution to explaining the importance of several EB attributes (culture that supports equality between sexes, culture that accepts (underrepresented) minorities, secure employment, and a performance-related bonus). On these grounds, there is huge potential to research gender-based differences in the employment expectations of Gen Yers of different nationalities, especially as more women now have an ambition to reach the top of organisational hierarchies. Such studies would guide both industry experts and academics in their attempts to better understand Gen Y.

In addition, future researchers should not only assess differences in mindsets based on nationality but consider the *ambitions* of graduates from developed as well as emerging nations. Such differences in ambitions might have numerous implications for the employer branding strategy. Moreover, there is potential for the cluster analysis[109] of different groups of Gen Yers: would career-oriented Gen Yers prefer completely different

109 A cluster is seen as a group of relatively homogeneous cases or observations that are similar to each other and differ from objects outside the cluster, especially objects in other clusters (cf. Sheppard 1996: 49 f.).

EB attributes than do work/life balance-oriented Gen Yers (see also Felser 2010: 26 f.)? In both cultural settings, attributes such as *job security, gender equality, flexible working hours,* and *continuing education* can justify cluster membership.

Referring to the interaction effects, which were shown by working with the present model, it should be noted than the theorising included only one binary moderator (nationality). There is thus research potential for testing three-way interactions (often thought of as a relationship between an IV X and DV Y, moderated by variables Z and W), which could also be continuous rather than binary moderators.

In addition, in terms of methodology, an endorsement of mixed methods research (a combination of qualitative and quantitative approaches) is welcome (cf. Kiessling/Harvey 2005: 22 ff.). These authors argue that strategic global HRM research in the 21st century[110] should use a mixed methods approach to "capture the fabric of global phenomena that include complex interactions of culture, institutions, societal norms and government regulations, among a few concerns" (Kiessling/Harvey 2005: 22). Pieper (1990: 24) also argues that to advance the research field on intercultural HRM, both quantitative and qualitative research approaches need to be combined "in order to get a more complex picture of nations and more realistic and differentiated comparisons". Hence, there is potential for endorsing the obtained results by conducting qualitative interviews with graduates and/or with the managers responsible for the employer branding strategies in the organisation.

When conducting a cross-sectional survey, one should thoroughly deliberate which additional influences might cause bias and try to control for these interferences. One possible idea for controlling for age and life-stage effects might be the utilisation of a preferably wide range of individuals

110 "Culture is now an important theoretical construct to incorporate in models of human behaviour and an important variable to consider in all areas of psychological research. Cross-cultural theories are now more complex, elegant, and sophisticated than ever before. [...] research methods must evolve to keep pace with theoretical developments; the methods by which researchers explore the linkage between culture and psychological processes need to evolve, as have those theories. [...] the field needs an evolution of methods that examine linkage, test competing cultural theories explaining between-country differences, and rule out rival hypotheses involving potential noncultural sources of those differences" (Matsumoto/Hee Yoo 2006: 245).

within a generation, i.e. in the case of Gen Y to survey students, young professionals, and individuals who have already been working for several years, and to include questions about their current life-stages and their perceived influence. Subsequent intergenerational comparisons may then show age and life-stage effects. Further, longitudinal studies (i.e. how expectations evolve over time) as opposed to the cross-sectional study of the importance of EB attributes should be performed by future researchers[111]. Jobseeking is a longitudinal process, and these expectations as well as the importance of certain EB attributes are likely to change as potential jobseekers have more information on their EOCs. For example, it would be interesting to study how the expectations of Gen Yers change in response to learning new information (e.g. because of changes in employer branding campaign or strategy) and whether they change as new information confirms or disconfirms previous expectations. Thom (2009: 187) argues that surveys on the initial employment expectations of graduates have to be repeated on a regular basis, since there is a tendency to reassess priorities. In addition, research should further investigate whether generational or national differences influence the appropriate use of preferred recruitment channels and social networking sites for employer branding decisions.

Further, organisations should continue to direct their attention to developments such as the emergence of a global culture and a global generation.

111 The design best suited to truly examining generational differences and characteristics is a time-lag or longitudinal design (cf. Levenson 2010: 258 f.; Twenge 2010: 202). A longitudinal design surveys the same respondents at different points in time, which allows for the observance of similarities or changes over time (cf. Lerner 2002: 497). A time-lag design surveys the attitudes of individuals at a particular age at different times in history (cf. Lerner 2002: 499). These two designs allow for the examination of the question of whether differences across generations are caused by generational, age, or life-stage effects (cf. Levenson 2010: 258 f.; Twenge 2010: 497). They even enable controlling for environmental effects (cf. Parry/Urwin 2010: 7). Examples of surveys using longitudinal and time-lag designs are those studies conducted by Smola and Sutton (2002), Twenge and Campbell (2008), Kowske, Rasch and Wiley (2010), and Twenge *et al.* (2010). However, such surveys are rare because they require a lot of time and money as well as a relatively strong commitment and effort from participants over a comparatively long period of time (cf. Lerner 2002: 497). Furthermore, longitudinal designs are subject to bias caused by decreasing response rates over time (cf. Lerner 2002: 497). In order to appropriately test hypotheses about Gen Yers, one has to collect data covering more than 30 years (cf. Levenson 2010: 258). Obviously, this is a very long time period considering that Gen Yers are entering the workplace at this very point in time and recommendations regarding the expectations of this generation of employees have to be given instantly and not retrospectively.

The closer examination of these phenomena is needed while monitoring how national attributes change over time and what influence this change has on the expectations of potential applicants. The development of a global culture and generation may be traced through the ongoing globalisation of markets, certain similarities in defining generational moments (events), and technological progress.

Throughout this study, much analysis has been carried out on Gen Yers and on how they have fully embraced the web era. As such, there is vast potential for performing similar analysis on generation Z – young people born between the late 1990s and late 2000s. This generation is considered to be the first that has not only grown up but also was born into a truly digital world.

REFERENCES

Accenture (2009): Talent Management at Peak Capacity. ‹www.accenture.com/usen/Pages/insight-talent-management-utilities.aspx›, accessed 30th January 2012.

Adachi, Barbara / Helfrich, Dan / Gretczko, Michael / DiMarzio, Marty / Schwartz, Jeff (2012): Human Capital Trends 2012. Leap ahead. Deloitte's annual report 2012.

Adecco (2008): Are Swiss companies prepared for the demographic crunch? Demographic Fitness Survey: Switzerland 2008, London 2008.

Aiken, Leona S. / West, Stephen G. (1991): Multiple Regression: Testing and interpreting interactions, Thousand Oaks 1991.

Alfes, Kerstin (2009): Einfluss der Kompetenzen von Personalverantwortlichen auf die strategische Rolle der Personalabteilung, Munich/Mering 2009.

Ambler, Tim / Barrow, Simon (1996): The Employer Brand. In: Journal of Brand Management, vol. 4 1996, no. 3, pp. 185–206.

Andratschke, Nadine / Regier, Stefanie / Huber, Frank (2009): Employer Branding als Erfolgsfaktor. Eine conjoint-analytische Untersuchung, Lohmar/Cologne 2009.

Arsenault, Paul M. (2004): Validating generational differences: A legitimate diversity and leadership issue. In: Leadership & Organization Development Journal, vol. 25 2004, issue 2, pp. 124–141.

Axelrod, Robert (1997): The Dissemination of Culture. A Model with local convergence and global polarization. In: Journal of Conflict Resolution, vol. 41 1997, no. 2, pp. 203–226.

Backhaus, Kristin / Tikoo, Surinder (2004): Conceptualizing and researching employer branding. In: Career development international, vol. 9 2004, issue 5, pp. 501–517.

Bakacsi, Gyula / Takács, Sándor / Karácsonyi, András / Imrek, Viktor (2002): Eastern European cluster: tradition and transition. In: Journal of World Business, vol. 37 2002, pp. 69–80.

Balmer, John (1998): Corporate Identity and the Advent of Corporate Marketing. In: Journal of Marketing Management, vol. 14 1998, no. 8, pp. 963–996.

Balmer, John / Gray, Edmund (2003): Corporate Brands: What are they? What of them? In: European Journal of Marketing, vol. 37, no. 7/8, pp. 927–997.

Barber, Alison E. (1998): Recruiting Employees: Individual and organizational perspectives, Thousand Oaks/London/New Delhi 1998.

Barber, Alison E. / Roehling, Mark V. (1993): Job postings and the decision to interview: A verbal protocol analysis. In: Journal of Applied Psychology, vol. 78 1993, issue 5, pp. 845–856.

Barney, Jay (1991): Firm Resources and Sustained Competitive Advantage. In: Journal of Management, vol. 17 1991, pp. 99–120.

Baron, Angela / Armstrong, Michael (2007): Human capital management: Achieving added value through people, London/Philadelphia 2007.

Barrow, Simon / Mosley, Richard (2005): The Employer Brand – Bringing the Best of Brand Management to People at Work, London 2005.

Bartscher, Thomas / Fritsch, Stephan (1992): Personalmarketing. In: Handwörterbuch des Personalwesens, eds. Eduard Gaugler and Wolfgang Weber, Stuttgart 1992, column 1747–1758.

Bauer, Susan (2003): Kienbaum High Potentials. ‹www.uni-kl.de/CONTACT/docs/presentation_uni_kl_20030507.pdf›, accessed 1st April 2009.
Bauer, Richard (2012): Ohne Arbeit und Perspektive. In: Neue Zürcher Zeitung, vol. 233 2012, no. 117, p. 23.
Baumueller, Martin (2007): Managing Cultural Diversity. An Empirical Examination of Cultural Networks and Organizational Structures as Governance Mechanisms in Multinational Corporations, Bern 2007.
Baskerville, Rachel F. (2003): Hofstede never studied culture. In: Accounting, Organizations and Society, vol. 28 2003, issue 5, pp. 1–14.
Beardwell, Julie / Claydon, Tim (2007): Human resource management: A contemporary approach, 5th ed., Harlow 2007.
Beechler, Schon / Woodward, Ian C. (2009): The global "war for talent". In: Journal of International Management, vol. 15 2009, pp. 273–285.
Beliaeva, Lidia A. (2006): A Social Portrait of Age Cohorts in Post-Soviet Russia. In: Russian Education and Society, vol. 47 2006, no. 5, pp. 23–45.
Behrens, William (2009): Managing Millenials. In: Marketing Health Services, vol. 28 2009, Spring 2009, pp. 19–21.
Bergstrom, Alan / Blumenthal, Dannielle / Crothers, Scott (2002): Why internal branding matters: the case of Saab. In: Journal of Communication Management, vol. 5 2002, no. 2/3, pp. 133–142.
Bernauer, Dominik / Hesse, Gero / Laick, Steffen / Schmitz, Bernd (2011): Social Media im Personalmarketing. Erfolgreich in Netzwerken kommunizieren, Cologne 2011.
Berry, Leonard L. / Parasuraman, A. (1991): Marketing Services. Competing through Quality, New York 1991.
Bersin, Josh (2011): Strategic Human Resources and Talent Management: Predictions for 2012. Driving Organizational Performance amidst an Imbalanced Global Workforce. Bersin & Associates research report, Oakland 2011.
Berthon, Pierre / Ewing, Michael / Hah, Li Lian (2005): Captivating company: dimensions of attractiveness in employer branding. In: International Journal of Advertising, vol. 24 2005, issue 2, pp. 151–172.
BFS (2006): Population growth and demographic aging: A view into the future. Hypotheses and results of the population scenario in Switzerland 2005–2050. (Bevölkerungswachstum und demografische Alterung: Ein Blick in die Zukunft. Hypothesen und Ergebnisse der Bevölkerungsszenarien für die Schweiz 2005–2050), Neuchâtel 2006.
Bird, Allan / Stevens, Michael J. (2003): Toward an emergent global culture and the effects of globalization on obsolescing national cultures. In: Journal of International Management, vol. 9 2003, issue 4, pp. 395–407.
Bleis, Thomas (1992): Personalmarketing. Darstellung und Bewertung eines kontroversen Konzepts, Munich 1992.
Blood, Milton (1969): Work Values and Job Satisfaction. In: Journal of applied psychology, vol. 53 1969, no. 6, pp. 456–459.
Boswell, Wendy R. / Roehling, Mark V. / LePine, Marcie A. / Moynihan, Lisa M. (2003): Individual job-choice decisions and the impact of job attributes and recruitment practices: A longitudinal field study. In: Human Resource Management, vol. 42 2003, issue 1, pp. 23–37.

Branham, Leigh (2000): Keeping the People Who Keep You in Business, New York 2000.
Branham, Leigh (2005): Planning to Become an Employer of Choice. In: Journal of Organizational Excellence, vol. 24 2005, issue 3, pp. 57–68.
Breaugh, James A. / Starke, Mary (2000): Research on employee recruitment: So many studies, so many remaining questions. In: Journal of Management, vol. 26 2000, issues 3, pp. 405–434.
Breaugh, James A. (2008): Employee recruitment: Current knowledge and important areas for future research. In: Human Resource Management Review, vol. 18 2008, pp. 103–118.
Breaugh, James A. / Macan, Therese H. / Grambow, Dana M. (2008): Employee recruitment: Current knowledge and directions for future research. In: International Review of Industrial and Organizational Psychology, vol. 23 2008, pp. 45–82.
Bretz, Robert D. Jr. / Judge, Timothy A. (1998): Realistic job previews: A test of the adverse self-selection hypothesis. In: Journal of Applied Psychology, vol. 83, issue 2, pp. 330–337.
Brewster, Chris (1993): Developing a "European" model of human resource management. In: The International Journal of Human Resource Management, vol. 4 1993, no. 4, pp. 763–784.
Brewster, Chris / Sparrow, Paul / Harris, Hilary (2005): Towards a new model of globalizing HRM. In: The International Journal of Human Resource Management, vol. 16 2005, issue 6, pp. 949–970.
Briedis, Kolja / Minks, Karl-Heinz (2007): Generation Praktikum: Mythos oder Massenphänomen?, ‹www.bayme.de/agv/downloads/11315@agv/HIS-Studie_generationpraktikum.pdf›, accessed 12th December 2009.
Bristow, Denny / Amyx, Douglas / Castleberry, Stephen B. / Cochran, James J. (2011): A Cross-Generational Comparison of Motivational Factors in a Sales Career Among Gen-X and Gen-Y College Students. In: Journal of Personal Selling & Sales Management, vol. 31 2011, issue 1, pp. 77–85.
Broadbridge, Adelina M. / Maxwell, Gillian A. / Ogden, Susan M. (2009): Selling retailing to Generation Y graduates: Recruitment challenges and opportunities. In: The International Review of Retail, Distribution and Consumer Research, vol. 19 2009, no. 4, pp. 405–420.
Brodbeck, Felix. C. (2006): Navigationshilfe für internationales Change Management: Erkenntnisse aus dem GLOBE Project. In: Organisationsentwicklung, vol. 25 2006, pp. 16–31.
Bruch, Heike / Kunze, Florian / Boehm, Stephan (2010): Generationen erfolgreich führen. Konzepte und Praxiserfahrungen zum Management des demographischen Wandels, Wiesbaden 2010.
Bryman, Alan / Bell, Emma (2003): Business research methods, New York 2003.
Burke, Ronald J. (2005): Human resources as a competitive advantage. In: Reinventing human resource management: Challenges and new directions, eds. Ronald J. Burke and Cary L. Cooper, New York 2005, pp. 17–34.
Burke, Ronald J. / Cooper, Cary L. (2005): The human resource revolution: Why putting people first matters. In: Reinventing human resource management: Challenges and new directions, eds. Ronald J. Burke and Cary L. Cooper, New York 2005, pp. 3–16.

Cappelli, Peter (2001): Making the Most of On-line Recruiting. In: Harvard Business Review, vol. 79 2001, no. 3, pp. 139–148.
Carless, Sally A. (2005): Person-job fit versus person-organization fit as predictors of organizational attraction and job acceptance intentions: A longitudinal study. In: Journal of Occupational and Organizational Psychology, vol. 78 2005, pp. 411–429.
Carless, Sally A. / Imber, Amantha (2007): Job and organizational characteristics: A construct evaluation of applicant perceptions. In: Educational and Psychological Management, vol. 67 2007, issue 2, pp. 328–341.
Cates, Karen / Rahimi, Kimia D. (2003): Algebra lessons for older workers. In: International Management: Cross-boundary Challenges, eds. Paul N. Gooderham and Odd Nordhaug, Oxford 2003, pp. 424–430.
Causey, Robert L. (1979): Theory and observation. In: Current research in philosophy of science, eds. Peter D. Asquith and Henry E. Kyburg, East Lansing 1979, pp. 187–206.
Cennamo, Lucy / Gardner, Dianne (2008): Generational differences in work values, outcomes and person-organization values fit. In: Journal of Managerial Psychology, vol. 23 2008, pp. 891–906.
Cheese, Peter (2007): The ABC of Generation Y. In: Best practice, vol. 61 2007, issue 5, p. 33.
Chambers, Elizabeth / Foulon, Mark / Handfield-Jones, Helen / Hankin, Steven / Michaels, Edward (1998): The war for talent. In: McKinsey Quarterly, vol. 7 1998, no. 3, pp. 44–57.
Chapman, Derek S. / Uggerslev, Sarah A. / Carroll, Sarah A. / Piasentin, Kelly A. / Jones, David A. (2005): Applicant attraction to organizations and job choice: A meta-analytic review of the correlates of recruiting outcomes. In: Journal of Applied Psychology, vol. 90 2005, issue 5, pp. 928–944.
Chen, Po-Ju / Choi, Youngsoo, (2008): Generational differences in work values: A study of hospitality management. In: International Journal of Contemporary Hospitality Management, vol. 20 2008, issue 6, pp. 595–615.
Chhokar, Jegdeep S. / Brodbeck, Felix C. / House, Robert J. (2007): Culture and Leadership Across the World. The GLOBE Book of In-Depth Studies of 25 Societies, New Jersey 2007.
Chiang, Flora (2005): A critical examination of Hofstede's thesis and its application to international reward management. In: International Journal of Human Resource Management, vol. 16 2005, issue 9, pp. 1545–1563.
Clare, Cindy (2009): Generational Differences: Turning Challenges into Opportunities. In: Journal of Property Management, vol. 18 2009, issue 5, pp. 41–43.
Clark, Terry / Knowles, Lynette L. (2003): Global myopia: Globalization theory in international business. In: Journal of International Management, vol. 9 2003, pp. 361–372.
Classen, Ina (1995): Personalmarketing. In: Personalmanagement in der Praxis. Unternehmerisches Handeln gestaltet die Zukunft, eds. Hans Böhm and Christoph Hauke, Cologne 1995, pp. 23–46.

Clayton, Glen (2012): Generation F "Facebook Generation" Future Workforce Research Whitepaper, London 2012.
Colbert, Barry (2004): The Complex Resource-Based View: Implications for Theory and Practice in Strategic Human Resource Management. In: Academy of Management Review, vol. 29 2004, no. 3, pp. 341–358.
Collins, Christopher. J. / Stevens, Cynthia Kay (2002): The Relationship Between Early Recruitment-related Activities and the Application Decisions of New Labor-market Entrants: a Brand Equity Approach to Recruitment. In: Journal of Applied Psychology, vol. 87 2002, no. 6, pp. 1121–1133.
Covri, Elizabetta / Bigi, Allessandro / Ng, Gabrielle (2007): The European Millennials versus the US Millennials: Similarities and differences. International Business Research Conference, Sydney 2007.
Cronbach, Lee J. (1951): Coefficient Alpha and the internal structure of tests. In: Psychometrika, vol. 16 1951, issue 3, pp. 297–334.
Davison, Kristl H. / Maraist, Catherine / Bing, Mark N. (2011): Friend or Foe? The Promise and Pitfalls of Using Social Networking Sites for HR Decisions. In: Journal of Business Psychology, vol. 26 2011, pp. 153–159.
Dawson, Jeremy (2011): Interpreting interaction effects. Excel worksheets ‹www.jeremy-dawson.co.uk/slopes.htm›, accessed 10th November 2011.
Dawson, Jeremy F. / Richter, Andreas W. (2006): Probing three-way interactions: The development and application of a slope difference test. Journal of Applied Psychology, vol. 91 2006, pp. 917–926.
Deal, Terrence E. / Kennedy, Allan A. (2000): Corporate cultures: The rites and rituals of corporate life, Cambridge 2000.
Deal, Jennifer J. / Altman, David G. / Rogelberg, Steven G. (2010): Millennials at work: What we know and what we need to know (if anything). In: Journal of Business and Psychology, vol. 25 2010, pp. 191–199.
DEBA (2007): Employer Branding Definition, ‹www.employerbranding.org/employer-branding.php›, accessed 8th September 2010.
DEGW (2008): Recruiting the next generation: Der Wettlauf um die besten Köpfe, ‹www.recruitingthenextgeneration.de/files/rng_executive _summary.pdf›, accessed 15th November 2010.
De Hauw, Sara / De Vos, Ans (2010): Millennials' career perspective and psychological contract expectations: Does the recession lead to lowered expectations? In: Journal of Business and Psychology, vol. 25 2010, pp. 293–302.
Delery, John (1998): Issues of fit in strategic human resource management: Implications for research. In: Human Resource Management Review, vol. 8 1998, no. 3, pp.289–309.
Deloitte (2010): Talent Edge 2020: Blueprints for the new normal. Global survey of Deloitte 2010.
Deloitte (2011): Talent Edge 2020: Building the recovery together – What talent expects and how leaders are responding. Global survey of Deloitte 2011.
De Mooij, Marieke K. (2003): Convergence and divergence in consumer behavior: Implications for global advertising. In: International Journal of Advertising, vol. 22 2003, pp. 183–202.
De Mooij, Marieke K. (2010): Global marketing and advertising: Understanding cultural paradoxes, 3rd ed., Thousand Oaks *et al.* 2010.

De Mooij, Marieke K. / Hofstede, Geert (2010): The Hofstede model. Applications to global branding and advertising strategy and research. In: International Journal of Advertising, vol. 29 2010, no. 1 pp. 85–110.
Derr, C. Brooklyn / Jones, Candace / Toomey, Edmond (1988): Managing High-Potential Employees: Current Practices in Thirty-Three U.S. Corporations. In: Human Resource Management, vol. 27 1998, no. 3, pp. 273–290.
De Saá-Pérez, Petra / Garcia-Falcón, Juan Manuel (2002): A resource-based view of human resource management and organizational capabilities development. In: International Journal of Human Resource Management, vol. 13 2002, no. 1, pp. 123–140.
Diekmann, Andreas (2007): Empirische Sozialforschung. Grundlagen, Methoden, Anwendungen, 18th ed., Reinbek bei Hamburg 2007.
Dietmann, Evelyne (1993): Personalmarketing. Ein Ansatz zielgruppenorientierter Personalpolitik, Wiesbaden 1993.
Dowling, Peter J. / Festing, Marion / Engle, Allen (2008): International human resource management: Managing people in a multinational context, 5th ed., Mason 2008.
Dries, Nicky / Pepermans, Roland (2008): "Real" high-potential careers: An empirical study into the perspectives of organizations and high potentials. In: Personnel Review, vol. 37 2008, issue 1, pp. 85–108.
Drucker, Peter (1974): Management. Tasks, responsibilities, practices, London 1974.
Dubin, Robert (1956): Industrial Workers' Worlds: a Study of the "Central Life Interests" of Industrial workers. In: Social Problems, vol. 3 1956, no. 3, pp. 131–142.
Duncan, Robert B. (1972): Characteristics of Organizational Environments and Perceived Environmental Uncertainty. In: Administrative Science Quarterly, vol. 17 1956, no. 3, pp. 313–327.
Edmunds, June / Turner, Bryan S. (2005): Global generations: Social change in the twentieth century. In: The British Journal of Sociology, vol. 56 2005, issue 4, pp. 559–577.
Eggers, Bernd / Ahlers, Friedel (1999): Schlüsselfaktoren eines erfolgreichen High-Potential-Personalmarketing. In: Innovatives Personalmarketing für High-Potentials, eds. Anke Thiele and Bernd Eggers, Göttingen 1999, pp. 39–45.
Egri, Carolyn P. / Ralston, David A. (2004): Generation cohorts and personal values: A comparison of China and the United States. In: Organization Science, vol. 15 2004, issue 2, pp. 210–220.
Eisner, Susan (2005): Managing Generation Y. In: SAM Advanced Management Journal, vol. 14 2005, Autumn 2005, pp. 4–15.
Esch, Franz-Rudolf (2003): Strategie und Technik der Markenführung, Munich 2003.
Ewing, Michael / Pitt, Leyland / de Bussy, Nigel / Berthon, Pierre (2002): Employment Branding in the Knowledge Economy. In: International Journal of Advertising, vol. 21 2002, no. 1, pp. 1–22.
Fang, Tony (2005): From "Onion" to "Ocean": Paradox and change in national cultures. In: International Studies of Management and Organization, vol. 35, issue 4 2005, pp. 71–90.
Fang, Tony (2010): Asian management research needs more self-confidence: Reflection on Hofstede (2007) and beyond. In: Asia Pacific Journal of Management, vol. 27 2010, pp. 155–170.

Fairchild, Amanda J. / MacKinnon, David P. (2009): A General Model for Testing Mediation and Moderation Effects. In: Prevention Science, vol. 10 2009, no. 2, pp. 87–99.
Farlex Financial Dictionary (2011): Labor intensity ‹financial-dictionary.thefreedictionary.com/Labor+intensity›, accessed 1st April 2012.
Farley, Catherine / Malkani, Deepak / Smith, David (2008): What Employers Need to Know about Recent University Graduates: Shaping Recruitment and Retention Strategies to Achieve High Performance. White Paper of Accenture, 2008.
Felser, Georg (2010): Personalmarketing, Göttingen 2010.
Field, Andy (2009): Discovering Statistics using SPSS, 3rd Ed., Los Angeles *et al.* 2009.
Franke, Nikolaus (2000): Personalmarketing zur Gewinnung von betriebswirtschaftlichem Führungsnachwuchs. Zur Positionierung von Unternehmen in studentischen Zielgruppen. In: Marketing Zeitschrift für Forschung und Praxis, vol. 22 2000, no. 1, pp. 75–92.
Franz, Julia (2009): Intergenerationelles lernen ermöglichen: Orientierungen zum Lernen der Generationen in der Erwachsenenbildung, Bielefeld 2009.
Fröhlich, Werner (1987): Strategisches Personalmarketing, Düsseldorf 1987.
Gadenne, Volker (2006): Empirische Forschung und normative Wissenschaftstheorie. In: Methoden der Sozialforschung, ed. Andreas Diekmann, Wiesbaden 2006, pp. 33–50.
Geertz, Clifford (1993): The interpretation of cultures, London 1993.
Gilly, Mary C. / Wolfinbarger, Mary (1998): Advertising's internal audience. In: Journal of Marketing, vol. 62 1998, no. 1, pp. 69–88.
Girschik, Stefan (2011): "Work-related differences between Russian and Swiss Gen Yers" Interview with the Group COO of REHAU, Bern, conducted on 7th April 2011.
Gonzales, Roberto (2008): Die Top-Arbeitgeber: Absolventen wissen, was sie wollen. In: Career step, no. 3, pp. 6–12.
Grochla, Erwin (1978): Einführung in die Organisationstheorie, Stuttgart 1978.
Grünig, Rudolf / Kühn, Richard (2005): Process-based Strategic Planning, 3rd ed., Berlin/Heidelberg 2005.
Grünig, Rudolf / Morschett, Dirk (2012): Developing International Strategies. Going and Being International for Medium-sized Companies, Berlin/Heidelberg 2012.
Gupta, Vipin / Hanges, Paul J. / Dorfman, Peter (2002): Cultural clusters: Methodology and findings. In: Journal of World Business, vol. 37 2002, pp. 11–15.
Guriev, Sergei / Tsivinsky, Oleg (2010): Ratio economica: Поколение Н. In: Ведомости, vol. 5 2010, no. 196, pp. 12–13.
Gursoy, Dogan / Maier, Thomas A. / Chi, Christina G. (2008): Generational differences: An examination of work values and generational gaps in the hospitality workforce. In: International Journal of Hospitality Management, vol. 27 2008, pp. 448–458.
Hauer, Gabriele / Schüller, Achim / Strasmann, Jochen (2002): Kompetentes Human Resources Management: Lösungen für Personalverantwortliche in einer veränderten Unternehmenswelt, Wiesbaden 2002.
Hall, Stuart / Jefferson, Tony (1993): Resistance through rituals: Youth subcultures in post-war Britain, 2nd ed., London/New York 1993.

Harris, Fiona / de Chernatony, Leslie (2001): Corporate branding and corporate brand performance. In: European Journal of Marketing, vol. 35 2001, no. 3/4, pp. 441–456.

Hart, Susannah / Murphy, John (1998): Brands: The New Wealth Creators, Basingstoke 1998.

Headhunter (2010): Online-survey of ‹hh.ru› and ‹www.career.ru› among university graduates in Moscow and St. Petersburg, Moscow 2010.

Herbison, Gerry / Bosemann, Glenn (2009): Here They Come – Generation Y. Are You Ready? In: Journal of Financial Service Professionals, vol. 63 2009, no. 5, pp. 33–34.

Herman, Roger E. / Gioia, Joyce L. (2000): How to become an employer of choice, Winchester 2000.

Hershatter, Andrea / Epstein, Molly (2010): Millennials and the world of work: An organization and management perspective. In: Journal of Business and Psychology, vol. 25 2010, pp. 211–223.

Hewitt Associates (2010): Employer Branding: Unternehmen investieren, aber nutzen Möglichkeiten unzureichend, ‹www.aon.com/germany/downloads/pressemitteilungen/pm20100707_employer-branding-unternehmen-investieren-aber-nutzen-moeglichkeiten-unzureichend.pdf›, accessed 26th December 2010.

Heyne, Ulrike (2011): Trendence Graduate Barometer 2011. European Business Edition, Berlin 2011.

Hieronimus, Fabian / Schaefer, Katharina / Schröder, Jürgen (2005): Using branding to attract talent. In: McKinsey Quarterly, vol. 14 2005, issue 3, pp. 12–14.

Hilb, Martin (2001): Glokales und integriertes m-HRM. In: Jahrbuch Personalentwicklung und Weiterbildung 2001, eds. Karlheinz Schwuchow and Joachim Gutmann, Neuwied/Kriftel 2001, pp. 9–11.

Hinkin, Timothy R. (1995): A review of scale development practices in the study of organizations. In: Journal of Management, vol. 21 1995, no. 5, pp. 967–988.

Hitt, Michael A. / Bierman, Leonard / Shimizu, Katsuhiko / Kochhar, Rahul (2001): Direct and Moderation Effects of Human Capital on Strategy and Performance in Professional Service Firms: A Resource-Based Perspective. In: Academy of Management Journal, vol. 44 2001, no. 1, pp. 13–28.

Hoecklin, Lisa A. (1995): Managing cultural differences: Strategies for competitive advantage, Edinburgh/Harlow/Essex 1995.

Hoepflinger, Francois (1999): Generationenfrage – Konzepte, theoretische Ansätze und Beobachtung zu Generationsbeziehungen in späteren Lebensphasen, Lausanne 1999.

Hofstede, Geert (1980): Motivation, Leadership and Organisation: Do American Theories Apply Abroad? In: Organisational Dynamics, vol. 9 1980, issue 1, pp. 42–62.

Hofstede, Geert (1983): National Cultures in four Dimensions. A Research-based Theory of Cultural Differences among Nations. In: Studies of Management and Organization, vol. 13 1983, no. 1–2, pp. 46–74.

Hofstede, Geert (1996): Riding the Waves of Commerce: A Test of Trompenaars' "Model" of National Culture Differences. In: International Journal of Intercultural Relations, vol. 20 1996, no. 2, pp. 189–198.

Hofstede, Geert (2001): Culture's consequences: Comparing values, behaviors, institutions, and organizations across nations, 2nd ed., Thousand Oaks 2001.
Hofstede, Geert (2006): Lokales Denken, globales Handeln. Interkulturelle Zusammenarbeit und globales Management, 3rd ed., Munich 2006.
Hofstede, Geert / Hofstede, Gert Jan / Minkov, Michael (2010): Cultures and Organizations: Software of the Mind. Intercultural Cooperation and Its Importance for Survival, 3rd ed., New York 2010.
Hole, David / Zhong, Le / Schwartz, Jeff (2010): Talking about whose generation? In: Deloitte Review, issue 6, pp. 84–97.
Holland, Peter / Sheehan, Cathy / De Cieri, Helen (2007): Attracting and retaining talent: Exploring human development trends in Australia. In: Human Resource Development International, vol. 10 2007, issue 3, pp. 247–262.
Homburg, Christian / Krohmer, Harley (2006): Marketingmanagement: Strategie – Instrumente – Umsetzung – Unternehmensführung, 2nd ed., Wiesbaden 2006.
Homburg, Christian / Kuester, Sabine / Krohmer, Harley (2009): Marketing Management: A Contemporary Perspective, Berkshire 2009.
House, Robert J. / Javidan, Mansour / Dorfman, Peter. (2001): Project GLOBE: An introduction. In: Applied Psychology: An International Review, vol. 50 2001, issue 4, pp. 489-505.
House, Robert J. / Javidan, Mansour / Hanges, Paul / Dorfman, Peter W. (2002): Understanding cultures and implicit leadership theories across the globe: an Introduction to project GLOBE. In: Journal of World Business, vol. 37 2002, no. 1, pp. 3–10.
House, Robert J. / Hanges, Paul J. / Javidan, Mansour / Dorfman, Peter W. / Gupta, Vipin (2004): Culture, Leadership, and Organizations. The GLOBE Study of 62 Societies, Thousand Oaks 2004.
House, Robert J. / Quigley, Narda R. / Sully de Luque, Mary (2010): Insights from Project GLOBE. Extending global advertising research through a contemporary framework. In: International Journal of Advertising, vol. 29 2010, no. 1, pp. 111–140.
Howe, Neil / Strauss, William (2000): Millennials rising: The next great generation, New York 2000.
hrm.ru (2011): Социальные сети в поиске и подборе персонала. Несколько срезов. ‹hrm.ru/socialnye-seti-v-poiske-i-podbore-personala-neskolko-srezov›, accessed 3rd March 2012.
Hubschmid, Elena (2011): Shaping Efficient Employer Branding. Generation Y's Employment Expectations: A cross-cultural Perspective on Human Resource Marketing. Working paper no. 96 at the Institute of Organisation and Personnel Management of the University of Bern, Bern 2011.
Hubschmid, Elena (2012): Shaping Efficient Employer Branding to Target Generation Y: A Cross-National Perspective on Recruitment Marketing. Results of the Study. Working paper no. 101 at the Institute of Organisation and Personnel Management of the University of Bern, Bern 2012.
Hubschmid, Elena / Thom, Norbert (2010): Управление персоналом в немецкоговорящих странах Европы и России. In: Труд за рубежом, vol. 12 2010, no. 1-2, pp. 115–129.

Hunt, Shelby D. (1984): Should marketing adopt relativism? In: 1984 AMA winter educators' conference. Scientific method in marketing, eds. Paul F. Anderson and Michael J. Ryan, Chicago 1984, pp. 30–34.

Hunt, Shelby D. (1990): Truth in marketing theory and research. In: Journal of Marketing, vol. 54 1990, no. 3, pp. 1–15.

Hunt, Susan / Landry, Rob (n/a): The Importance of Employer Branding. ‹www.sunlife.ca/static/canada/Customer%20Solutions/thefutureofwork/pdf/thefuture-of-work.pdf›, accessed 10th December 2011.

Huselid, Mark A. / Jackson, Susan E. / Schuler, Randall S. (1997): Technical and Strategic Human Resource Management Effectiveness as Determinants of Firm Performance. In: Academy of Management Journal, vol. 40 1997, no. 1, pp. 171–188.

Husted, Bryan W. (2003): Globalization and cultural change in international business research. In: Journal of International Management, vol. 9 2003, pp. 427–433.

Iadova, Maya A. (2007): The Behavioral Attitudes of Young People of the Post-Soviet Generation. In: Russian Social Science Review, vol. 48 2007, no. 5, pp. 25–46.

Ind, Nicholas (1998): An Integrated Approach to Corporate Branding, In: The Journal of Brand Management, vol. 5 1998, no. 5, pp. 323–329.

IOMA's Human Resource Department Management Report (2004): Why HR Branding Is a "Must Do" for Recruiting. In: Academy of Management Journal, vol. 3 2004, pp. 7–10.

Javidan, Mansour / House, Robert J. (2001): Cultural Acumen for the Global Manager: Lessons from Project GLOBE. In: Organizational Dynamics, vol. 29 2001, no. 4, pp. 289–305.

Javidan, Mansour / House, Robert J. (2002): Leadership and cultures around the world: findings from GLOBE. An introduction to the special issue. In: Journal of World Business, vol. 37 2002, no. 1, pp. 1–2.

Javidan, Mansour / Dorfman, Peter W. / Sully de Luque, Mary / House, Robert J. (2006): In the Eye of the Beholder: Cross Cultural Lessons in Leadership from Project GLOBE. In: Academy of Management Perspectives, vol. 20 2006, no. 1, pp. 67–90.

Javidan, Mansour / House, Robert J. / Dorfman, Peter W. / Hanges, Paul J. / Sully de Luque, Mary (2006a): Conceptualizing and measuring cultures and their consequences: a comparative review of GLOBE's and Hofstede's approaches. In: Journal of International Business Studies, vol. 37 2006, pp. 897–914.

Johns, Nick / Lee-Ross, Darren (1998): Research Methods in Service Industry Management, London 1998.

Johnson Controls (2010): Understanding the Generation Y in Germany: How would they like to work in 2010? ‹www.johnsoncontrols.com/publish/etc/ medialib/jci/be/global_workplace_innovation/oxygenz.Par.88160.File.dat/Oxygenz_report_Germany.pdf›, accessed 18th October 2010.

Jorgensen, Bradley (2003): Baby Boomers, Generation X and Generation Y? Policy implications for defence forces in modern era. In: Foresight, vol. 5 2003, issue 4, pp. 41–49.

Joshi, Aparna / Dencker, John C. / Franz, Gentz / Martocchio, Joseph J. (2010): Unpacking Generational Identities in Organizations. In: Academy of Management Review, vol. 35 2010, no. 3, pp. 392–414.
Josiam, Bharath M. / Reynolds, Johnny S. / Thozhur, Sumeetra / Crustinger, Christy / Baum, Tom / Devine, Frances G. (2009): An Empirical Study of the Work Attitudes of Generation Y College Students in the USA: The Case of Hospitality and Merchandising Undergraduate Majors. In: Journal of Services Research, vol. 9 2009, no. 1, pp. 5–30.
Jurgensen, C. E. (1978): Job preferences (what makes a job good or bad?). In: Journal of Applied Psychology, vol. 6 1978, no. 3, pp. 267–276.
Kalinina, Yulia (2010): Поколение Y. ‹www.business-magazine.ru/mech_new/staff/pub333609/›, accessed 22nd December 2011.
Kausel, Edgar E. / Slaughter, Jerel E. (2010): Narrow personality traits and organizational attraction: Evidence for the complementary hypothesis. In: Organizational Behavior and Human Decision Processes, vol. 114 2011, pp. 3–14.
Kelley, Braden (2012): Harnessing the Global Talent Pool to Accelerate Innovation. White Paper of InnoCentive Incorporated, Waltham 2012.
Kienbaum (2010): Was motiviert Generation Y im Arbeitsleben? Absolventenstudie 2007/2008. ‹www.personalwirtschaft.de/media/Personalwirtschaft_neu_161209/Startseite/Downloads-zum-Heft/0910/Kienbaum_GenerationY_2009_2010.pdf›, accessed 20th January 2012.
Kiessling, Timothy / Harvey, Michael (2005): Strategic global human resource management research in the twenty-first century: an endorsement of the mixed-method research methodology. In: International Journal of Human Resource Management, vol. 16 2005, no. 1, pp. 22–45.
Kitces, Michael E. (2005): The Millenials Are Coming. Are We Ready? In: Journal of Financial Planning, vol. 27 2005, no. 6, p. 16.
Knox, Simon / Freeman, Cheryl (2006): Measuring and Managing Employer Brand Image in the Service Industry. In: Journal of Marketing Management, vol. 22 2006, pp. 695–716.
Koc, Ed (2008): Myth of the Millennials: Is there really a Millennial generation? ‹ftp://ftp.cba.uri.edu/classes/beauvais/HPR341/Myth_Millennials_March_2008.pdf›, accessed 9th March 2012.
Kombacheva, Irina (2011): "What Russian Gen Yers are looking for in an employer?" Interview with the Director of the Employer Branding department of the Headhunter Group of Companies, Moscow, conducted on 11th April 2011.
Kotler, Philip (2000): Marketing Management. The Millennium Edition, New Jersey 2000.
Kopf, Elias (2008): Das Bewerbungs-ABC der Generation X/Y/Z. In: Careerstep, vol. n/a 2008, no. 3, pp. 14–19.
Koppelmann, Udo (2001): Produktmarketing: Entscheidungsgrundlagen für Produktmanager, 6th ed., Berlin 2001.
Kowske, Brenda J. / Rasch, Rena / Wiley, Jack (2010): Millennials' (lack of) attitude problem: An empirical examination of generational effects on work attitudes. In: Journal of Business and Psychology, vol. 25 2010, pp. 265–279.

Kroeber, Alfred L. / Kluckhohn, Clyde (1952): Culture: A critical review of concepts and definitions, New York 1952.

Kroeber-Riel, Werner / Weinberg, Peter (2003): Konsumentenverhalten, 8th ed., Munich 2003.

Kromrey, Helmut (2002): Empirische Sozialforschung. Modelle und Methoden der standardisierten Datenerhebung und Datenauswertung, 10th ed., Opladen 2002.

Kubicek, Herbert / Thom, Norbert (1976): Umsystem betriebliches (Corporate Environment). In: Handwörterbuch der Betriebswirtschaft, 4th ed., eds. Erwin Grochla and Waldemar Wittmann, Stuttgart 1976, column 3977–4017.

Kuhn-Spogat, Iris (2011): Globalization, Power and Fast-Moving Elites. Global Leaders of Tomorrow – Swiss Young People – A Comparison. In: Global Perspectives Barometer 2011. Bulletin – The Credit Suisse Magazine, vol. 117 2011, issue 3, pp. n/a.

Kunze, Florian / Boehm, Stephan A. / Bruch, Heike (2010): Generational leadership: How to manage five different generations in the workforce. In: From Grey to Silver: Managing the Demographic Change Successfully, eds. Sven Kunisch, Stephan A. Boehm and Michael Boppel, Berlin/Heidelberg 2010, pp. 87–100.

Kuper, Adam (1999): Culture – the anthropologists' account, London 1999.

Kupperschmidt, Betty R. (2000): Multigeneration employees: Strategies for effective management. In: Health Care Manager, vol. 19 2000, issue 1, pp. 65–76.

Kutschker, Michael / Schmid, Stefan (2006): Internationales Management, 5th ed., Munich 2006.

Lattmann, Charles (1998): Wissenschaftstheoretische Grundlagen der Personallehre, Bern *et al.* 2005.

Leung, Kwok / Bhagat, Rabi S. / Buchan, Nancy R. / Erez, Miriam / Gibson, Christina B. (2005): Culture and international business: Recent advances and their implications for future research. In: Journal of International Business Studies, vol. 36 2005, pp. 357–378.

Leisink, Peter / Steijn, Bram (2008): Recruitment, attraction and selection. In: Motivation in public management: The call of public service, eds. James L. Perry and Annie Hondeghem, New York 2008, pp. 118–135.

Leplin, Jarrett (1984): Introduction. In: Scientific realism, ed. Jarrett Leplin, Berkeley *et al.* 1984, pp. 1–7.

Lerner, Richard M. (2002): Concepts and theories of human development, 3rd ed., Mahwah 2002.

Levenson, Alec R. (2010): Millennials and the world of work: An economist's perspective. In: Journal of Business and Psychology, vol. 25 2010, pp. 257–264.

Lewis, Richard D. (2010): When cultures collide: leading across cultures, 3rd ed., Boston/ London 2010.

Lieber, Bernd (1995): Personalimage: explorative Studien zum Image und zur Attraktivität von Unternehmen als Arbeitgeber, Munich 1995.

Lievens, Filip / Highhouse, Scott (2003): The relation of instrumental and symbolic attributes to a company's attractiveness as an employer. In: Personnel Psychology, vol. 56 2003, pp. 75–102.

Lindner, Rainer (2009): Raum ohne Volk? In: Frankfurter Allgemeine Zeitung, vol. 60 2009, no. 43, p. 8
Lindner-Lohmann, Doris / Lohmann, Florian / Schirmer, Uwe (2008): Personalmanagement, Heidelberg 2008.
Lindquist, Tim M. (2008): Recruiting the millennium generation: The new CPA. In: The CPA Journal, 2008, pp. 56–59.
Lodahl, Thomas / Kejner, Mathilde (1965): The Definition and Measurement of Job Involvement. In: Journal of Applied Psychology, vol. 49 1965, no. 2, pp. 24–33.
Love, Linda F. / Singh, Parbudyal (2011): Workplace Branding: Leveraging Human Resources Management Practices for Competitive Advantage Through "Best Employer" Surveys. In: Journal of Business Psychology, vol. 26 2011, issue 5, pp. 175–181.
Lyons, Sean / Duxbury, Linda / Higgins, Chris (2005): An empirical assessment of generational differences in work-related values. In: Human Resources management, vol. 26 2005, issue 9, pp. 62–71.
Ma, Rong / Allen, David G. (2009): Recruiting across cultures: A value-based model of recruitment. In: Human Resource Management Review, vol. 19 2009, pp. 334–346.
Macky, Keith / Gardner, Dianne / Forsyth, Stewart (2008): Generational differences at work: Introduction and overview. In: Journal of Managerial Psychology, vol. 23 2008, issue 8, pp. 857–861.
Macleod, Alison (2008): Generation Y: Unlocking the Talent of Young Managers. The Chartered Management Institute's Report, London 2008.
Mahroum, Sami (2000): Highly skilled globetrotters: Mapping the international migration of human capital. In: R&D Management, vol. 30 2000, issue 1, pp. 23–31.
Mannheim, Karl (1963): The Problem of Generations. In: Psychoanalytic Review, vol. 57 1963, no. 3, pp. 378–404.
Mankoff, Jeffrey (2010): Generational change and the future if U.S.-Russian relations. In: Journal of International Affairs, vol. 63 2010, issue 2, pp. 1–17.
Marshall, Jeffrey (2004): Managing Different Generations at Work. In: Financial Executive Magazine, vol. 5 2004, July/August, p. 18.
Martin, Graeme / Beaumont, Phillip (2003): What's In a Name? Building a Relationship Between People Management and Branding, Wimbledon 2003.
Martin, Carolyn A. (2005): From high maintenance to high productivity. In: Industrial and Commercial Training, vol. 37 2005, issue 1, pp. 39–44.
Martin, Graeme / Beaumont, Phillip / Doig, Rosalind / Pate, Judy (2005): Branding: A new performance discourse for HR? In: European Management Journal, vol. 23 2005, no. 1, pp. 76–88.
Mathis, Robert L. / Jackson, John H. (2007): Human resource management, 12th ed., Mason 2007.
Matsumoto, David / Seung, Hee Yoo (2006): Toward a New Generation of Cross-Cultural Research. In: Perspectives on Psychological Science, vol. 1 2006, no. 3, pp. 234–250.
McGaughey, Sara L. / De Cieri, Helenn (1999): Reassessment of convergence and divergence dynamics: implications for international HRM. In: The International Journal of Human Resource Management, vol. 10 1999, no. 2, pp. 235–250.

McSweeney, Brendan (2002): Hofstede's model of national cultural differences and their consequences: A triumph of faith – a failure of analysis. In: Human Relations, vol. 55 2002, pp. 89–118.
McWilliams, Abagail / Van Fleet, David / Wright, Patrick (2001): Strategic management of human resources for global competitive advantage. In: Journal of Business Strategies, vol. 18 2001, no. 1, pp. 1–23.
Mead, Richard (2005): International management: Cross-cultural dimensions, 3rd ed., Malden/Oxford/Victoria 2005.
Mendenhall, Mark E. / Punnett, Betty J. / Ricks, David A. (1995): Global management, Cambridge 1995.
Mercer (2011): Inside Employees' Minds. Navigating the new rules of engagement. Mercer's What's Working Survey, New York 2011.
Mercer Bing, Catherine / Vastano, Jerry (2010): Webinar "Don't Worry – Be Happy!" An Explanation and Review of Hofstede's 6th Dimension. ‹https://www1.gotomeeting.com/join/328689153/106740575›, participated on 7th October 2010.
Michaels, Edward / Hanfield-Jones, Helen / Axelrod, Beth (2001): The War for Talent, Boston 2001.
Moroko, Lara / Uncles, Mark D. (2008): Characteristics of successful employer brands. In: Journal of Brand Management, vol. 16 2008, issue 3, pp. 160–175.
Moroko, Lara / Uncles, Mark D. (2009): Employer branding and market segmentation. In: Journal of Brand Management, vol. 17 2009, issue 9, pp. 181–196.
Moser, Klaus (2005): Recruitment sources and post-hire outcomes: The mediating role of unmet expectations. In: International Journal of Selection and Assessment, vol. 13 2005, issue 3, pp. 188–197.
Mosley, Richard W. (2007): Customer experience, organizational culture and the employer brand. In: Brand Management, vol. 15 2007, no. 2, pp. 123–134.
Motley, Apryl (2005): Bringing generation why into fold. In: Associations Now, November 2005, pp. 41–45.
Müller, Stefanie (2007): Junge Individualisten. In: Personal, vol. 59 2007, no. 10, pp. 38–39.
Myers, Karen K. / Sadaghiani, Kamyab (2010): Millennials in the workplace: A communication perspective on millennials' organizational relationships and performance. In: Journal of Business and Psychology, vol. 25 2010, pp. 225–238.
Narver, John / Slater, Stanley (1990): The effect of a market orientation on business profitability. In: Journal of Marketing, vol. 54 1990, no. 10, pp. 20–35.
Naumov, Alexander I. / Puffer, Sheila M. (2000): Measuring Russian Culture using Hofstede's Dimensions. In: Applied Psychology: An International Review, vol. 49 2000, issue 4, pp. 709–718.
Nederveen Pieterse, Jan (2009): Globalization & culture, 2nd ed., Plymouth 2009.
Ng, Eddy S. W. / Schweitzer, Linda / Lyons, Sean T. (2010): New generation, great expectations: A field study of the millennial generation. In: Journal of Business and Psychology, vol. 25 2010, pp. 281–292.
Nonaka, Ikujiro / Takeuchi, Hirotaka (1995): The Knowledge-Creating Company, New York 1995.

OECD (2012): OECD population pyramids in 2000 and 2050, ‹www.oecd.org/LongAbstract/0,3425,en_2649_33933_38123086_1_1_1_1,00.html› accesse 20th November 2011.
Oertel, Jutta (2007): Generationenmanagement im Unternehmen, Wiesbaden 2007.
Orlitzky, Marc (2007): Recruitment strategy. In: The Oxford Handbook of Human Resource Management, eds. Peter Boxall *et al.*, Oxford 2007, pp. 273–299.
Orr, Linda M. / Hauser, William J. (2008): A Re-Inquiry of Hofstede's Cultural Dimensions: A Call for 21st Century Cross-Cultural Research. In: The Marketing Management Journal, vol. 18 2008, issue 2, pp. 1–19.
Osland, Joyce S. / Bird, Allan (2000): Beyond sophisticated stereotyping: Cultural sensemaking in context. In: Academy of Management Executive, vol. 14 2000, issue 1, pp. 65–79.
Pallant, Julie (2007): SPSS Survival Manual. A Step by Step Guide to Data Analysis using SPSS for Windows, 3rd ed., Berkshire 2007.
Parment, Anders (2009): Die Generation Y – Mitarbeiter der Zukunft. Herausforderung und Erfolgsfaktor für das Personalmanagement, Wiesbaden 2009.
Parry, Emma / Urwin, Peter (2011): Generational differences in work values: A review of theory and evidence. In: International Journal of Management Reviews, vol. 13 2011, issue 1, pp. 79–96.
Penrose, Edith (1958): The Theory of the Growth of the Firm, New York 1958.
Petkovic, Mladen (2008): Employer Branding. Ein markenpolitischer Ansatz zur Schaffung von Präferenzen bei der Arbeitgeberwahl, 2nd ed., Munich/Mering 2008.
Petro, Nicolai N. (2008): The Putin Generation: How will its rise affect US-Russian Relations? In: Harvard International Review, Summer 2008, pp. 22–26.
Pieper, Rüdiger (1990): Human Resource Management: An International Comparison, Berlin 1990.
Pilbeam, Stephen / Corbridge, Marjorie (2006): People resourcing: Contemporary HRM in practice, 3rd ed., Essex 2006.
Popper, Karl R. (1974): Objective knowledge. An evolutionary approach, Oxford 1974.
Popper, Karl R. (1976): Logik der Forschung, 6th ed., Tübingen 1976.
Prašnikar, Janez / Pahor, Marko / Vidmar Svetlik, Jasna (2008): Are National Cultures Still Important in International Business? Russia, Serbia and Slovenia in Comparison. In: Management Journal of Contemporary Management Issues, vol. 13 2008, no. 2, pp. 1–26.
PricewaterhouseCoopers (2008): Managing tomorrow's people, ‹www.pwc.com/gx/en/managing-tomorrows-people/future-of-work/pdf/mtp-millennials-at-work.pdf›, accessed 10th September 2010.
PricewaterhouseCoopers (2011): Millennials at work: Re-shaping the workplace. PWC Publication 2011.
Raffée, Hans / Abel, Bodo (1979): Aufgaben und aktuelle Tendenzen der Wissenschaftstheorie in den Wirtschaftswissenschaften, eds. Hans Raffée and Bodo Abel, Munich 1979, pp. 1–10.
Ramachandran, Deepak / Artiuch, Paul (2007): Harnessing the Global N-Gen Talent Pool. Paper of the New Paradigm Learning Corporation, Toronto 2007.

Real, Kevin / Mitnick, Andrea D. / Maloney, William F. (2010): More similar than different: Millennials in the U.S. building trades. In: Journal of Business and Psychology, vol. 25 2010, pp. 303–313.
Ricardo, David (1817): Principles of Political Economy and Taxation, London 1817.
Robbins, Stephen P. / Odendaal, Aletta / Roodt, Gert (1998): Organisational Behaviour: Global and South African Perspective. 8th ed., New Jersey 1998.
Rofe, Matthew W. (2003): "I want to be global": Theorising the gentrifying class as an emergent elite global community. In: Urban Studies, vol. 40 2003, issue 12, pp. 2511–2526.
Roper, Stuart / Davies, Gary (2007): The Corporate Brand: Dealing with Multiple Stakeholders. In: Journal of Marketing Management, vol. 23 2000, no. 1–2, pp. 75–90.
Rothlauf, Jürgen (2009): Interkulturelles Management: Mit Beispielen aus Vietnam, China, Japan, Russland und den Golfstaaten, 3rd ed., Munich 2009.
Rottländer, Inga (2012): Ist der Ruf erst ruiniert. In: Personalwirtschaft, vol. 39 2012, no. 1, pp. 52–53
Ruane, Janet M. (2004): Essentials of research methods: A guide to social research, Malden/Oxford/Victoria 2004.
Ruettimann, Laurie (2011): The New Human Resources Department: Embracing Social Media and Being Smart About It. Achievers Survey, San Francisco 2011.
Rugimbana, Robert (2007): Generation Y: How Cultural Values Can Be Used to Predict Their Choice of Electronic Financial Services. In: Journal of Financial Services Marketing, vol. 11 2007, no. 4, pp. 301–313.
Rump, Jutta / Eilers, Silke (2006): Managing employability. In: Employability Management: Grundlagen, Konzepte, Perspektiven, eds. Jutta Rump, Thomas Sattelberger and Heinz Fischer, Wiesbaden 2006, pp. 13–76.
Rynes, Sara L. / Bretz, Robert D. Jr. / Gehart, Barry A. (1991): The importance of recruitment in job choice: A different way of looking. In: Personnel Psychology, vol. 44 1991, issue 3, pp. 487–521.
Sekaran, Uma (2003): Research methods for Business: A Skill Building Approach, 4th ed., New York 2003.
Schamberger, Ingo (2006): Differenziertes Hochschulmarketing für High Potentials. In: Schriftenreihe des Instituts für Unternehmungsplanung Band 43, eds. Harald Hungenberg and Günther Seliger, Norderstedt 2006.
Schanz, Günther (1988): Methodologie für Betriebswirte, 2nd ed., Stuttgart 1988.
Schein, Edgar H. (2004): Organizational culture and leadership, 3rd ed., San Francisco 2004.
Scherer, Andreas Georg (2006): Kritik der Organisation oder Organisation der Kritik? Wissenschaftstheoretische Bemerkungen zum kritischen Umgang mit Organisationstheorien. In: Organisationstheorien, eds. Alfred Kieser and Mark Ebers, 6th ed., Stuttgart *et al.* 2006, pp. 19–61.
Schewe, Charles D. / Meredith, Geoffrey (2004): Segmenting global markets by generational cohorts: Determining motivations by age. In: Journal of Consumer Behaviour, vol. 4 2004, issue 1, pp. 51–63.
Schiendorfer, Andreas (2011): Young People Are Showing Greater Environmental Awareness. In: Youth 2011. Youth Barometer: Hopes & Worries. Bulletin – The Credit Suisse Magazine, vol. 117 2011, issue 3, p. 8–13.

Schnorbach, Peter (2009): Gen Y for Hire. In: Material Handling Management, vol. 64 2009, no. 3, p. 34.
Scholz, Christian (1995): Personalmarketing. In: Handwörterbuch des Marketing, ed. Bruno Tietz, Stuttgart 1995, column 2004–2019.
Scholz, Christian (2000): Personalmanagement. Informationsorientierte und verhaltenstheoretische Grundlagen, 5th ed., Munich 2000.
Schreurs, Bert / Druart, Celina / Proost, Karin / De Witte, Karel (2009): Symbolic Attributes and Organizational Attractiveness: The moderating effects of applicant personality. In: International Journal of Selection and Assessment, vol. 17 2009, no. 1 pp. 35–46.
Schreyögg, Georg / Steinmann, Horst (1980): Wissenschaftstheorie. In: Handwörterbuch der Organisation, ed. Erwin Grochla, 2nd ed., Stuttgart 1980, column 2394–2404.
Schmidt, Simone (2007): Hochschulmarketing. Grundlagen, Konzepte, Perspektiven, Saarbrücken 2007.
Schmidtke, Corinna / Backes-Gellner, Uschi (2002): Personalmarketing: Stand der Entwicklung und Perspektiven. In: Wirtschaftswissenschaftliches Studium, vol. 31 2002, issue 6, pp. 321–327.
Schumpeter, Joseph (1934): The Theory of Economic Development, Cambridge 1934.
Schwab, Donald P. (1980): Construct validity in organizational behavior, in L. L. Cummings (ed.), Research in Organizational Behavior, Greenwich 1980, pp. 3–43.
Shaw, Sue / Fairhurst, David (2008): Engaging a new generation of graduates. In: Education + Training, vol. 50 2008, no. 5, pp. 366–378.
Sheppard, Anthony G. (1996): The sequence of factor analysis and cluster analysis: Differences in segmentation and dimensionality through the use of raw and factor scores. In: Tourism Analysis, vol. 1 1996, no. 1 pp. 49–57.
Sherry, Ann (2000): Put some branding iron into your image. In: Business Review Weekly, vol. 22 2000, no. 28, p. 66.
Shih, Win / Allen, Martha (2006): Working with Generation-D: Adopting and adapting to cultural learning and change. In: Library Management, vol. 28 2006, issue 1/2, pp. 89–100.
Simon, Hermann (1993): Industrielle Dienstleitung, Stuttgart 1993.
Simon, Hermann (1984): Die Attraktivität von Großunternehmen beim kaufmännischen Führungsnachwuchs. In: Zeitschrift für Betriebswirtschaft, vol. 54 1984, no. 4, pp. 324–345.
Simon, Hermann (1984a): Karriere ist wichtiger als Sicherheit. In: Manager Magazin, no. 8, 1984, pp. 82–88.
Simon, Hermann / Wiltinger, Kai / Sebastian, Karl-Heinz / Tacke, Georg (1995): Effektives Personalmarketing. Strategien – Instrumente – Fallstudien, Wiesbaden 1995.
Slaughter, Jerel E. / Greguras, Gary J. (2009): Initial Attraction to Organizations: The influence of trait inference. In: International Journal of Selection and Assessment, vol. 17 2009, issue 1, pp. 1–18.
Smith, Elroy / Krüger, Janine (2005): Perceptions of graduates regarding workplace expectations: An exploratory study. In: South African Journal of Business Management, vol. 36 2005, issue 1, pp. 23–31.

Smola, Karen Wey / Sutton, Charlette D. (2002): Generational differences: Revisiting generational work values for the new millennium. In: Journal of Organizational Behavior, vol. 23 2002, pp. 363–382.
Sokolov, Andrei (2006): Intellectual and moral difference among today's college students. In: Russian Education and Society, vol. 48 2006, issue 9, pp. 43–59.
Sokolova, Natalia (2010): Поколение игрек. In: Профиль, September 2010, pp. 50–53.
Soutar, Geoffrey / Clarke, Alexander (1983): Examining business students' career preferences: a perceptual space approach. In: Journal of Vocational Behavior, vol. 23 1983, no. 1, pp. 11–21.
Staffelbach, Bruno (1995): Strategisches Personalmarketing (Überblick). In: Strategisches Personalmanagement. Konzepte und Realisationen, eds. Christian Scholz and Mary am Djarrahzadeh, Stuttgart 1995, pp. 143–158.
StepStone (2011): StepStone Employer Branding Report 2011, Dusseldorf 2011.
Stevens-Huffman, Leslie (2006): Commitment, consistency are key to college recruiting. In: Workforce Management, vol. 85 2008, issue 6, pp. 42–43.
Strack, Rainer / Caye, Jean-Michel / Teichmann, Caroline / Haen, Pieter / Frick, Gerold / Bird, Stephanie (2011): Creating People Advantage 2011. Time to Act: HR Certainties in Uncertain Times. The Study of the Boston Consulting Group and the European Association for People Management, Boston 2011.
Stuart, Helen (2001): The role of employees in successful corporate branding. In: Thexis, vol. n/a 2001, no. 4, pp. 48–50.
Suchanek, Andreas (1999): Kritischer Rationalismus und die Methode der Sozialwissenschaften. In: Karl Poppers kritischer Rationalismus, eds. Ingo Pies and Martin Leschke, Tübingen 1999, pp. 85–104.
Sullivan, John (2012): An Open Letter to Mark Zuckerberg and Larry Page – Avoid the "Great to Good" Downward Spiral, ‹www.ere.net/2012/04/23/an-open-letter-to-mark-zuckerberg-and-larry-page-avoid-the-%E2%80%9Cgreat-to-good%E2%80%9D-downward-spiral-part-1-of-2/›, accessed 30th April 2012.
Sutherland, Margie M. / Torricelli, D. G. / Karg, Rail F. (2002): Employer-of-choice branding for knowledge workers. In: South African Journal of Business Management, vol. 33 2002, issue 4, pp. 13–20.
Tabachnik, Barbara G. / Fidell, Linda S. (1996): Using multivariate statistics, 3rd ed., New York 1996.
Tapscott, Don (2009): Grown Up Digital: How the Net Generation is Changing Your World, New York 2009.
Terjesen, Siri / Vinnicombe, Susan / Freeman, Cheryl (2007): Attracting Generation Y graduates. Organizational attributes, likelihood to apply and sex differences. In: Career Development International, vol. 12 2007, no. 6, pp. 504–522.
Thom, Norbert (1987): Personalentwicklung als Instrument der Unternehmungsführung. Konzeptionelle Grundlagen und empirische Studien, Stuttgart 1987.
Thom, Norbert (2001): Personalmanagement – Überblick und Entwicklungstendenzen. In: Excellence durch Personal- und Organisationskompetenz, eds. Norbert Thom and Robert J. Zaugg, Bern/Stuttgart/Wien 2001, pp. 117–131.
Thom, Norbert (2001a): Human Resource Management – Development Tendencies and Future Issues. In: Management Journal of Contemporary Management Issues, vol. 6 2008, no. 1-2, pp. 155–174.

Thom, Norbert / Luethi, David (2006): New Elites in South Africa and the Role of HR Management. In: Equity Skills News & Views, vol. 5 2006, no. 1, p. n/a.
Thom, Norbert / Moser, Regine (2006): Retention Management for High Potentials. In: Economy, Entrepreneurship, Science and Society in the XXI century, eds. Teresa del Val Núñez, Yolanda Ma Sánchez Jiménez and Cristina García Grewe, Universidad de Alcalá 2006, pp. 597–612.
Thom, Norbert / Friedli, Vera (2008): Hochschulabsolventen gewinnen, fördern und erhalten, 4th ed., Bern 2008.
Thom, Norbert (2009): Talente gewinnen, fördern und erhalten. In: Career Starter, vol. 13 2009, ed. Martine Willame, pp. 187–189.
Thom, Norbert (2010): Personalmanagement. Course manual of the lecture Personalmanagement at the Institute of Organisation and Personnel Management at the University of Bern, 7th ed., Bern 2010.
Thom, Norbert / Wenger, Andreas (2010): Die optimale Organisationsform. Grundlagen und Handlungsanleitung, Wiesbaden 2010.
Thom, Norbert / Hubschmid, Elena (2011): Le concept de marque employeur : la clé d'un recrutement efficace. In: Career Starter, ed. Martine Willame, vol. 15 2011, pp. 171–173.
Thom, Norbert / Hubschmid, Elena (2011a): Potenzielle Mitarbeiter weltweit rekrutieren. In: io management, vol. 80 2011, no. 4, pp. 18–21.
Tomlinson, Michael (2007): Graduate employability and student attitudes and orientations to the labour market. In: Journal of education and work, vol. 20 2007, no. 4, pp. 285–304.
Tremmel, Joerg (2008): Was ist eine Generation? In: Soziokulturelle Konstruktion des Alters: Transdisziplinaere Perspektiven, eds. Dieter Ferring *et al.*, Wuerzburg 2008, pp. 149–168.
Trompenaars, Fons / Hampden-Turner, Charles (2010): Riding the waves of culture. Understanding cultural diversity in business, 2nd ed., London 2010.
Trost, Armin (2009): Employer Branding. In: Employer Branding. Arbeitgeber positionieren und präsentieren, ed. Armin Trost, Cologne 2009, pp. 13–77.
Tulgan, Bruce / Martin, Carolyn A. (2001): Managing Generation Y. Global Citizens Born in the Late Seventies and Early Eighties, Amherst 2001.
Tulgan, Bruce (2009): Not Everyone Gets a Trophy: How to Manage Generation Y, San Francisco 2009.
Twenge, Jean M. / Campbell, Stacy M. (2008): Generational differences in psychological traits and their impact on the workplace. In: Journal of Managerial Psychology, vol. 23 2008, issue 8, pp. 862–877.
Twenge, Jean M. (2010): A review of the empirical evidence on generational differences in work attitudes. In: Journal of Business and Psychology, vol. 25 2010, pp. 201–210.
Twenge, Jean M. / Campbell, Stacy M. / Hoffman, Brian J. / Lance, Charles E. (2010): Generational differences in work values: Leisure and extrinsic values increasing, social and intrinsic values decreasing. In: Journal of Management, vol. 36 2010, no. 5, pp. 1117–1142.
Tylor, Edward B. (1871): Primitive culture, London 1871.

Ullman, Jeffrey D. (1996): Employee referrals: Prime tool for recruiting workers. In: Personnel Psychology, vol. 43 1996, pp. 30–35.
Ulrich, David (1997): Human resource champions: The next agenda for adding value and delivering results, Harvard 1997.
Ulrich, David (2002): Assessing Human Resource Effectiveness: Stakeholder, Utility, and Relationship Approaches. In: Human Resource Planning, vol. 12 2002, no. 4, pp. 301–315.
Universum (2011): Results of 2010 and 2011 student surveys on Russian and Swiss graduates in comparison provided by Universum employees for scientific use only (confidential).
Universum (2011a): EB Insights 2011. Spring Edition, Stockholm 2011.
Van der Sluis, Lidewey / Van de Bunt-Kokhuis, Sylvia (2009): Introduction. In: Competing for Talent, eds. Lidewey van der Sluis and Sylvia Bunt-Kokhuis, Assen 2009, pp. 1–7.
Verhoeven, Helen / Chansarkar, Bal / Williams, Sue (2009): Convergence, Divergence or "A Middle Way"? The influence of Culture on Internet Recruitment. In: International Review of Business Research Papers, vol. 5 2009, no. 1, pp. 87–96.
Viel, Oliver (2007): Was Hochschulabsolventen in Europa suchen – ein Vergleich. In: HR Today, vol. 6 2007, no. 11, pp. 5–7.
Wannacott, Thomas M. / Wannacott, Ronald J. (1990): Introductory Statistics, 5th ed., Ontario 1990.
Wang, Edgar (2010): Generation Y: Die Arbeit zählt, ‹archiv.personalwirtschaft.de/wkd_pw/cms/website.php?id=/de/index/jahrgang2010/personalwirtschaft092010.htm›, accessed 10th November 2010.
Wang, Heli C. / He, Jinyu / Mahoney, Joseph T. (2009): Firm-specific knowledge resources and competitive advantage: the roles of economic- and relationship-based employee governance mechanisms. In: Strategic Management Journal, vol. 30 2009, pp. 1265–1285.
Wanous, John P. (1992): Organizational entry: Recruitment, selection and socialization of newcomers, 2nd ed., Reading 1992.
Werner, Jon M. / DeSimone, Randy L. (2009): Human resource development, 5th ed., Mason 2009.
Wernerfelt, Birger (1984): A Resource Based View of the Firm. In: Strategic Management Journal, vol. 5 1984, no. 2, pp. 171–180.
Wilson, Alan (2001): Understanding Organisational Culture and the Implications for Corporate Marketing. In: European Journal of Marketing, vol. 35 2001, no. 3–4, pp. 353–367.
Wilton, Petra (2008): Unlocking the Talent of Generation Y. In: Engineering and Technology, vol. 3 2008, issue August–September, pp. 80–83.
Wiswede, Günter (1998): Soziologie. Grundlagen und Perspektiven für den wirtschafts- und sozialwissenschaftlichen Bereich, 3rd ed., Landsberg am Lech 1998.
Wollack, Stephen / Goodale, James G. / Wijting, Jan P. / Smith, Patricia Cain (1971): Development of the Survey of Work Values. In: Journal of Applied Psychology, vol. 55 1971, no. 2, pp. 331–338.

Wong, Melissa / Gardiner, Elliroma / Lang, Whitney / Coulon, Leah (2008): Generational differences in personality and motivation: Do they exist and what are the implications for the workplace? In: Journal of Managerial Psychology, vol. 23 2008, issue 8, pp. 878–890.
Wright, Patrick / McMahan, Gary / McWilliams, Abagail (1994): Human resources and sustained competitive advantage: a resource-based perspective. In: International Journal of Human Resource Management, vol. 5 1994, no. 2, pp. 301–326.
Wright, Patrick / Dunford, Benjamin / Snell, Scott (2001): Human Resources and the Resource Based View of the Firm. In: Journal of Management, vol. 27 2001, September, pp. 701–721.
Wunderer, Rolf (1991): Personalmarketing. In: Die Unternehmung, vol. 45 1991, no. 2, pp. 119–131.
Yaeger, Therese F. / Head, Thomas C. / Sorensen, Peter F. (2006): Global organization development: Managing unprecedented change, Charlotte 2006.
Yoo, Boonghee / Donthu, Naveen (2001): Developing and validating a multidimensional consumer-based brand equity scale. In: Journal of Business Research, vol. 52 2001, issue 1, pp. 1–14.
Zaugg, Robert J. (1996): Integrierte Personalbedarfsdeckung. Ausgewählte Gestaltungsempfehlungen zur Gewinnung ganzheitlicher Personalpotentiale, Bern/Stuttgart/Vienna 1996.
Zaugg, Robert J. (2002): Bezugsrahmen als Heuristik der explorativen Forschung: Grundlagen – Bezugsrahmen – Forschungsstrategien – Forschungsmethoden. Working paper no. 57 at the Institute of Organisation and Personnel Management at the University of Bern, Bern 2002.
Zaugg, Robert (2009): Nachhaltiges Personalmanagement: Eine neue Perspektive und empirische Exploration des Human Resource Management, Wiesbaden 2009.
Zhang, Yingying / Straub, Caroline / Kusyk, Sophia (2007): Making a life or making a living? Cross-cultural comparisons of business students' work and life values in Canada and France. In: Cross Cultural Management: An International Journal, vol. 14 2007, issue 3, pp. 174–195.
Zottoli, Michael A. / Wanous, John P. (2000): Recruitment source research: Current status and future directions. In: Human Resource Management Review, vol. 10 2000, issue 4, pp. 353–382.

www.ingramcontent.com/pod-product-compliance
Ingram Content Group UK Ltd.
Pitfield, Milton Keynes, MK11 3LW, UK
UKHW021922120926
8556IPUK00042BA/1150

9 783034 312462